M000217178

Truth-Spots

Truth-Spots

How Places Make People Believe

THOMAS F. GIERYN

The University of Chicago Press ❋ *Chicago and London*

The University of Chicago Press, Chicago 60637
The University of Chicago Press, Ltd., London
© 2018 by The University of Chicago
All rights reserved. No part of this book may be used or
reproduced in any manner whatsoever without written
permission, except in the case of brief quotations in
critical articles and reviews. For more information,
contact the University of Chicago Press, 1427 E. 60th St.,
Chicago, IL 60637.
Published 2018
Printed in the United States of America

27 26 25 24 23 22 21 20 19 18   1 2 3 4 5

ISBN-13: 978-0-226-56195-0 (cloth)
ISBN-13: 978-0-226-56200-1 (e-book)
DOI: https://doi.org/10.7208/chicago
/9780226562001.001.0001

Library of Congress Cataloging-in-Publication Data

Names: Gieryn, Thomas F., author.
Title: Truth-spots : how places make people believe /
    Thomas F. Gieryn.
Description: Chicago ; London : The University of
    Chicago Press, 2018. | Includes bibliographical
    references.
Identifiers: LCCN 2017044664 | ISBN 9780226561950
    (cloth : alk. paper) | ISBN 9780226562001 (e-book)
Subjects: LCSH: Heritage tourism. | Tourism—Social
    aspects. | Tourism—Anthropological aspects. | Culture
    and tourism.
Classification: LCC G156.5.H47 G54 2018 |
    DDC 306.4/819—dc23
LC record available at https://lccn.loc.gov/2017044664

♾ This paper meets the requirements of ANSI/NISO
Z39.48-1992 (Permanence of Paper).

For my desk, office, study, atelier
Ballantine Hall 754
Indiana University
Bloomington

Contents

1

Oracular Tourism

Being shown how to locate, to place, any account is what does most toward making us believe it, not merely allowing us to, may the account be the facts or a lie.

«EUDORA WELTY[1]»

Not long ago, I visited the oracle at Delphi, in Greece, to consult with the Pythia about my prospects for writing a book on how places lend credibility and legitimacy to beliefs and claims. Following custom, I first cleansed myself in waters gushing from the Castalian Spring, beneath the "shining ones" (Phaedriades) on Mount Parnassus. I climbed the Sacred Way, passing by treasuries and monuments built by the great city-states (Athens, Sparta, Corinth, and Thebes) to recognize the prophecies they received, and with their gratitude. I arrived at the Temple of Apollo, and waited my turn—as a non-Greek, at the end of a long line. At last, there was the Pythia before me, seated on her tripod, holding laurel leaves and sacred water, with the omphalos nearby and also the two golden eagles of Zeus—intoxicating vapors emanated from a little fissure at her feet. I put my money down, and a sacrificial cake, which was promptly burned on the altar.

I got no immediate response from the oracle, and sensing that the priestess might need a little background, I recited the passage from Eudora Welty that works as an epigraph for the book. Still no prophecy. Maybe the Pythia needed examples of places that have become truth-spots: pondside hut, wild nature, botanical garden, university lectern, outdoor historical museum, art institute, pilgrimage destination, courthouse, commemorated birthplaces, laboratory. Silence. Oh yes, I continued, then there is the oracle at Delphi—indeed, it is the Mother of All Truth-Spots. Now obviously ecstatic, the priestess began to speak, channeling Apollo himself. I had hoped for something like "#1 on the nonfiction bestseller list" or "hit series on public television." Instead, she told me this: "To be read, the book must be written." Her attendants smiled with satisfaction at the prophecy, and I left the Temple content with what I surmised as oracular encouragement to write on.

——•——

What was it about Delphi—as a place—that made ancient Greeks believe that prophecies received there possessed predictive accuracy? What is it about Delphi today—as a place—that affirms the ordinary tourist's supposition that such oracular consultations really did happen on this very spot way back then? Delphi *as a place* consists of three essential and inseparable ingredients:[2]

- a unique location in geographic space: Delphi is precisely *here* (latitude 38°28′45″ N, longitude 22°29′36″ E) and not there, rising 1,837 feet above sea level, near to some places but far from others, with inevitably elastic and porous[3] borders
- material stuff gathered at this spot, both natural and human made, objects and geological features made or found there that give the place a solid physicality
- narrations, interpretations, and imaginations that give the place distinctive meaning and value

Take away any one of these ingredients, and Delphi ceases to be Delphi—indeed, it ceases to be a place at all. The premise of this book is that place matters mightily for what people believe to be true. We can better understand why some assertions or propositions or ideas become for some people credible and believable by locating them somewhere on the skin of the earth—and by asking what things are to be experienced at that spot and how this place is culturally understood.

To locate an account is to return it to a place where it was discovered or manufactured, where it is displayed and celebrated, where it gets enacted and reproduced, where it is contested or obscured. Such places may become truth-spots—and the place itself is not merely an incidental setting where some idea or assertion just happens to gain credibility, but a vital cause of that enhanced believability. To be sure, the acceptance of a claim as true (or its affirmation for oneself) is never a matter of place alone. Whether or not someone is perceived to be speaking the truth is an upshot of many factors, including the qualities he or she brings to the judgment: pertinent expertise and training (especially if accompanied by institutional "insignia of affiliation," like academic degrees and professional recognition[4]), a history of integrity, absence of a dog in the fight. My suggestion is that perhaps these many determinants of credibility are modulated or inflected in various ways by the places where an account and a potential believer intersect.

Not all truth-spots visited in this book will work just like Delphi: the combination of those three ingredients (location, materiality, and narration) into a fount of perceived truth never follows the exact same recipe. Walden Pond as a place gave credence to Thoreau's pronouncements via pathways that are different from how an ultra clean laboratory did the same for Clair Patterson's factual assertions about human-made sources of lead in the environment. These diverse pathways to the probable— exactly *how* places make people believe—will become the target of our explorations.

———•———

Somehow in Delphi . . . what is here, one feels, is *intact* in its purity. . . . Perhaps *today* the oracle is due to make its re-entry into the world. If it did, if from the

heart of the rock we heard one of those terrific and yet ordinary judgments upon the world of affairs, would we be ready to receive it, act upon it?
«LAWRENCE DURRELL[5]»

The ultimate question about an oracle . . . is not whether it tells the truth but what we will allow to count as the truth.
«MICHAEL WOOD[6]»

Delphi's very existence, then or now, as something more than a forgotten unvisited peasant village hung on the side of Parnassus depends crucially on its success as a truth-spot. Through the last twenty-six centuries or so, diverse allies have worked hard to make it so. Between the sixth century BC and the fourth century AD, the actual residents of Delphi, leaders of distant Greek city-states, invaders from Macedonia, conquering Persians, Roman emperors, and ambivalent Christians variously sustained the place as the center of the universe where mortals could receive divine wisdom. After the late nineteenth-century AD excavations of the site began in earnest, classical archaeologists, the restaurateurs, hotel owners, and shopkeepers of Delphi, the Greek National Tourist Organization, and countless travel agencies and tour-bus operators keep alive the belief that what happened at the oracle at Delphi is real history and culturally important.

The spectacular landscape of Delphi has always been remarkable, and for that reason it has never been unnarrated. Vincent Scully finds there "a very conscious drama between the natural and the manmade . . . calculated to embody the eventual victory of Apollo over the earth's cataclysmic power":[7] the orderly columns of his Temple stand defiant against the menacing horns of the Phaedriades looming above, with all their instability and force (Parnassus is indeed prone to earthquakes). The earliest stories about the origins of the oracle and sanctuary were written centuries after cultic activities began there, as later archaeological evidence would suggest.[8] But these accounts should not be disqualified as inaccurate simply because their authors were less interested in historical verisimilitude than in legitimating Delphi as the superior source of divine guidance and sanction. Legends do as much to make a truth-spot as stone, raw or dressed. Delphi figures in tragedies by Aeschylus, Sophocles, and Euripides and in Herodotus's *Histories* from the fifth century BC, and still appears in the first century AD with Plutarch, who lived there for a time. The tales are tall. Delphi was home to Gaia, Earth Mother, one of the primordial Greek deities—which extends the cosmic significance of this spot back to the beginning of everything. Or, if you prefer a celestial origin myth, Sky Father Zeus, seeking the location of Gaia's home, is said to have released two eagles from the ends of the earth—and flying toward each other, they met exactly above Delphi, where Gaia's belly button (omphalos) was taken to signify that here was the navel of the world.

Pride of place among the deities celebrated at Delphi goes to Apollo, son of Zeus, who wanted Gaia's precinct for himself. The place had been guarded by her serpent or she-dragon, which Apollo slew, leaving its carcass to rot in the sun on the mountainside among mortals; "to rot" in Greek is *pythō*, hence Apollo Pythios and his priestess medium, the Pythia. Once liberating the place from the snake, Apollo needed humans to populate it, whose life mission would be his veneration. According to the *Homeric Hymn to Apollo* (seventh–sixth centuries BC), he assumed the form of a dolphin (*delphis* in Greek) and pushed Cretan sailors toward the northern coast of the Corinthian Sea, getting them to land quite unexpectedly at a spot just below Parnassus. At landfall, Apollo assumed human form, and told the sailors to climb 600 meters up the mountain and build an altar where humans could consult the God of Truth and Prophecy. Upon arriving at a cleft between the peaks, the sailors suspected that Apollo had surely made a most ungodlike mistake: the stony mountainside was barren, offering no viable means of livelihood.

But of course Apollo's moment of Eureka! was well founded. In the *Homeric Hymn*, Apollo is seen wandering around looking for the perfect spot for his Temple, rejecting one place because it is rich with wheat and forests, rejecting another because it has no footpaths or roadways, and rejecting a third as bothered by "the clattering of the swift horses and of the mules." But on a "ridge of the mountain; . . . underneath snow-covered Parnassos; . . . is a slope that is turned toward the west wind; high up above is hanging a cliff overhead, and beneath it runs a deep valley, hollow and rugged," Apollo found a spot just right: bereft of natural resources, somewhat accessible (to mortals) and tranquil. After the Cretan leader reminds Apollo that "this is a land not pleasing for vineyards or good for its pastures," the god responds: "Simpletons truly you are . . . if in your right hands each of you taking a knife were to slaughter sheep incessantly here, unstinted the victims would all yet be, so many the glorious nations of mankind bring me"—or, if you play by my rules, the hordes of worshippers making the trek up the mountain will bring more sheep than you could possibly raise yourself (eternal sustenance will be no problem).[9]

I might be agnostic about whether Apollo ever existed or ever issued those exact words—but sociologically, he was on the money. This location (and its bleak but awesome natural geographic features) turns out to be exactly the right place for the job of an oracular truth-spot. I suspect that when Apollo sought a tranquil place, he had something more on his mind than clattering hooves. Delphi is tranquil because it is located *away*, far enough from the noisy Greek city-states rising in the archaic period (roughly, seventh to early fifth centuries BC), and thus (at least initially) not attached to or owned by any one of them. The place could become neutral and autonomous territory, where Greeks from all over could come to seek Apollo's wisdom without worry of trespassing on the turf of a rival city-state. Moreover, no city-state would covet the immediate territory around Delphi because, as Apollo insisted, it had no natural resources to exploit. At least until the oracle was up and running, there was little reason for any mortals to be especially interested in the place for economic or strategic reasons. An unproductive spot far from anybody's immediate control allowed Delphi to find its legs as a politically independent home for Apollo—which did wonders for the perceived credibility of the Pythia's prognostications. How so?

The sacred sanctuary at Delphi managed to last, with varying intensity of oracular activity, from about the seventh century BC until roughly the fourth century AD because of a permanently precarious symbiosis between the Delphians who actually lived on-site and the city-states, ethnic peoples, and empires from around the Mediterranean who valued the place. This mutually beneficial interaction depended upon Delphi's position as a truth-spot, a place that afforded credibility to the oracle's messages. Inhabitants of Delphi hoped to gain their own freedom as a town and protection from conquest, but most important they needed a steady flow of resources (e.g., sheep—and emphatically, it was "no fee, no consultation")[10] in order to survive on the tough mountainside—and these would be provided by seekers trekking to worship there and, later, to participate in athletic competitions and artistic festivals. Visiting devotees and inquirers, in turn, hoped to enjoy unimpeded access to the site and to the priestess whose pronouncements had to be unsullied by ulterior motives or distracting interests. Delphians, in effect, traded objectivity and believability for edibles and prosperity. Supplicants provided protection and resources in exchange for prophecies accepted as legitimate because barren and remote Delphi was initially beyond anybody's outside control and thus free from suspicions that its predictions were politically motivated or constrained. Smart guy, Apollo: by encouraging those Cretan sailors to put their altar at inhospitable and distant Delphi, he insured that believers from everywhere would come to venerate him at a spot so neutral that his wisdom came through mortals whose only real stake was to preserve a reputation for clean hands.

Archaeological evidence suggests that Greeks from far and wide beat a path to Delphi, despite significant vertical challenges for those arriving at sea level, starting in the late eighth century BC. Pottery shards show stylistic signatures of objects made to the north in Thessaly and also from the south in the

Peloponnese, suggesting that Delphi sat on a developing north-south trade route whose traffic would intensify as the oracle's legitimacy and utility grew. The place was accessible. Leaders of the city-states had increasingly good reason to consult with the Delphic oracle. Classical historian Michael Scott suggests that Athens, Sparta, Corinth, and the rest were just beginning to develop processes of deliberative decision-making that were potentially accountable to their citizens. Oracular advice was sought to guide or legitimate decisions about whether or not to colonize new settlements[11] or to initiate war against a foreign power or a rival Greek city-state. The prophecies were ambiguous: typically they lacked decisive yea/nay recommendations and instead offered a range of possible interpretations for city leaders and citizens to mull over. However fuzzy or unfalsifiable their substance may have been, Delphic predictions were ascribed credibility so that they could be used effectively in arguments over what course of action to take and later to justify eventual outcomes.[12] "The ritualized environment in which divination takes place helps to confirm its validity."[13]

In a world rife with competing oracles, Delphi assiduously protected its brand of superior wisdom—straight from Apollo, and no cajoling. Although scholars continue to disagree about so much of what may have happened at Delphi long ago, "what is not in dispute is the position of pre-eminence it achieved and sustained."[14] The words of the faraway Pythia possessed a greater legitimacy than those received from a local oracle around the corner because of her assumed independence of mind ("no prophet has honor at home"). So important was the protection of Delphi's autonomy (and objectivity) that the Greek city-states came together in a rare moment of Panhellenism to defend the independent sanctuary against a would-be usurper. In the late sixth century BC, residents of the town of Crisa (located on the fertile plain below Delphi) were ripping off travelers heading up to the oracle and even had the temerity to attack the Delphians themselves. An association of Greek cities and states known as the Amphictyony (led, in this instance, by Thessaly, Athens, and

Sicyon) came together to crush Crisa in battle—seizing booty and declaring that the fertile plain between the Corinthian Sea and the base of Parnassus would remain forever uncultivated (and thus neutral ground traversable without risk).[15]

Some of that booty allowed members of the Amphictyony to construct a variety of buildings and infrastructural improvements at Delphi (which, before the mid-seventh century or so, probably consisted only of the steaming fissure, the Pythia on her tripod, and whatever residences were needed to house the few Delphians). In 650 BC, Corinth built the first of what would become a string of "treasuries" lining the paths up to the eventual Temple of Apollo, first built shortly thereafter. These treasuries (and the columns, monuments, stadium, and stoa that would follow) served various functions vital to securing the reputation of Delphi as a source of preferred truth about the future. They were storehouses for gold, silver, and other valuables gifted to Delphi by members of the Amphictyony as thanks for Apollo's guidance in urging a successful holy war (for example) on the greedy Crisans. They allowed cities and states to have a presence at the oracle without implying possession or control: they were built to display gratitude, not dominance. In the ensuing centuries, however, monumental buildings at Delphi played a crucial part in ancient pissing matches (or, more politely, "the hubris of humans"[16]) as cities (and later empires) sought to display their wealth or power, to commemorate their role (sometimes exaggerated) in achieving victory on a battlefield, and to prevent rivals from monopolizing the sacred place. Built-Delphi became a simulation of international power-relations in the wider Mediterranean world: ever more lavish treasuries and monuments were built by ascending cities and empires, and they crumbled (or got replaced) as the power of their builders declined. There was also something tit-for-tat here: cities, states, and even individual beneficiaries who built the most sumptuous displays of gratitude were allowed to jump the line as they sought to consult the Pythia, a practice known as promanteia (the priestess was available only nine times per year, and the lines evidently could get very long, even when three Pythia were on call).

Moreover, visiting city-states and residents of Delphi together invested in material improvements that would make the site more accessible and convincing—like terracing the steep slope. Boundary walls were erected to demarcate spaces reserved for sacred activities, clearly marked off from the secular, domestic, and commercial activities of a growing town. But most important, the treasuries and monuments served as testaments in stone, prominent and durable affirmations of the wise and helpful guidance received from the oracle at Delphi. After Corinth completed its treasury, Athens just had to follow, at an even more conspicuous spot and demanding greater investments of wealth and labor. Visitors to Delphi could not help but be reassured by these monuments that the prophecy they were about to receive emanated from a believable source and without subterfuge: just look at the material evidence left by those demonstrably satisfied by their consultation with the priestess.

See how places make people believe? There sits Delphi, given meaning through stories connecting this sublime spot to Zeus and Gaia, with a location that separates its sacred activities from compromising politics, and consisting of human edifices that serve as a heartening scorecard of successful prophecies past. For centuries, says historian Julia Kindt, "the oracle of Apollo at Delphi was regarded as a rare seat of authority, an authority that . . . served as an important source of truth and orientation."[17] Delphi had a good long run, but no truth-spot is forever. Its stature began to decline in the fourth century BC, even though oracular forecasting, festivals, monumental building projects, and pissing matches continued into the fifth century AD and beyond. Oracular consultations became less frequent (and suspicions of graft increased) as the place became less autonomous and impartial. Aetolians from the east seized control over Delphi in the third century BC, and although the town and sanctuary were later liberated, successive waves of global powers looted valuables for their own gain and/or threatened the objectivity of the

Pythia, who survived by twisting in the wind and keeping happy whomever was in power. Gauls invaded from the north, and seized valuables but left little behind; Macedonians and Romans gave Delphi greater respect and used the place to announce their own superiority while allowing the enduring Amphictyony to manage the place; Christians eventually denounced Delphi as pagan, and Theodosius I shut the place down in AD 390–91; and after enduring repeated earthquakes, fires, conquests, and rockslides, the onetime center of the universe finally melted into the mountainside for more than 1,000 years.

———•———

Truth markers function to cement the bond of tourist and attraction by elevating the information possessed by the tourist to privileged status. . . . Sustaining a firm sense of social reality requires some *mystification*.
«DEAN MACCANNELL[18]»

Actually, tourism began at Delphi even before its big sleep. Plutarch tells us that in the first century AD "there were enough people coming to Delphi to ensure the need for guides to lead tours." The site was increasingly appealing for visitors as a place where important things had happened for a very long time, not simply an occasion for veneration and prophecy but now as "commercial theatre" for celebrating "cultural memory and history."[19] All that business dwindled away starting in the fifth century AD, when ordinary people of Delphi began to use the stones once part of treasuries and monuments to build their houses over the sacred spaces. When the Slavs laid waste to much of Greece in the early seventh century AD, Delphi showed "signs of destruction and wholesale abandonment."[20] The place even lost its identity, for the emerging settlement on the spot was known as Castri, and there were no priestesses around to presage the future, no grand displays of veneration and gratitude, no festivals or games, and after a while nobody local who even remembered what the place had once been.

Delphi remained submerged under falling stones and peasant dwellings for about eight to ten centuries, essentially unnoticed and amazingly forgotten about. In the fifteenth century, Cyriac of Ancona, sometimes called the father of classical archaeology, used textual traces to make his way to where Delphi once was, in search of engraved stone that might reveal stories about the disappeared oracle.[21] A few intrepid scholars poked around the place in the seventeenth and eighteenth centuries, and when Englishman George Wheeler arrived in 1676, "no trace was left of the ancient monuments."[22] Following clues in the scattered stones and engravings, sustained excavations began with various German and French teams in the 1840s.[23] In 1891, permission was granted to the French School of Archaeology in Athens to begin excavation of the entire sanctuary, and soon the village of Castri was moved from the sacred site to the nearby location of the modern town with the name of Delphi.[24] Had the archaeologists not rediscovered and unearthed ancient Delphi, we would have been left only with textual accounts (like the *Homeric Hymns* and Plutarch) and an undistinguished village amidst the once-distinguished rubble. The activity of these scholars is an essential part of the resuscitation of Delphi as a truth-spot for tourists whose numbers would swell after the Second World War. At one time the place for mortals to receive the wisdom of Apollo, Delphi gets remade as a research site for inquiry and discovery, an object of study by experts in archaeology as well as history, geology, and philology—and it is in this guise that the oracle and sanctuary appear to tourists today.

Scholars' annotation and selective reconstitution of Delphi transfer the responsibility for understanding the place from tourist to expert. The throngs of visitors are dependent upon scientific representations of the place, and probably very few of those just passing through possess the acumen to challenge the facts and stories presented. The full armament of scholarship and curatorial skill is used to persuade visitors from our disenchanted world (where Apollo is a myth, and Oracle is a global corporation selling database management systems) that at this very place where they are standing, people long ago believed that they could communicate with the gods and receive prophecy from the Pythia that would be used to deliberate and ratify civic policy—and that this center of the universe, incredulously, was then wiped off the side of Parnassus for more than eight centuries! The same ingredients of place that once convinced ancient Greeks that the oracle had credibility are now assembled to affirm tourists' beliefs that such claims about the practices of ancient Greeks at Delphi are equally credible: location, materiality, and narration (guidebooks written by professors are available in many languages).

Not all tourist sites make claims about historical realities, but those that do manage the visitor's experience and understanding of the place with exquisite attention. For the typical tourist who comes around the mountain and catches that unforgettable first glimpse of Delphi wedged into Parnassus, the word that might first come to mind is "ruin." At its heart, the ruin is a remnant of the struggle between culture and nature, as the once-built bends to the ravages of wild time.[25] As archaeologists began to unearth monumental structures and detritus encrusted at Delphi, they faced strategic choices about how the excavated materials should be handled, choices that are consequential for the capacity of the site to persuade tourists of its own authenticity. Some artifacts would not survive if left exposed on the mountainside, and many of these have ended up in a modern museum immediately adjacent to the sanctuary. Other remains are reconstituted outdoors into the form they might have taken when the oracle was a going concern. But the vast majority of wrought stones are just lying around the place in a jumble—not just because it would cost incalculable amounts of money to rebuild the entire place in situ, and not just because some of the key pieces are missing or severely damaged.

The Delphic story for tourists has two chapters—center of the universe, then oblivion—and equal attention during excavation and rebuilding must be given to both constructive culture and destructive nature if tourists are to accept the whole story as true.

Too little reconstruction leaves the place looking like the aftermath of an earthquake with little human or cultural significance; too much reconstruction creates a Disneyland theme park that is more about amusement than edification and lacks the gravitas needed to make people believe. So the Temple of Apollo gets six of its majestic columns rebuilt, with the remainder left for imagination. The Athenian Treasury is displayed with all four walls intact and even an entablature, triangulated pediment, and roof, while treasuries from rival city-states are "totally ruined,"[26] marked by grass, stones flat on the ground, and an interpretive plaque. Tourists are marched up the Sacred Way believing that this is the very path taken by supplicants from the sixth century BC as they approached the Pythia at the Temple, and it probably does not matter for them if they happen to notice that the present Sacred Way did not took shape until almost the very end of the game in the sixth century AD.[27] Welty wrote that places do most to make us believe any story or claim—"may the account be the facts or a lie."

Signage abounds at Delphi, in the sanctuary and the museum, telling tourists what they are looking at—for sociologist John Urry, "the tourist gaze."[28] There are very few opportunities for visitors to form their own impressions of the place: Delphi comes preinterpreted, narratively sealed up as tight as a drum. Walking up the first switchback on the Sacred Way, just left of the Athenian Treasury, the tourist comes upon a cone of stone—remarkable because it is the only cone around (but looking just like Dan Aykroyd's head in that movie). Its significance is all found in the adjacent twenty-seven-line caption that starts out: "The sacred omphalos of Delphi, believed to have fallen from the heavens . . . was also identified with the stone thrown by Zeus from the heavens to discover the center of the universe." In the English-language version, something in Greek is parenthetically inserted just after the word "heavens," which reassures casual tourists that scholars who wrote the caption know more than they do. "The omphalos held an important place in divination at the oracle," which is not offered up as mere opinion, but as something authoritative: "We learn from the ancient sources that the sacred tripod, prophetic laurel and omphalos were in the adyton of the Temple of Apollo." The tourist may not know that the "adyton" is a restricted area within a temple, the word itself meaning "do not enter" (I didn't), but trusts classical archaeologists who know that this is important. So that cone is the actual stone thrown by Zeus? Only at the very end of the caption do we get this: "There were many copies of the sacred omphalos at the sanctuary, among them the one exhibited here." Copy? Whose copy? From when? Is there an original? The tourist today, hungry for signs of the authentic, probably decides that the inability to answer these questions (left unaddressed by the interpretive signage) reflects his or her ignorance, not the lack of knowledge among scholars—like when Apollo called the Cretan sailors "simpletons."

Ancient Delphi simulated power struggles among Greek city-states and other empires, as real battlefields got transmuted into a pacific and sacred space festooned with a succession of monuments each bigger and more luxurious than those erected by vanquished rivals. The archaeological museum at Delphi, most recently renovated at the turn of the twenty-first century and located just a few minutes walk from the sanctuary itself, relies on simulations of its own to convince tourists about the veracity of what used to happen here. There are collections of small artifacts, carefully classified, labeled, and explained, whose significance would be lost if they were left in place on the mountainside (even if that would have been a more authentic thing to do). Next to a case showing corroded metal objects carefully grouped by shape (round, pointed, with a shaft or without), visitors read the caption explaining that these came from "repositories" of objects, made from precious materials ("gold, ivory, silver, copper") and dating from the eighth to the fifth century BC: "Thanks to a years-long restoration project" (i.e., archaeologists worked long and hard to make this discovery), "thousands of fragments from the two pits were reassembled to take the form of the exhibits we see today"—i.e., this is not how they were found outside, "intermingled with earth, charcoal and ashes," but doing a better job there in the vitrine to give us a "vivid picture of the opulence of the dedications to the sanctuary." Objects in the museum are rearranged not just for scholarly accuracy but to maximize convincing effects on audiences walking through.

Sometimes, such restorations go to great lengths. One star of the museum at Delphi is the Charioteer, from the fifth century BC. The statue is missing only a left arm and is stunning in its detail: the folds of fabric in his girdled chiton and the use of contrasting black stone for the pupils of his eyes are worth the price of admission. But this guy was once part of a much larger composition that probably included multiple riders, grooms, horses, and chariots. Along one wall, curators have assembled about eight scattered pieces including three lower legs of a horse, one arm of a boy holding the horse, and incomplete reins—an "ethnographic fragment" like everything else at Delphi today.[29] These bits are suspended immediately in front of a complete drawing of the whole shebang: it certainly looks plausible, even though the caption suggests that "the scholars involved are not unanimous" in deciding how the entire composition might originally have looked. Tourists are not provided evidence of dissenting experts' opinions. Deeper in the museum, the visitor comes upon complete scale models of the entire Delphi site in a detail that would have been absolutely goofy had it been rendered outside, on the mountain, in stone, life-size. Instead, we have a miniature cardboard simulation in a glass case, and then a digital one with touch-screen features. How difficult it would be for a skeptic to deny that something very special— involving cleansing waters, the cone stones (there is a second omphalos inside the museum), gold and silver, laurel leaves, tripod, and authoritative oracular messages—really did come together centuries ago at this very place. Scholars and curators who create truth-spots like Delphi as credible windows on history are not disingenuous, but it can be easy to forget how their noble intentions, professional integrity, skillful work, and materials on display *manufacture* powerfully persuasive stories of life long ago. As a tourist myself at Delphi, never once did I feel cheated or deceived—just won over by the place to believe that ancient Greeks believed that Apollo spoke truth through the Pythia.

Ancient ideas about divination, deities, and prophecies remain abstract until the practices that sustain them are located in geographic space. Just as the ancients constructed stone walls to demarcate their sacred sanctuary, modern curators of the site put fences around Delphi not just to exclude nonpaying visitors but to mark out the limits of oracular and devotional activity. By emplacing the elusive features of cultures long gone, by respectfully arranging the accoutrements of their practices, by interpreting it all through signage—and most important, by doing all of that at a discrete bounded location where presumably the stuff all happened first time through—scholars and curators put together a powerfully affirming narrative for their visiting tourists. It helps, of course, that the location of Delphi (after construction in 1935 of a highway across the mountains from the east, with a turn-around for monstrous buses) is reachable from Athens on a convenient day trip, complete with expert guide: "Immerse yourself in the myths and monuments of classical Greece," with tickets starting at about $95. The charming village of Arachova, marketed big time by the Greek National Tourism Organization for its skiing, clean air, mountain views, tony shops, and traditional restaurants lies on the road to Delphi, a perfect stop for lunch and souvenirs. At least for truth-spots welcoming the masses to important sites of history, such touristic amenities become part of the draw.

I did not lie to the Pythia: Delphi is indeed the Mother of All Truth-Spots. It is a place found, a place built, and a place narrated to make people believe—to believe that here is the fount of oracular wisdom, or much later, here is the fount of scholarly wisdom about oracular wisdom. It is a place where people once visited to receive an authoritative consultation about the future; it is now a place where people visit to receive an equally authoritative depiction of the past.

———•———

This book stands firm against two ideas trending now: post-truth and post-place. With a title like *Truth-Spots*, how could it be otherwise? It is hardly the case that we have run out of truth, or moved beyond the desire for it. Rather, there are too many truths out there to choose from, so that the issue comes down to this: on what grounds do some people (but rarely everybody all at once) accept a claim or assertion as true? The available but often disputed grounds are as many as the flavors of truth itself: consistency with observational or experimental data, congruence with theory, outcome of logical reasoning, fidelity to a sacred text, embodiment of long-standing and cherished values or principles, alignment with political ambitions, fit with memory, upshot of an experiential aha, reflection of what "everybody knows." Based on how the word "truth" is variously used in common parlance, no privilege can be given to any one of these—not even point-for-point correspondence to natural or historical reality, not even timeless and transcendent verities. It just happens that some claims about some slice of the universe become more believable for some people—that is, those people are inclined to see in those claims something real (not illusion). Other accounts get dismissed as error, lies, heresy, retrograde, politically incorrect, claptrap, or simply unworthy of any attention at all. Rather than wish for a universal and absolute Truth lurking behind these culture-bound judgments, we would do better to figure out why the inevitably partial and situated truths of some people—and vitally, not other people—assume the appearance of "the way it must be" and thus become the operative reality for decisions that affect us all.

The grounds for assigning credibility to some claims but not others just might involve putting that assertion on the ground somewhere—literally, taking it back to its geographic and material provenance, like a fine wine, where it was found, made, deliberated, adjudicated, announced, displayed, stored, or challenged (or maybe lost, hidden, disguised, or forgotten). Places are not idle backdrops—they have agency and exert a force of their own on the direction and pace of knowledge and belief, on what becomes true. I may be swimming upstream here against those who believe that the digital mediation of everything or the homogenization of everyplace makes *where* you happen to be insignificant or even irrelevant. Perhaps we can all get along. Even the advent of "virtual reality" need not necessarily result in the declining significance of place, as if the two—cyberspace and physical place—stood in a zero-sum relationship. Some of you may have looked at pictures of Delphi online as you read this chapter, and maybe those free-floating images inclined you toward accepting my premises and arguments. The instant availability of infinite images on the web—and claims and assertions too—might make it even more vital these days to anchor our beliefs (our truths) in a place somewhere with slightly more permanence than a nanosecond. The ease of declaring truths online (with accountability often absent) regularly sends skeptics scurrying away from their screens and back to Real Places where the claims might have come from—possible truth-spots where a fact was evidenced or a belief confirmed.

Eudora Welty certainly got the conjecture right, but so much work, so many travels, will be needed to find out *how* different kinds of places make people believe different kinds of accounts. The journey ahead will visit truth-spots selected for their variety, both in the kinds of places they are geographically and physically, and in the kinds of claims they help to affirm (metaphysical lessons, taxonomies of nature, assertions about the historical past and future, the meaning of life, faith, renderings of justice, political ideology, collective identity-claims, and empirical facts of science will all find their spots in the chapters to come). "Place makes a poor abstraction. Separated from its materializations, it has little meaning," writes anthropologist Clifford Geertz.[30] We must pay visits to Walden Pond and to Clair Patterson's ultra clean lab, to see up close how the particulars of each place lend credibility to beliefs and claims rooted there. Pack your bags.

2

Ground-Truthing at Walden Pond

It has no name in my mind except the Place. . . . It's a spot in which to wonder about things. . . . Now, sitting in the Place, out of the wind, seeing under the guardian lights the tide creep in, black from the dark sky, I wondered whether all men have a Place, or need a Place, or want one and have none. . . . I call whatever happens in the Place "taking stock."

«JOHN STEINBECK[1]»

The writer of *Walden* is not counting on being believed; on the contrary, he converts the problem or condition of belief into a dominant subject of his experiment.

«STANLEY CAVELL[2]»

I have read The Book more times than I have been to The Pond. By coincidence, both times I visited Walden it was on a bitterly cold winter's day when I had the place almost to myself—just as it was for Thoreau, whose solitude there was interrupted only occasionally by a human visitor. My visits were separated by two decades, long enough for me to confirm what he wrote about the changing shoreline: "The pond rises and falls, but whether regularly or not, and within what period, nobody knows, though, as usual, many pretend to know."[3] On my second walk, I noticed that the flat beach between where the water stopped and the permanent vegetation began had increased considerably in width from twenty years before (perhaps because of recent drought, or maybe it rained a lot in 1997). I couldn't stay very long on either occasion, and took refuge from impending frostbite inside Haute Coffee at 12 Walden Street in Concord. Thoreau would have disapproved on two counts: water is simpler to drink, and coffeehouses epitomize the news and gossip and "society" that compelled him to build his hut out of town.

From the pond, Thoreau asserted all kinds of claims: philosophical, scientific, literary, poetic, ethical, mystical, and political (*Walden* was written before these pursuits had been professionalized into tidy boxes).[4] He instructs us on diverse matters such as the real necessities of life, how to measure the depth of a body of water, how to escape from lives of quiet desperation, how to grow beans, proper diet, why Brits and old people are often misguided, the value of reading and the folly of fashion—but above all, the need to "simplify, simplify" (136). He urges his Concord neighbors to get out of their warm coffeehouse and into Nature, but seems to doubt that they will muster the patience needed to find reality outside on their own. So he wrote a book for them, as if he knew that the words themselves would assume responsibility for persuading us of his truths. His literary burden is to get readers to trust what he writes by giving a provenance to his wisdom, a place for his experiences, grounds for his lessons. *Walden* presumes "that Thoreau had some better way of discerning the truth than other people did."[5] Thoreau knew from the start what he hoped to tell his readers, but still he needed "to establish his right to declare it"[6]—to extract credibility and moral authority from the pond and his studio[7] in the woods.

———•———

People in the city often wonder whether one gets lonely up in the mountains among the peasants for such long and monotonous periods of time. But it isn't loneliness, it is solitude. . . . Solitude has the peculiar and original power of not isolating us but of projecting our whole existence out into the vast nearness of the presence of all things.

«MARTIN HEIDEGGER[8]»

Solitude . . . rarely meant absolute aloneness [but] . . . disengagements from specific institutions or sectors of society.

«STEVEN SHAPIN[9]»

The location of Walden Pond matters considerably. The place must be close enough to Concord for Thoreau to be able to influence his neighbors, but far enough away from town so that his neighbors could not influence him. If he had lit out for the American frontier, his readers back east might have lost touch with him or cast him as an outsider whose life lessons could not possibly apply to Concord or Boston. Walden Pond was presumably familiar for those living in Concord in a way that Indiana or Wisconsin was not, and a few of Thoreau's neighbors actually stopped by his cabin in the woods to see what he was up to. Accessibility (even if just a potential) was vital for Thoreau to elicit curiosity from his neighbors and to establish that he really did build a hut beside Walden Pond where he maintained residence for about two and one-half years (1845–47, starting at age twenty-seven). Skeptics could always hike out south from Concord center, to see for themselves (although by the time the book appeared in 1854, Thoreau had moved back into town).

It was even more important for Thoreau to get away from his neighbors; in 1845, in exurban Massachusetts, three miles from Concord (it seems) would do the trick. The book begins with the author giving a location for himself and his assertions: "When I wrote the following pages, or rather the bulk of them, I lived alone, in the woods, a mile from any neighbor, in a house which I had built myself, on the shore of Walden Pond, in Concord, Massachusetts" (45). I must dwell on the obvious: Thoreau could surely have come up with his wise maxims from *anywhere*—or *nowhere*. There is nothing inherently emplaced about that bumper-sticker favorite: "If a man does not keep pace with his companions, perhaps it is because he hears a different drummer"

(374). The drum has no particular location, but Thoreau heard its beat clearly at Walden Pond. There is no necessity that the book put its author in a place, or that its very title becomes the name of the chosen place—but in making these choices, Thoreau makes us believe. "No American writer has been more closely identified with a single place," writes Robert Gross.[10] Thoreau's proof of concept was to be in a place. What makes this particular place—Walden Pond—so right for discovering and crowing truth is captured by one word in the opening sentence: "alone." Thoreau invites readers to share his temporary solitude in the woods, his life of epistemic self-reliance. "I preferred the solitary dwelling" (115), Thoreau writes. "I find it wholesome to be alone the greater part of the time" (180).

Plainly, for Thoreau, the society he left behind was anything but wholesome for getting reality straight. His move away to the pond measured an "obstinate disengagement from the social," Lawrence Buell suggests,[11] and Thoreau tells us exactly what he is running from:

> Let us settle ourselves, and work and wedge our feet downward through the mud and slush of opinion, and prejudice, and tradition, and delusion, and appearance, that alluvion which covers the globe, through Paris and London, through New York and Boston and Concord, through church and state, through poetry and philosophy and religion, till we come to a hard bottom and rocks in place, which we can call *reality*, and say, This is, and no mistake. (142)

Thoreau finds his neighbors in town to be a "society of our gossips" (180), people easily "distracted" (147) who "soar but little higher in our intellectual flights than the columns of the daily paper" (153). They are beset by one sin or another: "Every generation laughs at the old fashions, but follows religiously the new" (68), and yet, "how deep the ruts of tradition and conformity" (371). Either way, "public opinion is a weak tyrant compared with our own private opinion" (50). It is far better to leave the dinner table of society for the remote woods: "Rather than love, than money, than fame, give me truth. I sat at a table where were rich food and wine in abundance, and obsequious attendance, but sincerity and truth were not; and I went away hungry from the inhospitable board" (379). This place persuades readers by being located a distance away from the hustle and bustle of Concordian fantasies. The author goes solo with "stones in place" (101), preferring what Robert Thorson calls "rock reality," or the "conviction that bedrock and truth are one in the same."[12]

Thoreau is especially unimpressed by received expertise: "Instead of calling on some scholar, I paid many a visit to particular trees" (248–49). He has little good to say about "professors" and the books they write, distancing himself (professionally and geographically) from those who make a good living from their supposed intellect: "The success of great scholars and thinkers is commonly a courtier-like success, not kingly, not manly. They make shift to live merely by conformity" (57). Thoreau's lessons depend upon his seeing things fresh and autonomously, which he can do better in solitude, without assistance from learned types: "If I wished a boy to know something about the arts and sciences, for instance, I would not pursue the common course, which is merely to send him into the neighborhood of some professor, where any thing is professed and practised but the art of life" (94). A Harvard man himself (class of 1837), Thoreau recalls his residence at Hollis Hall, where "the occupant suffers the inconvenience of many and noisy neighbors" (93). In his class book, Thoreau wrote in 1860: "Those hours that should have been devoted to study have been spent in scouring the woods, and exploring the lakes and streams of my native village."[13] In *Walden*, he reflects on his bean crop: "I learned from the experience of both years, not being in the least awed by many celebrated works on husbandry" (98). The local "wild men" (indigenous native people) "never consulted with books," and because of that they "instinctively follow other fashions and trust other authorities than their townsmen . . . as wise in natural lore as the citizen is in artificial" (331). Books *can* be useful, and *Walden* would be especially so, but maybe only if read in solitude: "My residence was more favorable, not only to thought, but to serious reading, than a university" (144). The very process of discovering new knowledge is thus shifted away from a communal process (of scholars) to the work of an isolated observer: "They are the highest reality. Perhaps the facts most astounding and most real are never communicated by man to man" (264).

To be alone is anything but lonely, if one is willing to expand the idea of engagement to include intercourse with natural things. Thoreau has many friends and neighbors at Walden Pond, like the loon or the lake: "I have a great deal of company in my house; especially in the morning, when nobody calls. . . . I am no more lonely than the loon in the pond that laughs so loud, or than Walden Pond itself. What company has that lonely lake, I pray?" (182). In the absence of interfering and distracting human visitors, he can see and hear these natural friends more clearly and learn more from them than in the "overcultivated and overstuffed parlors of Concord."[14] "So many autumn, ay, and winter days, spent outside the town, trying to hear what was in the wind, to hear and carry it express!" (60). He takes in the "pines and hickories and sumachs [sumacs], in undisturbed solitude and stillness" (156–57). He desires "to explore the private sea, the Atlantic and Pacific Ocean of one's being alone" (370), and because "it is as solitary where I live as on the prairies . . . I have, as it were, my own sun and moon and stars, and a little world all to myself" (175). Thoreau (and Heidegger) make an epistemic virtue out of being solitary in Nature—it is not a suffering caused by the absence of other people: "I have never felt lonesome, or in the least oppressed by a sense of solitude. . . . I was suddenly sensible of such sweet and beneficial society in Nature. . . . Every little pine needle expanded and swelled with sympathy and befriended me" (176–77). Thoreau's solitude created an author with a mind of his own, and for that reason we still read the book today.

———•———

Nothing—no laboratory result or field-camp speculation—can replace the rich, complex texture, the credibility, of something that takes place "out there."
«BARRY LOPEZ[15]»

The pathless world of wild nature is a surpassing school and those who have lived through her can be tough and funny teachers. Out here one is in constant engagement with countless plants and animals.
«GARY SNYDER[16]»

Nowhere could be more distant from Thoreau's Walden Pond than the Lesche of the Knidians, part of the oracular sanctuary at Delphi—geographically for sure (about 4,700 miles away), but more importantly in the different conditions they present for making and discerning believable claims. The people of Knidos, an ancient Greek city on the southwest coast of Asia Minor, built a *lesche* at Delphi during the fifth century BC to thank the gods for victory over the Persians in the battle of Eurymedon. Little of the building remains, and so its actual uses are a matter of speculation, but the Ionic Greek word *lesche* generically refers to a place for council or common conversation, ideally with seats facing the sun (the one at Delphi might have been a club or restaurant). Quite possibly, the Lesche of the Knidians was a site for deliberating the meaning of oracular messages received at the Temple of Apollo, before the recipients returned home from Delphi. The Lesche afforded a built-in reality check premised on the idea that the utility of the Pythia's prognostications depended upon a collective and public ventilation of their substance and implications.

The Lesche of the Knidians exposes an epistemic risk that Thoreau takes by locating himself and his claims at the solitude of Walden Pond. Where is *his* reality check—with nobody around but loons and whippoorwills? An isolated knower might more easily be deceived by tricks or deluded by hopes than a bunch of knowers debating the evidence among themselves (groupthink[17] notwithstanding). For Thoreau, though, the loons and whippoorwills (along with the entirety of Nature "out there") are sufficient to rein in his soaring imagination, to bring his

thoughts back down to the ground. Walden Pond is not a fig-
ment of Thoreau's fertile mind; indeed, it is made into a place
outside human artifice and history altogether. Thus, the reader
gets the impression that the author came upon a preexisting and
autonomous reality at Walden, sitting there waiting for his patient observations and thick descriptions, available as affirmation
(or not) of his conjectures. We believe *Walden* because its assertions and lessons are *found* at Walden, grounded in the reality of
a place that was not invented for purposes of persuading us or
making Thoreau famous: "I stood in the laboratory of the Artist
who made the world and me" (354).

At Walden, Thoreau confronts what Buell describes as the
"implacable *thereness* of the external world," a place to be approached with "the conviction that the natural world was real
on its own terms," adds Laura Dassow Walls.[18] The process of
observing—immersion in an externalized natural reality experienced with all the human senses—is described meticulously
throughout the book because it is exactly the thing missing from
the lives of Thoreau's busy but unseeing neighbors in Concord:
"For many years I was self-appointed inspector of snow storms
and rain storms, and did my duty faithfully" (60). Recalling earlier times when he was a hunter, Thoreau is "now inclined to
think that there is a finer way of studying ornithology than this. It
requires so much closer attention to the habits of the birds, that, if
for that reason only, I have been willing to omit the gun" (259). He
has no purpose now in interacting with birds except to learn from
them: "I heard the lark and pewee and other birds already come
to commence another year with us" (84). The "soundest truths"
are within our grasp "if men would steadily observe realities only,
and not allow themselves to be deluded" (139–40)—adding: "We
crave only reality" (142). Observation becomes the basis for a
personal experience of Nature, in Nature—the author becomes
a "witness" (275) of all the things that surround him at the pond:
"You only need sit still long enough in some attractive spot in
the woods that all its inhabitants may exhibit themselves to you
by turns" (275). Thoreau's reason for getting out into Nature is to

"know it by experience, and be able to give a true account of it" (135). No claim "can be trusted without proof" (51), and verification comes from seeing the world and listening carefully: "Wisdom clarified by experience" (274). Nature (studied attentively) is its own check on folly.

Thoreau is so committed to presenting Walden as a pristine place that he becomes suspicious of any contrivance created to mediate between the human senses and stars or trees. The "professor" must "survey the world through a telescope or a microscope, and never with his natural eye" (94), impoverishing what is seen. Far better to watch "from the observatory of some cliff or tree" (60), where we could "spend more of our days and nights without any obstruction between us and the celestial bodies" (71). His cabin may be necessary for shelter from the elements, but it interferes with clear-sighted observations of "Nature herself" (59): "So much more interesting most familiar objects look out of doors than in the house" (158), and for that reason, he "would rather sit in the open air" (79). Marilyn Chandler imagines Thoreau's cabin this way: "The ideal house would simply be a perching place; real living, the best living, takes place outdoors, as close to nature as it is possible to dwell."[19]

But the implication that humans have never ever affected Walden is something of a charade, however vital it remains for Thoreau to give the place a reality that sits outside human designs. "We need the tonic of wildness" (365), because unspoiled nature stimulates the eye and mind toward profound (and true) insights otherwise unimaginable. He watches for a long time the edge of the pond: "There are few traces of man's hand to be seen. The water laves the shore as it did a thousand years ago" (233). He locates himself in a "forever new and unprofaned part of the universe" (132), an assertion that may only be accurate when the woods are contrasted to Concord coffeehouses (where nothing sacred could possibly happen). Wild? Thoreau could concentrate on the "vespers" "chanted" by the "whippoorwills" only "after the evening train had gone by" (169) on the line from Boston through Concord to Fitchburg, the tracks running up against the pond's bank—right through his idyll. Humans long ago logged these woods, and Thoreau admitted that he had also cut down a tree or two: "since the woodcutters, and the railroad, and I myself have profaned Walden" (245). He apologizes for the intrusion, and moves on: "Before I had done I was more the friend than the foe of the pine tree, though I had cut down some of them, having become better acquainted with it" (85). The place was wild enough for Thoreau's purposes, and it cannot be forgotten that *Walden* remains a book of "determined authorship and personal myth making," writes David Robinson.[20]

"Thoreau makes his reader believe that . . . he has not appropriated [the Pond's] 'facts' to his symbolic convenience, but," writes Walls, "has let nature articulate herself, through him, the poet of Walden."[21] But his challenge in the book is not merely to record a few observations about fish and fowl, but to change the lives of his readers in Concord and beyond—offering a "manual for self-reform."[22] "Each observation, each understanding was imbued with [moral] judgment," Alfred Tauber suggests.[23] How can his tale of a meadow mouse snug in a snow bank (312) render actionable lessons for human conduct? His painterly accounts of the wild become meaningful parables because humans are just as much the creation of "the Artist" as ants; what we see in nature is us: "Shall I not have intelligence with the earth? Am I not partly leaves and vegetable mould myself?" (183). "I go and come with a strange liberty in Nature, a part of herself" (174). The recommendation to "simplify, simplify" gets justified by its grounding in a life pattern that humans (if only wiser) could choose to share with wild animals and plants: "Let us first be as simple and well as Nature ourselves" (122). "A lake . . . is earth's eye; looking into which the beholder measures the depth of his own nature" (233). Thoreau wants to give his readers fresh understandings that they have not already devised or learned for themselves, even though (in a way) they have always had those "same" woods, trees, birds, mice, and fish all around them. The familiar must become strange: "Not till we are completely lost, or turned around—for a man needs only to be turned around once with his eyes shut in this world to be lost—do we appreciate the vastness and strangeness of Nature" (217). The pond has always been "out there," but "we must see [it] as new,"[24] so that "the known becomes the unknown, . . . strange to us, in the very midst of the familiar."[25]

———•———

Becoming Native to this Place
«WES JACKSON[26]»

The stranger . . . often receives the most surprising revelations.
«GEORG SIMMEL[27]»

The water of Walden Pond is unique, but so is every other body of water, or drop, or place; and as universal.
«STANLEY CAVELL[28]»

If you "turn around" too many times with your eyes closed, you get dizzy. Some Concordians probably believed that this is exactly what had happened to Thoreau, after more than two years living as a hermit in the woods. To observe the familiar as strange runs the risk of making everything look baffling, and the author does not help matters by writing: "We require that all things be mysterious and unexplorable, . . . unsurveyed and unfathomed by us because unfathomable" (365–66). Thoreau has an antidote for the reasonable conclusion that he has lost his bearings—he gives Walden Pond and Concord another credibilizing feature: it is home.

Thoreau was born in Concord in 1817, lived almost all of his life there, and died there in 1862. He draws on this lifetime familiarity with the place to establish himself as a reliable observer, capable of noticing changes in nature that can be seen only after extended periods of time: "When I was four years old, as I well remember, I was brought from Boston to this my native town, through these very woods and this field, to the pond. It is one of the oldest scenes stamped on my memory" (201). The pond held different attractions for him back then: "Formerly I had come to this pond adventurously, from time to time, in dark summer nights, with a companion, and making a fire close to the water's edge, which we thought attracted the fishes, we caught pouts with a bunch of worms strung on a thread. . . . But now I had made my home by the shore" (221–22). He converts nativity into believability: "I can speak from an unusually complete experience" (261), having "travelled a good deal in Concord" (46). Travel to more distant places was rare. He sauntered off to the Maine woods and to Cape Cod, and wrote up his findings, but Concord remained his center of gravity for a lifetime. He is less sure of himself, less sure of his grasp on reality, the farther away he gets from Walden Pond: "He who is only a traveller learns things at second-hand and by the halves, and is poor authority" (258). Thoreau does not trust travelers, having "read one or two shallow books of travel . . . till that employment made me ashamed of myself, and I asked where it was then that *I* lived" (145). The answer is always Concord and its close but wild environs, the only place where he could become an "expert in home-cosmography" (369).

Having hung around Walden Pond for so long, Thoreau is in a position to detect changes over time—but it isn't exactly clear what might have changed: the pond or Thoreau, neither or both? Its shoreline has been part of his life for "more than twenty years" (240): "I have spent many an hour, when I was younger . . . having paddled my boat to the middle, and lying on my back across the seats, in a summer forenoon, dreaming awake, until I was aroused by the boat touching the sand" (239). Later in life, the more observant student of shorelines notices change: "I can remember when it was a foot or two lower, and also when it was at least five feet higher, than when I lived by it" (227). For Thoreau to conclude that the shoreline of pond "out there" really did move, year to year, relative to terra firma, would be consonant with his preference for learning directly from "Nature herself" without intrusion from human imagination or technical contrivance. At the same time, in order for this native place that is so familiar to become strange enough to be knowable with fresh eyes, the observer (and the author) must change—implying perhaps that the pond and its shoreline do not: "It is itself unchanged, the same water which my youthful eyes fell on; all the change is in me. . . . Why, here is Walden, the same woodland lake that I discovered so many years ago" (240). Thoreau is playing both sides of the fence. As a native, he knows this place like the back of his hand (so he is a trustworthy guide, with a "narrator's authority"[29])—but he needs it also to be strange (or at least different) in order to go beyond a desensitizing familiarity that would yield only conformity with received wisdom. Buell suggests that Thoreau must simultaneously keep "alive a sense of strangeness" about the pond and its inhabitants, while at the same time emphasizing that he knows the place so well because it has always been home: "Without novelty, place would lapse into banality; but without the element of repetition, Thoreau would not have thought so consciously about the muskrats as part of the spirit of the place."[30] It may not be "worth the while to go round the world to count the cats in Zanzibar" (370) if one has the ability to become a stranger on his own homeground.

Staying home, however, raises the possibility of provincialism (itself a place-saturated affliction). Maybe the rest of the world is just not like Concord. Maybe Walden Pond is a poor bellwether for reality. Thoreau admits as much: "Thank Heaven, here is not all the world. The buck-eye does not grow in New England, and the mocking-bird is rarely heard here" (368). And he worries about it: "I fear chiefly lest my expression may not be *extravagant*[31] enough, may not wander far enough beyond the narrow limits of my daily experience, so as to be adequate to the truth of which I have been convinced" (372). But he rights the ship by making "here" ubiquitous, and sails ever more confidently toward credibility: "Olympus is but the outside of the earth every where" (129). Walden is as good as any place for accessing divine truth, because its essential discoverable features are not only typical but universal: "I cannot come nearer to God and heaven / Than I live to Walden even" (241). Having drawn on his home-familiarity to establish the authenticity of his claims (as opposed to those of mere travelers), Thoreau now hopes to avoid being hemmed in by the place: "I desire to speak somewhere *without* bounds" (373), to find "Nature's universal" (183). Walden's beach has innumerable grains of sand, so to speak, and "thus it seemed that this one hillside illustrated the principle of all the operations of Nature" (356). Walden *is* Zanzibar, and everywhere else, in terms of what one can learn there: "Men esteem truth remote, in the outskirts of the system. . . . In eternity there is indeed something true and sublime. But all these times and places and occasions are now and here" (141).

————·————

"Thoreau" is today an industry, complete with quotable T-shirts and coffee mugs. The Thoreau Society convenes annual meetings to discuss *Walden* and other works, and runs a shop where you can buy souvenirs. The pond and surrounding woods are a state reservation, without much development. In 1967, the US Postal Service put Thoreau on a five-cent commemorative stamp, designed by the celebrated artist Leonard Baskin. Erudite books on Thoreau appear annually, each trying to find something new in what he wrote. Don Henley of the Eagles called the place "a cultural treasure," and raised money to keep it sacred.[32] The Book is required reading for students everywhere. The Pond has become a pilgrimage destination for old hippies, political nonconformists, environmentalists, stray philosophers, and ordinary fans—who all compete for nearby parking with locals seeking cool waters on a hot summer's day.

We trust Thoreau—but why? We believe what he says about loons even if we have never seen one in the feathers, but only through his sedulous account. Simply put, he found the perfect place to rest his case. The pond is far enough away from society to enable apprehension without convention: fresh eyes. The author textually constructs a place made to confront him as a reality that forces itself upon his mind and pen: he is not making up this stuff.

And it is his home, with all of its up-close familiarity but none of its parochialism, for here becomes everywhere. Walden does not make us believe the way that Delphi convinced the ancient Greeks of the oracle's truth. Thoreau built a hut and not a temple, a modest place designed more to blend in with the natural surrounds than to defy the threatening power of Parnassus. The connections between place and truth do not always line up the same way, from case to case. So . . . next comes a man who moves around a lot among different kinds of places, and in doing so, acquires the same measure of credibility for his ideas that Thoreau acquired by staying put.

3

Linnaeus's Credibilizing Transit

Anna Pavord's resplendent book on botanical taxonomy—*The Naming of Names*—ends its history just when things get really interesting. To be sure, there is nothing uninteresting about the previous two millennia of attempts to attach a nomenclature to the world of plants, from Theophrastus in classical Greece to the early modern Cambridge plantsman John Ray. But by the mid-eighteenth century, Pavord is plainly bored, allowing Carl Linnaeus to enter her book only "grudgingly" on page 395. Linnaeus's sin is science, his systematic pursuit of logical and orderly standardization, which brought to an end the preceding "superstition" that Pavord finds fascinating.[1]

The enticing question for me is how Linnaeus (a.k.a. Carl von Linné) managed to create a taxonomic system that soon achieved near-universal application, in the face of rival scientists from rival places offering viable alternative classifications. His Latinized binomial code for naming plants—genus and species, *Tulipa cypria*—is more or less what everybody uses today, though DNA analysis has replaced very careful comparisons of a flower's sexual organs as the scientific basis of sorting.[2] To rush to the conclusion that Linnaeus triumphed because his taxonomy inherently did a better job at giving order to plants than any other system begs the question: how did Linnaeus's system for naming plants come to be accepted by experts and eventually by everybody as preferable and authoritative? Or, simply, *where* did Linnaeus get his credibility?

Some say that Linnaeus succeeded because his system was simple to use, his rules and instructions for sorting were easily applied by anybody with a modicum of botanical training; others say that success followed from the generative and almost limitless character of his system, which could find the right space for any and all of the new genera and species arriving almost daily in eighteenth-century Europe from around the globe;[3] still others say that his system captured the zeitgeist "with the ruthless efficiency of a computer program."[4] Linnaeus's system was not created out of the blue: key elements were borrowed from other botanists (including Sébastien Vaillant's emphasis on the sexual parts of plants and Gaspard Bauhin's anticipation of the binomial classification).[5] But these virtues—utility, simplicity, accessibility, elasticity, precision, corrigibility,[6] and at least a little originality—are not intrinsic aspects of Linnaeus's classifications so much as latterly attributions by those who joined his growing legion of devotees. Explanation of Linnaeus's triumph is less likely to be found inside the substance of his taxonomy than in the moments of his life and in particular the places he traveled.

Linnaeus's system was not the only game in town, nor was it instantly embraced by all (slowest among the French). There may have been as many as fifty rival taxonomic systems floating around Europe in the eighteenth century, based on different principles for clustering living organisms, each with its enthusiasts, and each assigning different labels to plants and animals. Joseph Pitton de Tournefort's classification, which Linnaeus learned in school, was based on the arrangement of a flower's petals—but it was soon to be "neatly demolished" by the sexual system.[7] Linnaeus's early works were burned by the Vatican, and excoriated by pious readers throughout Europe, because of their indelicate discussions of the sex lives of plants and Linnaeus's penchant for describing reproduction of flowers in steamy anthropocentric ways (or because of the pretense of assuming that any human categorization could capture God's own orderings[8]). St. Petersburg academician Johann Siegesbeck denounced the system as "lewd" and full of "loathsome harlotry": "Who would have thought that bluebells, lilies and onions could be up to such immorality?"[9] Georges-Louis Leclerc, Comte de Buffon's philosophical criticism was more serious, accusing Linnaeus "of the primary error of confusing arbitrary genera, as entities of reason, with physical and real genera."[10] Was order in nature or in the mind of the naturalist? Oxford botanist Johann Jacob Dillenius joins the critics: "A new botanist is arisen in the North, founder of a new method, based on the stamens and pistils, whose name is Linnaeus. . . . He is a Swede, and has travelled over Lapland. He has a thorough insight and knowledge of Botany, but I am afraid his method will not hold."[11] Though Dillenius was not convinced, and his prediction completely off the mark, his references to the places where Linnaeus came from (Sweden, Lapland) offer a clue about how and why opponents were eventually won over, or forced to go along with the tidal wave of adherents. Even a new pope in Rome adopted Linnaeus's system in his public lectures.

How can we explain Linnaeus's triumph, besting rivals, vanquishing opponents, overcoming criticism? The massive historical literature on Linnaeus provides few straight answers. Biographies veer toward hagiography (especially Swedish ones: Linnaeus adorns the 100 kronor note, still) or exposé. For every work that finds the man to be a faultless seeker of truth and a steadfast advocate for a prosperous Sweden, we have Linnaeus as mired in masculinist fantasies of his day and all too eager to impose gendered assumptions about men and women on helpless plants (some plant marriages were clandestine);[12] or as an ethnocentrist who saw the "happy Lapps" as lazy primitives; or as contributor to the pernicious pursuit of empire in which the naming of plants is less about scientific tidiness and more about colonial exploitation—a kind of "bioprospecting" and "linguistic imperialism";[13] or (as biographer Lisbet Koerner puts it) as one "who understood his science to be a legitimation and a technique of state governance"; or as one focused on "the economy of nature"[14] (exotic plants grown in Sweden could become new agricultural cash crops); or as a "second Adam," an arrogant self-promoter of his own prowess with an insatiable lust for fame (Linnaeus described his own *Species plantarum* [1753] as "the greatest achievement in the realm of science");[15] or (in a very different register) a rude country bumpkin from the uncivilized Nordic regions.[16] Linnaeus is probably all of that and more, but none of these characterizations explain how he succeeded in getting his own systematics accepted by almost everybody everywhere.

It helps to examine how Linnaeus pursued, acquired, and displayed credibility—within the scientific community and beyond—to better understand how his nomenclature eventually commanded assent. I pick up a suggestion by David N. Livingstone that we examine the "life geography" of scientists: "Greater awareness of the spaces of biography, of the places of identity, of the geography of selfhood, would enormously enrich our understanding of the mutual making of science and scientist."[17] I follow Linnaeus as he transits through a series of credibilizing spaces, acquiring and accumulating—with the time passed in each—perceived expertise and trustworthiness that lent legitimacy to his proposed conventions for naming plants. I shall consider how Linnaeus's identity as the authoritative "prince of plants" was shaped in and through his stay in Lapland; in (and around) Leiden; and back in Sweden, at Uppsala. Each specific place illustrates a more general category of truth-spot: Lapland is a field site; Leiden is a collection of both natural specimens and discerning experts; Uppsala is a demonstration and pulpit. Each spot affords credibility in different ways—via its geographic location, material conditions assembled there, spatial organization and reputation—and Linnaeus's peripatetic genius was his ability to gather believability from all three.

———•———

I damn near died.

«CLIFFORD GEERTZ *on his fieldwork at Java in 1952*[18]»

Each experience of a wild place jabs us in the ribs and takes us by surprise.
«EDWARD S. CASEY[19]»

To fieldworkers, it was *presence*, not absence, *closeness*, not distance, that underwrote their claims to authenticity.
«DAVID N. LIVINGSTONE[20]»

In 1732, at age twenty-five, and as a student of medicine at Uppsala University, Linnaeus headed north, into Lapland—wild Sweden, its mythological heart and soul, home of the Sami people, home also to flora (and fauna) waiting to be discovered by science, and named. Nobody before him had sought to be scientific about Lapland, and while tramping about the woods, he collected seeds, pressed flowers, and made copious drawings with descriptive annotations. His notes contextualized the plants, providing details about their exotic growing conditions and requirements in situ (even though his goal in gathering them up was to recontextualize them later in an artificial and contrived place: botanical gardens in Holland and eventually Uppsala).[21] He experienced unadulterated nature in its pristine state, unblemished by experiment or theory, up close and personal—and unlike Thoreau at the Pond, for there was no railroad running through Lapland. He returned to Uppsala with new knowledge about previously unknown plants, in his possession alone—at a historical moment when the collection and identification of new specimens were, within the scientific community, at a fever pitch. In Lapland, Linnaeus laid the groundwork for his later reputation by contributing firsthand to what was valued most by the community of naturalists throughout Europe: increasing the number of plants "known to science." These specimens would open doors at Leiden three years later, once he came in from the wild and moved on to the epicenter of all things botanical.

Linnaeus was no "armchair theorist" who sorted and named only from the comfort of a botanical garden or herbarium (like some of his rivals), but rather a "hero" who endured the risks and privations of spending time in the dangerous wild—for the cause of science: "Field naturalists . . . [are] validated by their heroism in physically encountering and overcoming distance from metropolitan centres."[22] Although historians of Linnaeus, even those given to hero worship, admit that he imaginatively trumped up his survival struggles in Lapland (and exaggerated the number of kilometers he walked—supposedly 4,000 km!—because, quite literally, he would be recompensed for each step taken), such depictions of harsh conditions and perilous moments would do wonders to establish him as "Linnaeus of the North" (*Linnaea borealis*—common name: Twinflower). His published version of the journey is full of trials: "I, who was already ill and exhausted from such great exertions and long journeying, from carrying my own baggage (for the Lapp carried the boat), from sleepless nights, from having no cooked food and from drinking too much water (since there was nothing else to drink and nothing to eat but unsalted and often maggoty fish)—I would have died had it not been for a scrap of dried and salted reindeer's flesh which the pastor's wife had given me, though without bread it was very bad for the stomach and was evacuated undigested."[23] For Linnaeus, as for the anthropologist Clifford Geertz, exposing oneself to the risks of the wild field site, even facing death, makes hard-won claims from there all the more believable (things of real value come at a price).

Why do scientists go to "the field"—and what exactly do they bring back? Think of other famous field scientists and their exotic place-attachments: Margaret Mead in Samoa; Jane Goodall at Gombe Stream in Tanzania; Charles Darwin in the Galápagos Islands;[24] John Tyndall scaling the Alps.[25] Whether for botanical, anthropological, ethnological, geophysical, or any other scientific purpose, fieldwork at its core involves "physically leaving 'home' (however that is defined) to travel in and out of some distinctly *different* setting," "taking distance" "to get out of the house."[26] It requires changing places, movement to a location that holds potentially revealing mysteries important for science. Going to the field offers "privileged access to nature, to reality, and to knowledge," and allows the researcher "to lay claim to entire *categories* of natural objects and phenomena."[27] That privilege is earned in part by the "proximate and intimate" nature of fieldwork: "because we have lived some part of our lives there."[28] Moreover, field scientists assert objectivity for their observations in the wild because of the "'pregiven' status of nature in its pure form—untouched by human hands."[29] Objects in the field appear to have been simply come upon in their pristine state of nature. Scientists return from the field with specimens and data, but also with an authority won by "being there"—presenting themselves (in some cases) as the only scientist to have been to that unique spot, seen the stuff then and there, which is then fashioned into a scientific treasure trove for which the intrepid visitor becomes the sole interlocutor, all the while enduring risk and hardship. They bring back from terra incognito scientific chops and formerly unknown specimens and facts—the wherewithal of persuasiveness and later fame.

The ability of "the field" to serve as an authoritative place for making credible scientific knowledge has, especially in the natural sciences, declined since Linnaeus walked through Lapland. No truth-spot can secure permanent and universal believability for claims attached to that place (there are limits). With the rise of the laboratory as a preferred site for scientific discovery starting in the nineteenth century, the constraints and liabilities of field science were exposed: a pristine state of nature becomes something messy and uncontrollable; the up-close and personal witnessing of nature by the field investigator becomes a single set of fallible eyes perhaps biased or out of focus; the unique particulars found right there become a shaky foundation on which to build generalized understandings that apply everywhere; collecting and comparing specimens become less revealing of nature's secrets than experimental intervention in a lab; the fleeting venture to the field becomes an inability to replicate the process of discovery; even the wild becomes, with technological prowess, tame and less exotic. Fifty-five years after Margaret Mead published *Coming of Age in Samoa*, Derek Freeman questioned the credibility of Mead's fieldwork, raising the possibility that she may have been duped by her informants into believing things about Samoan adolescent sexuality that were just not so (but conveniently aligned with Mead's politics and cultural relativism). Freeman went back to Mead's field, back to Samoa, and talked to contemporary informants who implied that Mead had got it wrong—but *his* news from the field was itself vigorously challenged, in part through a rereading of Mead's own field notes.[30] We have today become suspicious of the field as a truth-spot (and for that reason, going to the field has become more like moving the lab outside, a point explored in chapter 8).

Linnaeus had fewer worries. He carried Lapland with him as a badge when he prepared for his next way station in Holland. He brought specimens and notebooks, of course, as well as incipient taxonomies based on variations among the new plants that he observed and gathered in the Swedish woods. It would be vital for Linnaeus to connect both specimens and taxonomies to his stay in Lapland as a place of provenance, in order to establish their authenticity and believability: "Field observations . . . without clear provenance had greatly diminished value."[31] *Flora Lapponica* includes an engraved frontispiece that undeniably situates brave Linnaeus among the Sami natives, and among the reindeer and exotic plants found in the Nordic north. It is an embarrassingly fanciful depiction, surely seen as contrived even by eighteenth-century readers—but no matter. Who would doubt that Linnaeus was really there and so spoke with the experiential authority of confronting plants and dangers in the wild? For good measure, Linnaeus also brought to Holland the accoutrements of Sami life—native garb, the hat, skins, pointy-up boots, shaman's drum, and the Twinflower—which he dons to sit for a portrait commissioned by his Dutch patron George Clifford. Patricia Fara writes in her book *Sex, Botany, and Empire*:

> Linnaeus was masquerading as an exotic indigenous person, a tactic that had the effect of reinforcing his true status as an imperial possessor. Any Sami could (if foolhardy enough) have told Linnaeus how ridiculous he looked. His beret, a present from a Swedish tax collector, was suitable for women in the summer. His winter fur jacket, which he had bought in Uppsala, came from a different region, and

his reindeer leather boots were made not to wear but to export for rich, gullible southerners. His shaman's drum—another gift—was an illegal possession. To complete the look, Linnaeus dangled assorted tourist souvenirs from his belt.[32]

However fake, the "look" convinced George Clifford for one, and served as an authentic foundation on which Linnaeus would build his reputation as botanical maven.

———•———

If I can make it there, I'll make it anywhere.
«FRANK SINATRA *on New York*»

Scientists who go to the field must return from there in order to cash in on the credibility obtained by facing the special challenges and opportunities of the wild. Geertz writes: "In itself, Being There is a postcard experience ('I've been to Katmandu—have you?'). It is Being Here, a scholar among scholars, that gets your anthropology read . . . published, reviewed, cited, taught."[33] Same for Linnaeus (and his botany), who just had to go to Leiden in 1735, now age twenty-eight (where he would pick up a medical degree). It will become for him a "locus imprimatur," a place of approval and distinction enabled by the fact that Leiden then was a research epicenter: bringing together a collection of plant specimens second to none as well as a collection of naturalists who were the global experts in the medicinal uses and morphology of those plants.

It seems anachronistic to use a conceptual framework devised for the twenty-first-century global information network to describe the scene at Leiden three centuries before—but it works. Manuel Castells suggests that information flows through communication networks linking specific nodes or hubs that agglomerate and concentrate the business services, the entrepreneurs, and the skillful scientists and engineers on which a postindustrial economy depends—think New York or London for finance or real estate, Silicon Valley for biotechnology.[34] These "global cities"[35] or "milieux of innovation"—mapped out to form a "geography of genius"[36]—are increasingly designed and built to serve as docking stations for the ideas, data, and prototypes that circulate globally at warp speed. With videoconferencing and other digitally mediated forms of communication, it may be less vital that any individual player is corporeally *there* in the magnet city—but in that respect, Leiden in the eighteenth century is rather unlike Shanghai today. In a way, you had to be there.

Instead of terabytes and DNA strands whooshing across the planet and settling at a node only for as long as it takes to capitalize on them, it was—in Linnaeus's time—plants, seeds, dried flowers, and their scientific descriptions from everywhere that made their way back mostly to the Netherlands (and largely for the same reason: money). Although tulipomania had taken Holland by storm just a century before, the eighteenth-century global circulation of plant matter that made Amsterdam and Leiden its preferred destination was less about the ornamental value of pretty flowers (and the status of their owners) than about their potential utility for medicine (herbals were big then). The Dutch exploited their mastery of the high seas and spice monopolies granted to the United (Dutch) East India Company to gather up from exotic places anything of possible value that could fit on a ship and survive the journey back to the metropole.[37] As a result, by the time Linnaeus arrived, Dutch gardens had assembled the largest number of plant species in Europe—more than 3,000 different kinds by 1685. Leiden's *hortus academicus* dates to 1587, and under Clusius's direction starting in 1593, it crammed more than 1,000 different plants into a space 35 by 40 meters.[38] With specimens brought from Lapland, Linnaeus added to that stock, but in exchange, he got access to the raw materials he would need to show that his classification system actually worked, uniquely collected for him in the unparalleled gardens of Leiden.

Botanical gardens belong to a category of truth-spots best labeled "collections," along with zoos and libraries (museums are also collections, and those are explored in chapter 4). Gardens collect specimens of plants, to be sure, but how exactly do they make people believe claims about nature that come from there?[39] Collections lend credibility precisely through their contrivance and, ironically, their artificiality. They sacrifice the contextuality of a plant in the wild—the soil in which it grows, altitude, orientation to the sun, hours of light, available water—but in exchange for powerfully persuasive epistemic gains. Collections allow side-by-side comparisons of specimens no longer separated by ocean or continent, with presumably less privation and risk than in the field, and in a more patient manner because the botanist is not a transient in this place (as Linnaeus was in Lapland). Specimens in gardens are preserved, so that repeated comparisons can extend over long periods of time and as new additions to the collection arrive from all over (a stand-in for experimental replication).

But there is more, as Michel Foucault suggests in his analysis of classical "natural history," a kind of science dependent on observation, comparison, and classification. Gardens arrange and give order to plants based on whatever the botanist considers interesting as a basis of same/different (for Linnaeus, sexual organs)—an order altogether invisible when one looks at a field of wildflowers: "The documents of this new history are not other words, texts or records, but unencumbered spaces in which things are juxtaposed: herbariums, collections, gardens; the locus of this history is a non-temporal rectangle in which, stripped of all commentary, of all enveloping language, creatures present themselves one beside another, their surfaces visible, grouped according to their common features, and thus already virtually analyzed, and bearers of nothing but their own individual names." The power of the garden as a site of truth-making rests on a classic Foucauldian paradox: "This process of obliteration, they allow to emerge: they screen off anatomy and function, they conceal the organism, in order to raise up before the eyes of those who await the truth the visible relief of forms, with their elements, their mode of distribution, and their measurements."[40] Qualities of the plant in its natural home are hidden in order to put in high relief the features that define its orderly spot in some imposed taxonomy. The materiality of a botanical garden carries a believability all its own (but not exactly like Delphi or Walden): plants actually found in Suriname or Sweden but grown out in Leiden carry an authenticity more difficult for a skeptic to challenge than, say, an account of what some field-worker saw in the wild. However contrived the assemblage and ordering of specimens, the plants themselves have a palpable reality, available for anyone's inspection: "Only the keenest and most experienced observer—who had, like Linnaeus, inspected thousands of different specimens—was qualified to distinguish genuine species from mere varieties, to identify the true specific characters imprinted in the plant, and to separate accidental from essential features."[41]

Dutch gardens, then, become Linnaeus's taxonomic playground and surely the right place for the job of pitching his sexual system of classification. One garden in particular paid the freight. Not far from Leiden, George Clifford built an estate named Hartekamp, with riches gained from his role as director of the Dutch East India Company—a position that afforded Clifford the means to amass an impressive garden and herbarium with specimens from all over. Clifford hired Linnaeus to bring order to his collection of plants (and possibly to cure his depression and other ailments, with herbal remedies). Bolstered by the publication of *Systema naturae* in 1735 (just twelve pages long, but with the germ of all that would came later), Linnaeus fully appreciated the opportunities that Clifford's patronage allowed. He was almost broke, and plainly he preferred to stay in comfort in Holland than go collecting in southern Africa, the alternative. Clifford's collection allowed an opportunity to reconstruct a garden that could exhibit his budding taxonomy in the plants themselves—row after row of different genera and species, arrayed by Linnaeus's understanding of their pistils and stamens. "Clifford was much impressed by Linnaeus's ability to classify Indian plants that were new to him, simply by opening a flower and examining its parts. As for Linnaeus, he was seized with a sudden longing to be in-vited to take charge of this wonderful garden and its hothouses and to have the run of Clifford's fine library and herbarium."[42] Clifford's collection allowed for Hartekamp to become the material embodiment in paths, dirt, and flowers of an otherwise abstract table of categories in a catalogue, as it "provided both the stimulus and the material for the construction of systems of taxonomy and naming."[43] It was a tangible and visitable place available for personal witnessing by those who might doubt the legitimacy of Linnaean nomenclature. And the skeptics, soon to be won over, were formidable.

Leiden accumulated not only the widest array of plant species, but also the most influential and demanding bunch of botanists in Europe. It did not start out so well for Linnaeus. The celebrated chemist, physician, and botanist Herman Boerhaave initially "considered the young Swede bumptious and pushing," and he turned down Linnaeus's invitation to write a preface for *Flora Lapponica*. Two years later, having been convinced by "Linnaeus of the North" and by the rearrangements of plants at Hartekamp, Boerhaave consented to have *Genera plantarum* dedicated to him—"thus assuring it of an auspicious start."[44] Jan Frederik Gronovius, another Dutch botanist, who eventually blessed the sexual system and provided support for publication of *System naturae*, wrote in Linnaeus's *liber amicorum*: "With this parting gift I bid farewell to the most famous and learned man, Doctor CAROLUS LINNAEUS—pre-eminent on account of the several very dangerous journeys which he has undertaken for the benefit of the community—journeys during which he so felicitously investigated the three kingdoms of Nature."[45] Leiden is a pivotal place for Linnaeus, marking his transition from Swedish collector of Lapland specimens to famous author of the book of names for all plants. How so? "By the influence of Leyden I mean, of course, the power exerted *here* through the teaching and example of such men (Boerhaave, Gronovius), by the spoken word and demonstrations of living plants in the botanic garden."[46]

As the toughest court Linnaeus would face on his way to fame and glory, Leiden at the time was an example of a scholarly epicenter that required "being there" to prove one's mettle. Göttingen (Germany) in the 1920s was another such place for the discipline of mathematics, with Felix Klein and David Hilbert ruling the roost: "Even budding geniuses, like Norbert Wiener and Max Born, could be scarred by the daunting experience of facing the hypercritical audiences that gathered at the weekly meetings of the Göttingen Mathematical Society."[47] The place itself mattered fundamentally in the creation of credible mathematical claims.

Physical copresence was vital in a culture of knowledge-making that relied more on oral communication than print, on the immediate give-and-take of the latest fresh idea (perhaps during hikes in the surrounding countryside or in the Schwarzer Bär bar), and on the cultivation of trust and real-time emergence of reputations. Sociologists have generalized the point: "Copresence is 'thick' with information. . . . For actors . . . to achieve solidarity and truth, there must be a minimum amount of space between them."[48] Young mathematicians "flocked to Göttingen from everywhere"[49] for the same reason that Linnaeus had to go to Leiden: to earn their spurs. Such recognized centers of specialized inquiry—inevitably a temporary kind of truth-spot—are places where believable claims (and believable scholars) can be sorted out from the dross by those present who already possess sufficient standing in a field to pull it off: "In order to achieve the status of knowledge, claims had to be produced in the right place and had to be validated by the right public."[50]

A measure of the extent to which Linnaeus "made it" in Leiden is the number of gardens that were eventually dug up and rearranged so that the plants could be properly relocated in the taxonomic niches that Linnaeus named. That happened even at the Oxford Botanic Garden, founded in 1621, attesting to an English ratification of the sexual system. In 1790, the French put a statue of Linnaeus in the Jardin des Plantes, which the critic Buffon had supervised for years.[51] Linnaeus's success is also evident in a remark by one of his Swedish epigones, the botanist Adam Afzelius: scientists "sought him as a small oracle."[52] But in order to make his taxonomic conquest complete, Linnaeus needed to build his own Delphi, in Uppsala.

———·———

Intellectual sacred objects can be created and sustained only if there are ceremonial gatherings to worship them.

«RANDALL COLLINS[53]»

The truth of the lecturer's knowledge was established through observing a demonstration.

«ANDREW BARRY[54]»

With the publication of *Hortus Cliffortianus* in 1737 (a catalogue of the collection arranged by the sexual system), Linnaeus's exploitation of the plants and people assembled in Leiden was complete. He returned to Sweden in 1739, first to Stockholm for a short unsatisfying stint as a practicing physician (specializing in gonorrhea), then two years later to a university post at Uppsala, where he continued to enlarge *Species plantarum*, his masterwork of taxonomy. He replicated (on a smaller scale) the "table" of plants that he had arranged for Mr. Clifford, constructing the University's first botanical garden and orangerie, immediately adjacent to his residence (which also served as a herbarium, library, laboratory, lecture hall, and seminar room). His challenge now was different: to attract young scientists who would carry his increasingly authoritative taxonomic system to the ends of the earth, and bring back still more exotic specimens—to be named by Linnaeus, of course, the "final single arbiter of flora,"[55] and to be studied for possible medical, agricultural, or other economic benefits.

For that purpose, Linnaeus built at Uppsala a third kind of truth-spot: a site for disseminating the "sacred object" to those who would universalize his sexual system. He fashioned a "pulpit" for himself, a special place that lends credibility to those who speak from there (rather than from any old street corner)—like the bishop at Uppsala Cathedral not far from Linnaeus's new garden (where the botanist would be buried in 1778). He had to attract potential converts to Uppsala (and thus make it into a magnet, a new node in the global network of circulating plants and correspondents), and once they arrived, convince them to believe. Linnaeus needed a place for show-and-tell. The garden materialized his abstract classifications (in effect, a mimesis of nature): the plants were arranged according to Linnaean rules, and starting in the nineteenth century, each one was labeled with a Roman numeral (I–XXIV) to indicate its order, which (along with the genus and species) was penned on a slate, and stuck in the soil beside the path (many of them with a big *L* to indicate that Linnaeus himself was the first to provide its scientific description). It was a site for demonstration and instruction: see, it works! Linnaeus at Uppsala could show his students exactly how the stamens and pistils on these flowers were different from those, and also give lessons to prepare them for their global foraging (for example, how to fold paper into a sealed envelope so that seeds collected from afar would not fall out on the way home).

Even within the circumscribed world of "botany," Linnaeus's gardens at Uppsala are hardly unique as a demonstration place that makes people believe the truth about a scientific theory or practice. Sir Albert Howard, Imperial Economic Botanist, was stationed in India (with his wife, Gabrielle, also a scientist) during the first three decades of the twentieth century, and charged with improving the quality and maximizing the quantity of foodstuffs and cotton shipped back to Britain. In 1924, the Howards designed and built the Institute of Plant Industry at Indore as an embodiment of their growing commitment to "holistic" agriculture—and, in particular, as a place where scientific methods of composting organic waste could be demonstrated for area cultivators and zamindars (who would, presumably, emulate what they saw and learned there).[56] In the United States, starting at roughly the same time, the cooperative extension program of the University of California established plots for conducting field trials (actually called "demonstrations") of preferred agricultural practices—located on sites near the places where commercial farming happened. One grower told sociologist Christopher Henke: "While we trust extension . . . there's nothing like seeing it with your own eyes to, to say, 'This really does work.' . . . Like turning a light on in a dark room."[57] Starting in 1980, Charles, Prince of Wales, decided to bring Sir Albert Howard's message closer to home, by adopting and displaying organic principles at Highgrove House, his estate in Gloucestershire, complete with compost pits. Prince Charles realized that his green efforts at Highgrove are "one very small attempt to heal the appalling short-sighted damage done to the soil, the landscape and our own souls"; but about 30,000 people visit the gardens and pits each year, taking away souvenirs and credible lessons.[58] *Do* try this at home!

Those who came to Uppsala and left for the world with diverse skills—how to fold envelopes for collecting seeds, how to inspect a flower to decide if its reproductive organs indicated a plant new to science—were known as Linnaeus's "apostles" (he called them that himself). The risks and potential rewards of going out to the field had shifted from Linnaeus to his students: he stayed home and gathered credit for having devised the one true system for naming plants. He demanded a lot from his students: they must be willing to sleep "on the hardest bench as on the softest bed, but to find a little plant or moss the longest road wouldn't be too long"[59]—but he sometimes repaid them by naming a genus after a favored apostle. Daniel Solander sailed with Captain James Cook on his first trip around the world. Two died in transit from tropical fevers in the South Pacific, making very real the risks of "going to the field." Pehr Kalm spent more than two years collecting specimens in eastern North America, and "returned to Stockholm with a magnificent collection of pressed plants and seeds. Linnaeus, ill though he was with a sharp attack of gout, waited 'as impatiently as a bride awaits one in the morning' for a sight of these treasures; so excited was he that he quite forgot his aches and pains and rose from his sickbed to welcome his pupil."[60] Linnaeus directed 186 completed doctoral dissertations (he wrote them himself),[61] and twenty-three

of those scholars went on to become university professors themselves, with their own pulpit for spreading the word. Uppsala
was always with them, no matter where they went (and indeed,
they touched every continent). For Johann G. Acrel, an apostle,
"[Linnaeus] never failed to captivate his audiences. He knew
how to emphasize certain words in his short sentences so ex-
pressively that no one could possibly fail to be convinced by his
argument. Those who heard him speak about his Introduction
to the *Systema Naturae*—about God, Man, the Creation, Nature
and so on—were more moved than by the most eloquent ser-
mon."[62] Pulpit indeed!

Uppsala had become a place of cultivation, for plants and for the
next generation of botanists—a place of demonstration, dissemi-
nation, and dispersion. Imagine those "ceremonial gatherings" in
the garden, on the steps of his home: Linnaeus surrounded by devoted students, being made to believe the man's every word. The
journey was complete, and so would be the triumph of Linnaean
botanical nomenclature.

———.———

The place of knowledge lays down conditions for the appearance of the objects
of science, for their validation as real, and for the terms on which they are
knowable.

«ADI OPHIR AND STEVEN SHAPIN[63]»

Scientific truths begin as local things, going global only after
much effort and occasional luck along the way. The eventual uni-
versalization of Linnaeus's system for classifying plants makes it
easy to forget its origins and its dependency upon Lapland wilds,
Leiden gardens, and the demonstrative "gatherings" at Uppsala.
There are two transits here: one took Linnaeus through those
credibilizing places—and because of his accumulating authority on that path, his taxonomic system moved from these three
places of provenance to the entire world, where it stuck. Were it
not for Linnaeus's itinerary, a rose might be called by any other
name (but would smell as sweet).

4

Ford's Potemkin Villages

Impression management: the *successful* staging of . . . false figures involves use of *real* techniques—the same techniques by which everyday persons sustain their real social situations.

«ERVING GOFFMAN[1]»

Which was the greater deceit? In 1787, Prince Grigory Potemkin builds fully artificial and transient villages, complete with painted screens, apparently happy serfs and their livestock, which he constructs, deconstructs and reconstructs five or six times along the Dnieper River, just in advance of Empress Catherine the Great's flotilla, and designed to convince her that Russia's strategy for colonizing and developing the southern provinces is a complete success; *or* Potemkin's courtly rivals and enemies elsewhere who *made all of that up*? So it is that the tag we routinely use today to describe a bogus façade contrived to deceive—"Potemkin Village"—rests precariously on a sham of its own.

Here is probably what happened. Potemkin had actually done a decent job of bringing economic development and stability to Russian territories reaching south to the Black Sea. He anticipated the visit from Catherine, his lover, and began preparations for it as early as 1784, building palaces and sprucing up old houses, perhaps with a fresh coat of paint. His biographer writes:

"One could argue that Potemkin was the inventor of modern political spectacle—but not that he was a fairground huckster."[2] Cattle and sheep evidently would not have survived the repeated migrations down the Dnieper at a pace required to stay in front of the Empress's eighty boats. The peasants, happy or not, would surely have turned out in droves to see Catherine and her 3,000 troops in all their splendor, and probably did not need coaxing from Potemkin. Still, an "embittered Saxon envoy Georg von Helbig . . . coined the phrase 'Potemkinsche Dörfer'" well before Catherine's eyewitness inspection: perhaps he and others were jealous of Potemkin's privileged place in Catherine's court and heart, or perhaps (being inclined to oppose Russian expansion to the south) they suspected that Potemkin had squandered the rubles she lavished upon him.

In a way, it did not matter whether or not Potemkin faked the appearance of successful colonization: pasteboards or brick-and-mortar could have done equally well. What mattered is whether Catherine took those riverside villages as evidence of his successful colonization of the south. And she did, writing to Potemkin on July 13, 1787: "We've been exercising our brains discussing the delightful condition of the places—the provinces and regions—entrusted to you, your labors, successes, effort, zeal and care, and the order that you have established everywhere."[3] Even if von Helbig was right, though, that the villages were all make-believe, what matters is that those villages made Catherine believe. Real or fake, Potemkin's villages served as a truth-spot, validating for Catherine at least that her lover's strategy for Russian expansion was working. It is thus no surprise at all that "Potemkin Villages" have continued to pop up everywhere, discursively and materially, compelling (and sometimes duping) people to believe, ever since the "original." Villages are not especially easy to fake, and for that reason these places work effectively to convince people about the supposed "reality" of some social project or event. Henry Ford knew that it takes a village.

———•———

... true history. These relics of days that are gone tell only truthful tales. They cannot lie.

«HENRY A. HAIGH, *writing in* Michigan History *magazine in 1925, upon seeing objects gathered for what would become Greenfield Village* [4]»

The exhibition . . . creates an effect *called* the real world.

«TIMOTHY MITCHELL[5]»

Why would a man who famously declared that "history is bunk" bother to invest a sizable chunk of his admittedly vast fortune to gather up relics on the cusp of the industrial era—machines and tools of all kinds, and the buildings in which they were used— and move them all to Dearborn, Michigan, where he would establish an immersive open-air museum dedicated to preserving and presenting the past? Actually, Henry Ford used the words "history" and "bunk" conjointly on repeated occasions, sometimes as in "après moi, le déluge," telling the *Chicago Tribune* on May 25, 1916: "History is more or less bunk. It's tradition. We don't want tradition. We want to live in the present and the only history worth a tinker's dam is the history we make today."[6] Elsewhere, the bunkiness of history results from the subjective bias of its teller: "You read a book and it may be just one man's misunderstanding or prejudices. Most history as written is bunk."[7] Or "History is being rewritten every year from a new point of view; so how can anybody claim to know the truth about history?"[8] Ford railed against the emphasis placed upon politics and war in official history-as-written, two endeavors for which he had little admiration, while the lives and accomplishments of those who really shaped history, inventors and industrial entrepreneurs (like himself), were ignored.

Ford built Greenfield Village not because history was unimportant for him, but because it mattered so much that he needed to get it told truthfully and persuasively. Starting in the mid-1920s, on 240 acres not far from the cradle of mass production— the enormous assembly line at River Rouge, downriver from Detroit—Ford spent millions to acquire and move to Michigan the remnants of technological change. Smaller implements like stoves and clocks, but some as large as automobiles (of course) and steam engines, would be housed inside next door at what is now called the Henry Ford Museum of American Innovation. At Greenfield Village, Ford built a replica of a New England town common, surrounded by what one would expect to find in such a village: the chapel at its head, an inn, a school, a doctor's office, a courthouse, the town hall, the general store and other shops, residences, and small factories—each building outfitted with "period" artifacts and some with role-playing interpretive guides. Many buildings were moved lock, stock, and barrel from their original location to Dearborn, while others are replicas constructed on-site. Some buildings are associated with Ford's heroes and their feats: Edison's laboratory and boarding house from Menlo Park, the Wright brothers' home and cycle shop from Dayton, Luther Burbank's birthplace and garden office, and, among recent additions, the entire farmstead where Harvey Firestone grew up, transported from Columbiana, Ohio. To tell his own story, Ford pulled together his home, the Bagley Avenue workshop where it all began, and an early small Ford factory. The Village and Museum were inaugurated in 1929 with a reenactment of Edison's invention of the electric light bulb, and were fully opened to the public in 1933. They attract enormous numbers of tourists and schoolchildren every year. One visitor remarked: "I never knew that Henry Ford, Thomas Edison, and the Wright brothers all lived on the same street."[9]

Ford wanted his visitors to leave Greenfield Village convinced that unending technological progress is the defining feature of American history—and, implicitly, of its future. This would not necessarily be an easy sell during the depths of the Depression, when Ford Motor Company had laid off workers and reduced pay for the rest. The message of the place could not be nostalgia— although, at least in the early years, many visitors were reminded of their own biographical pasts as they wandered among familiar buildings and machines. Rather, Ford's statement at Greenfield Village is that things are better now than ever before, thanks largely to the ingenuity and doggedness of inventors and industrial entrepreneurs. Early tools and simple machines are celebrated mainly for what they augur: improved devices that accomplish the same product or process, only better—faster, more efficiently, and with less human drudgery. With horses and buggies trotting down Main Street, even the casual visitor is made to believe in the linear advancement of human transportation, culminating with the automobiles parked just outside the Village walls (initially, Ford did not allow cars in the Village, but now the place is filled with the put-puts of flivvers and tin lizzies). "To lift farm drudgery off flesh and blood and lay it on steel and motors has been my most constant ambition," Ford said in the twenties.[10] Whom should one thank for such progress? Certainly not politicians or financiers: Greenfield Village has no bank, and government buildings are strictly for local proceedings rather than national or global. Edison, the Wright brothers, Burbank, and Ford are here because *they* changed history for the better, or so the visitor is led to believe.

At the same time, Ford was profoundly ambivalent about progress in the early twentieth century—and specifically, about the human consequences of the mass production and rapid urbanization that he himself had set in motion. In Ford's mind, and in the design of his Village, steady improvements in tools and machines are distinguished from the values and dispositions of heroes who made those improvements possible. His choice to spatialize the history of technological innovation as a *village* is Ford's way of calling attention to the crucible or "cradle"[11] of values such as hard work, self-reliance, curiosity, thrift, and determination. Edison, the Wright brothers, Burbank, Firestone, and Ford himself came from village roots, close to the land, familiar with the chores of the farm, in or near small towns with houses close by the simple shops where residents worked, and where the children (maybe) attended a one-room school (Ford's own Scotch Settlement School is at the Village, along with his collection of McGuffey's Readers). The captains of American industry came from such humble origins—a lesson that is important for

Ford to tell those who suffered in the Great Depression (there is hope for Horatio Alger's impoverished boys). The proximity of domestic dwellings (homes, boardinghouses) to workplaces (stores and early industrial machine shops) is designed to emphasize that these villages made not only goods but boys disposed to those Ben Franklin values that would permit them, as adults, to transform American society for the better through their ingenuity and entrepreneurship. By implication, Ford cautions that the cultivation of these necessary values is less likely to happen in dense sprawling cities—which Detroit had become under his watch. Such values are even less likely to be nurtured along the mind-numbing mass-production assembly line epitomized by megafactories like the Rouge complex, captured unforgettably by Charlie Chaplin in *Modern Times* (1936).

Greenfield Village freezes American society on the eve of modern industrial mass production and intense urbanization, and so conveys a double meaning. It signals our escape from the body-draining drudgery of the farm, from the slow and sweaty craft production of goods, and our arrival at the technological cornucopia of consumer goods with its abundance of labor-saving devices that make ordinary lives easier and more comfortable. But the possibility that such changes could destroy the very conditions that unleashed technological progress was not lost on Henry Ford. The *New Republic* remarked: "Mr. Ford might be less interested in putting an extinct civilization into a museum if he had not done so much to make it extinct."[12] Ford built a Village to show where modern industrial society was born in the experiences of his heroes, fully aware that by putting farm, small town, and Main Street inside a museum—at a distance from the Rouge plant and the Detroit metropolis outside—he was also signaling a worry that the society he had brought into reality could not sustain the human values on which its commencement depended.[13]

The credibility of Ford's account of American society is secured by what museums do best as truth-spots. They gather up authentic "stuff" and give those objects significance by embedding them in a "story" whose narrative makes that material into the star of the show. Historical museums affirm the truth of their message in a circular or self-referencing way. By attaching a provenance to each object or building, and giving visitors every reason to believe that the object has been in proper custody throughout the journey from its native place to here, museums persuade us that this stuff is the real thing. *"That chair right there is the chair Thomas Edison sat in"*[14] as he tinkered with a light bulb, and Ford later had the chair nailed down to the floor after the inauguration celebration, so that it could never be moved from its truthful spot where history was made. Ford saved these monuments to American technological history by putting them "outside of time and inaccessible to its ravages,"[15] making "perfect and whole objects that existed in an incomplete and fragile state outside the imaginary world of the museum."[16] Visitors' "reactions would not be as they are . . . if the object were not what it is."[17]

A historical museum without authentic objects becomes a theme park with little epistemic force. But a museum full of stuff without obvious historical significance is a flea market or somebody's attic. So Ford's story—of technological progress dependent upon men with certain values acquired in the village and on the farm of their humble beginnings—makes the stuff gathered in Dearborn consequential and meaningful (not just any cycle shop but the one where the possibility of aviation was hashed out). The putative authenticity of *stuff* in museums lends credibility to a *story* on which the special significance of those objects depends.

When Greenfield Village was first opened to the public, interpretive signage was rudimentary, something like "Luther Burbank's garden office from Santa Rosa, California." Presumably every visitor knew who Burbank was and what he had done for potatoes, and stating the point of origin for the building was sufficient to achieve its perceived authenticity—along with its material there-ness. The garden office looks, well, like an outbuilding that might have been sitting in a field of test plots; the floors creak as you walk in; it smells old. Nothing more need be said or written—because the relocation of Burbank's office to Greenfield Village filled in all of the remaining details. There it was, just off Main Street near the Village Green, near similarly humble beginnings of Ford and Edison, in an obvious shrine to the industrial heroes of the American Century. Its "exhibition" alone, sans interpretation, "embodies ordering propositions."[18] In fact, Ford believed that additional textual embellishment could have compromised the building's authenticity and credibility. He told the *New York Times* on April 5, 1931: "For by looking at things that people used and that show the way they lived, a *better and truer impression* can be gained than could be had in a month of reading."[19] Ford believed that "objects more powerfully conveyed historical meaning than words."[20] Historical museums trade on the authenticity of their collection of objects, and when those objects are presented not in halls filled with glass cases but in a *place*, with buildings and streets that give a self-evident narrative context to the objects, their authenticity becomes unassailable, and the story itself becomes that much more believable: "The proximity of things to one another perhaps has more authority, more readable meaning than the things themselves."[21]

But historical museums like Greenfield Village are thoroughly inauthentic and fully artificial places (not unlike a botanical garden when compared to an open field of wildflowers, discussed in chapter 3), and their ability to make visitors believe depends as much on contrivance as on the real thing. Potemkin haunts this Village. Ford materialized an audacious compression of space and time, assembling in one easily walkable spot a seventeenth-century Cotswold cottage from England that sits anachronistically not far from an early nineteenth-century courthouse from Postville, Illinois, where young Abraham Lincoln argued a case. Some buildings are not originals but constructed from scratch on-site, based on Ford's sense of what reality in the past should have looked like (historical liberties were taken in the interest of impression management). His faux New England town is located more than 700 miles from its geographic referent, on a plot of land known mostly as the world headquarters of the Ford Motor Company (how different it is for Delphi today: its authenticity rests on the location of the reconstruction at the site where the original events took place). Gathering these homes and shops of multiple famous American inventors around an archetypal New England town with other civic buildings does a better job than the scattered or decaying originals-in-place to convince visitors about the truth of American technological progress and where it came from. Richard Handler and Eric Gable suggest that "authenticity . . . becomes as much a question of creating and maintaining the right appearance as the truth itself."[22]

Greenfield Village also persuades by leaving so much out. The culmination of Ford's story of technological progress—his own Rouge factory and urban Detroit itself—is conspicuously absent from the grounds, separated from the collection by endless brick serpentine walls. The Mack Avenue plant included in the Village captures "the period before Ford began using moving assembly lines [where] . . . workers had assembled Ford cars one at a time."[23] The building pays homage to the craft work, the intimacy, the skilled workers, and the ingenuity that were the emplaced preconditions of mass industrial capitalism. A bigger workplace that might have brought the story of technological progress up to the minute would have compromised Ford's desire to recover and preserve the village origins of the great inventors. Inside the bubble, nothing is wrong in the Village—but surely every New England town has a dark side, as the fate of Hester Prynne reminds us, though Ford's romanticized replica comes off as utopia. Authenticity and strategically plotted artificialities work together to lend credibility to Ford's messages, and the line between them becomes unimportant if visitors (like Catherine) see nothing but the truth.

———•———

What I had represented on their Garden walls was reality.
«DIEGO RIVERA[24]»

The Mexican muralist and socialist Diego Rivera spent an entire day at Greenfield Village in 1932—and loved the place. Shortly after, his wife, the artist Frida Kahlo, whose politics also ran to the left, danced with Henry Ford himself—more than once! These two improbabilities open a new window on Greenfield Village, and how it was interpreted and used by at least this one famous visitor. Rivera would paint a series of murals that in effect covers the same ground as Ford's historical village, but in a different medium and with a different message. It also relies on a different sort of truth-spot for the believability of its assertions about "Detroit Industry" (the title of the murals).

Rivera's communist politics were surely well-known to Wilhelm R. Valentiner, director of the Detroit Institute of Arts in the early 1930s, even though Rivera had recently been booted out of the Mexican Communist Party for continuing to work on murals for the country's government after it had made the Communist Party illegal (and perhaps because he preferred Lenin and Trotsky to Stalin). Rivera's political baggage would not pose a serious obstacle for Valentiner, himself disposed to leftist currents, and hell-bent on attracting one of the world's recognized great muralists to adorn the walls of the Garden Court at his museum on Woodward Avenue. The artist's ties to communism might have posed a greater obstacle for Edsel Ford, Henry's only son, who had agreed to bankroll the project. But Edsel trusted Valentiner, and gave Rivera free rein to interpret the theme of "Detroit Industry" as he wished, modestly insisting only that the murals not limit themselves to the city's automobile industry, but surely hoping for a little positive "PR" for the Ford Motor Company.

With the commission in hand, Rivera and Kahlo moved to Detroit in 1932, and Diego immediately begins his fieldwork, spending several months at Ford's River Rouge assembly plant, collecting ideas about how to portray mass industrial production at the scale of this gargantuan factory. Rivera made "literally thousands of sketches of towering blast furnaces, serpentine conveyor belts, impressive scientific laboratories, busy assembling rooms; also of precision instruments, some of them massive yet delicate; and of the men who worked them all."[25] But he also made time to spend a day at Greenfield Village, adjacent to the Rouge complex but serene by contrast, and judged it in glowing terms: "organized not only with scientific clarity, but with impeccable, unpretentious good taste."[26] As Rivera inspected the old machines and tools that might somehow figure in his mural, Henry Ford secretly turned out the lights in one of the buildings—leaving Rivera momentarily in the dark—just to tease. The two had lunch the next day, and, despite the epochal rift between socialism and capitalism, hit it off.

Ford and Rivera shared a love for machines. Rivera recounts that his visit to Greenfield Village rekindled a "childhood passion for mechanical toys . . . transmuted to a delight in machinery for its own sake."[27] Ford described himself as a tinkerer at heart, and perhaps was never happier than when he fiddled around with a machine: "Machines are to a mechanic what books are to a writer."[28] After the Model As began to roll off the assembly line in the late twenties, Ford spent as much or more time at Greenfield Village than at Rouge, perhaps because of his firsthand familiarity with the relatively simple machines and tools at the museum—the ones he himself had used to build Ford automobiles, now eclipsed by the overpowering technological wonders at Rouge.

Ford and Rivera also shared a belief in technological progress: machines had liberated humankind from the drudgery of manual labor and presented us with comforting consumer goods (like cars). Ford and Rivera found common ground in their love for machines and their confidence that technological progress had made life better for all—on display at Greenfield Village, and materialized as well at Rouge. In Rivera's words: "I thought of the millions of different men by whose combined labor and thought automobiles were produced, from the miners who dug the iron ore out of the earth to the railroad men and teamsters who brought the finished machines to the consumer, so that man, space, and light might be conquered, and ever-expanding victories be won against death."[29] Bertram Wolfe, Rivera's biographer, wrote that "he would paint the human *spirit* that is embodied in the machine . . . ; the *hope* that is in the machine that man, freed by it from servitude to nature, need not long remain in servitude to hunger, exhausting toil, inequality, and tyranny."[30] Ford put it this way, on several different occasions: "Machines were devised, not to do a man out of a job, but to take the heavy labor from man's back and place it upon the broad shoulders of the machine." "The machine is the best servant man has ever had and will perform still greater tasks for him, making life more comfortable, refined and humane, more worth the living." "Man minus the machine is a slave. Man plus the machine is a free man."[31] Perhaps finding in Rivera a fellow traveler, who appreciated what machines have done to improve humanity, emboldened Henry, a devotee of American folk dances, to ask Frida Kahlo for a twirl or two, despite her occasional caustic remarks about rich people.[32]

The sheer power of man + machine working in tandem is at the heart of the two largest panels of "Detroit Industry." On the north wall, Rivera presents "the manufacture of the 1932 Ford V-8 engine and transmission. There are scenes in the foundry, with molten steel pouring from the blast furnace into molds; then there are the conveyor belts, the assembly lines and the honing of the newly cast engine block." On the opposite wall, "Rivera showed the body shop, with stamping press, welders and paint oven, and the final assembly line."[33] Elaborately detailed machines hover above the men who work them, mostly silvery, in contrast to the sepia tones of their multiracial human tenders. The writer Pete Hamill suggests that "as portrayed by Rivera, machines were benevolent and triumphant, the redeeming engines of the utopian future."[34] Surrounding these two principal panels are depictions of the extractive labor needed to gather the raw materials that go into every Ford car, along with a paean to agriculture as the occasion where technological innovation initially eased the burden of humankind (and a way to mark progress—as Ford had done at Greenfield Village by juxtaposing sweaty and strenuous hand production to the ease of its machine successor).

Although Greenfield Village and "Detroit Industry" were fully opened to the public within the same year, the time horizons at the two places differed. Ford retrieved an imagined past in the Village, in order to show how much better life really is in the present (thanks to those machines), but also to expose a risk that rapid mass production and unchecked urbanization might prevent the cultivation of individualist values on which technical ingenuity and self-reliant entrepreneurship rest. Rivera's eye is squarely on the present as evidence of a future diametrically opposed to Ford's (although some scholars suggest that the murals are more accurate as a depiction of Rouge before the economy went haywire in 1929). In "Detroit Industry," the factory at Rouge has now displaced the New England town as a crucible of values and dispositions—it produces a different historical subject than those who grew up on farms and in small towns, like Ford or the Wright brothers. When asked in an interview "whether or not he had painted the 'Philosophy of Moscow' on the walls of the Detroit Art Institute, [Rivera] answered, 'Of course, because it is the only ultimate form of social life among civilized people.'"[35] According to Marx, the concentration of workers in massive factories creates the necessary revolutionary conditions where their immiseration and degradation under wage-labor capitalism would become palpable and where mobilization into a revolutionary force would be facilitated. Rouge would manufacture workers with a socialist ethic, whose ability to bring capitalism to its inevitable end depended upon class solidarity rather than Horatio Alger's gumption. In his autobiography, Rivera recalls meeting a worker in Russia who had four portraits framed on his wall at home: Marx, Lenin, Stalin, and Henry Ford. At Rouge, Rivera found the segué to communism.

From their vantage in the depths of the Great Depression, Ford and Rivera—simpatico on the progressive role machines had played historically—imagined discrepant futures. Apart from an explicitly future-facing experimental Soybean Laboratory,[36]

Greenfield Village encourages visitors to conclude that the idealized small town might be the best model for tomorrow. Ford had confidence that inventors and entrepreneurs would eventually pull the world out of its present economic doldrums, if only speculative bankers, parasitic lawyers, and meddling politicians would stay out of the way (an opinion that was a by-product of his notorious anti-Semitism).[37] He was surely naïve in his understanding of the effects of capitalist mass production on his workers. Though Ford admits that he himself "could not possibly do the same thing day in and day out"[38] like those on his assembly line at Rouge, the future of labor is for him decidedly not immiseration and degradation. "You can drive a machine until it breaks—you must not drive men that way," he said; and "We believe in making 20,000 prosperous instead of a few slave-drivers rich"; "my ambition is to employ still more men; to spread the benefits of this industrial system to the greatest possible number, to help them build up their lives and their homes."[39] Even in 1931, Ford believed that a return to prosperity was just around the corner: "The man of tomorrow can have luxuries unknown today, by reason of the machine and what the machine can do for him"; "the promise of the future makes the present seem drab."[40]

Ford further pursued his commitment to "the village" as both past and possible future by creating nineteen small factories in towns located no more than sixty miles from Detroit—he called them "village industries." Each was created to produce parts, supplies, or instruments for the mass-production plants like the Rouge, and most were located along streams or rivers affording a source of hydroelectric power (many were repurposed grist- or sawmills). A 1938 article in *Life* magazine noted that "a farm boy who has kept his love of the land, Ford now visions the 'little factory in a meadow' as the future shape of American industry."[41] Ideally, the village industries would provide work and income for farmers, especially in the fallow winter months, and, true to Ford's theories of socialization, would provide the proper environment for the cultivation of small-town and agrarian values and dispositions. This decentralization of production facilities was perhaps also a move against growing threats of unionization. The village industries were plainly an experiment, a pet project of Henry Ford himself, and "utopian" in their vision.[42] The Ford Motor Company phased out almost all of the properties after Henry's retirement in 1945.[43]

Ford's village industries illustrate another truth-spot: "prototypal places" that materialize a vision of the future. By actualizing a dream or an ideal, such places present by their very construction the possibility that such ambitions could be scaled up and realized elsewhere or even everywhere. "I never prophesy," said Ford, which did not keep others from seeking out the great man "as the oracle of Delphi."[44] The experimental Soybean Laboratory, originally a barn built by Henry's father in 1863, was (before assuming its final resting place at Greenfield Village) reconstructed at the Chicago Century of Progress World's Fair in 1934 and "filled not with hay but with various tools and machines to process the patch of soybeans surrounding the structure itself."[45] As a physical model for others to emulate, Ford's barn/laboratory made his ideas about decentralizing factories seem more believable as a possible agro-industrial tomorrow. World's fairs in general[46] are prototypal places, along with built environments at utopian communities,[47] company towns like Pullman outside Chicago,[48] new cities seeking to be ahead of their time like Shanghai's Pudong[49] and Celebration, Florida—a Disney application of neo-urbanist planning principles to create a "village" of sorts[50] (Walt Disney himself visited Main Street at Greenfield Village in the 1940s,[51] and plainly picked up a few pointers).

Rivera was less sanguine than Ford about the possibility of prosperity under industrial capitalism, and those village industries would have been, for him, a step backward from the intensification of capitalist production sure to hasten the proletariat revolution. But the rhetorical challenge he faced was the same as Ford's: how to find or make a *place* where audiences could experience his message—and believe it. By "moving" the River Rouge assembly plant to the Garden Court at the Detroit Institute of

Arts, he could achieve what Ford had achieved by moving the homesteads and machine shops of American inventors to Greenfield Village: a rendering of social reality prone to selective inclusion and occasional exaggeration, all for effect.

Rivera had to prevent any details from getting lost in translation. Accuracy to the realities at Rouge verité would stand in for the authenticity attached to objects and buildings at Greenfield Village—each is a condition of the believability of the finished place. Ford himself gave "Detroit Industry" his seal of approval: "Every inch of his [Rivera's] work is technically correct. That's what is so amazing."[52] Valentiner said that "the function of the machinery was so well understood that when engineers looked at the finished murals they found each part accurately designed."[53] On the other side of the class divide, workers praised the murals for their accuracy and respect. Rivera recounts a worker describing "Detroit Industry" as a "classic example of proletarian art created exclusively by you for the pleasure of the workers of this city" and as "your excellent portrayal of our life."[54] Jerry Herron suggests that the murals are "like hanging a plasma screen up there, if there had been plasma screens in 1933, beaming in a live feed of the River Rouge plant."[55] Wolfe wrote that the machines in the murals were "so true to the logic and precision of the models that they would 'work.'"[56] That's a double entendre: "work" to make an V8 engine, "work" to convince viewers of the accuracy and fidelity of Rivera's rendering of the now and future of "Detroit Industry."

Art museums (like those for history or natural science) have their own legitimating capacity. The expertise of curators powerfully aligns with the refined tastes of elite patrons to insure that nothing inside is either bogus or gauche. "Detroit Industry" takes its place among the treasures of the Detroit Institute of Arts, on the wall (not off) with Caravaggio, Poussin, and Bruegel. The Garden Court is at once the perfect and an extremely awkward place to relocate a mass-production industrial plant. The substance and exuberant style of Rivera's murals clashed with the Court's Beaux-Arts Italianate Renaissance getup (he asked for a fountain to be removed). Rivera recalled that he wanted "to represent the life of an age which had nothing to do with baroque refinements—a new life which was characterized by masses, machines, and naked mechanical power. So I set to work consciously to overpower the ornamentation of the room."[57] A disappointed Rev. H. Ralph Higgins of Detroit's St. Paul's Episcopal church pointed out that the "murals are about as appropriate to the classical court of our art museum as a jazz band in a medieval cathedral."[58] But (bully) pulpit is exactly what Rivera wanted and needed—a Court variously described as Detroit's "temple of culture"[59] with "sacrosanct walls,"[60] a place that could sanctify his art and his message: "Rivera Court has become the sanctuary of the Detroit Institute of Arts, a 'sacred' place dedicated to images of workers and technology. . . . To Rivera, Valentiner, and Edsel Ford, technology was Detroit's true deity."[61] "Rivera's aim was a transformation from the pseudo-sacred to a secular ideal."[62] The "rarefied aesthetic atmosphere"[63] of the Garden Court attracted Detroit's elite patrons, affording Rivera the opportunity to speak truth to power. He recalled telling a group of wealthy ladies (who objected to a factory in their museum) "that the growth and wealth of the city of Detroit which they enjoyed came from the subjects and substances to which they were objecting."[64]

The epigraph above the Woodward Avenue entrance to the Detroit Institute of Arts reads in stone: "Dedicated By the People of Detroit to the Knowledge and Enjoyment of Art." The Garden Court was public space, which very quickly became contested terrain even before the paint was dry. Local newspapers quoted religious and civic leaders who found Rivera's work blasphemous and defamatory (the Holy Family is caricatured in a panel showing the vaccination of a child), pornographic (voluptuous nudes!), shameless publicity for the Ford Motor Company, insulting to Detroit (which was not to be defined only by its factories and workers), and an "anti-American communist plot."[65] Some wanted the murals whitewashed, like the grimy peasant houses along the Dneiper River (Valentiner squelched that possibility when he announced that "Edsel Ford, the donor, was completely satisfied").[66] The museum itself had been "politicized."[67] To judge from the prodigious numbers of people who paid to see the murals starting on March 21, 1933—by the thousands, patrician and proletariat alike—it seemed as if all Detroit suddenly had a stake in what had gone up on the walls of their Garden Court. Ironically, according to one witness, "Detroit talked itself out of the recession by talking about the Rivera frescoes."[68] The attention paid to the murals was perhaps even more than Rivera could have hoped for: if you want to make a statement, make a place to lure the crowds.

But what they saw was not quite a plasma-screen feed from the Rouge. Although the murals were received as technically accurate by those in the know, the encompassing message about the future of American society required Rivera to take liberties with reality (as Ford did when he ripped inventors' homes and shops from their native places and reassembled them—or built replicas—around a New England town common in Michigan). "Detroit Industry," like Greenfield Village, is an imaginary, and as Jean Baudrillard said of Disneyland: it "is neither true nor false: it is a deterrence machine set up in order to rejuvenate in reverse the fiction of the real."[69] Success for both creators would not be measured by fidelity to the original but by the numbers of people persuaded that the reality served up there is true. Rivera's political ambitions required several embellishments of the Rouge: "He saw himself as a Communist provocateur in the home of capitalism,"[70] who "foresaw a new society in which the bourgeoisie would vanish."[71] "He was painting a future for the industrial world as he believed it would appear. . . . He was a believer, and he wanted to make other people believers too."[72] So, although the human workforce along the Rouge assembly line was actually "sparse" according to a contemporary photograph, Rivera clusters the proletariat cheek by jowl, pulling together toward the revolution.[73] According to Linda Downs, the painted size of the workers relative to the open-hearth ladle is exaggerated considerably in order to "monumentalize the worker."[74] And in a mural where nobody seems to be smiling, goons posing as "grim-faced supervisors" appear especially ominous, "hinting . . . at the degree to which the workers were policed both at home and at work by Henry Ford's organization."[75] Did the embellishments work? Eighty years later, the International Committee of the Fourth International posted on its World Socialist website: "Detroit Industry" "would instead inspire and become an active agent in the revolutionary transformation of society. In this Rivera continues to be proven correct."[76]

Just as interesting is what Rivera leaves out. On March 7, 1932, workers at the Rouge plant orchestrated a hunger march—four strikers were killed. When Rivera and Kahlo arrived in Detroit on April 21, according to Mark Rosenthal, "they did not mention a word about it" or the ensuing funeral procession involving tens of thousands of people.[77] A predella under one of the main panels in "Detroit Industry" shows workers walking toward the entrance of the Rouge plant, where police and Ford's security force fired shots into the crowd. Despite this hint, Rivera plainly pulled his communist punches. There is little evidence in the murals of the 300,000 or so autoworkers recently laid off, the reduction in wages from $33 to $22 per week or the bloody risks of working in the "colossal machinery" at Rouge.[78] Patrick Marnham suggests that "the only hint of the Depression . . . is in the paper hat worn by one of the workers on the south wall. It bears the words 'We want'; the back of the hat, not shown, carried the word 'beer,'" an objection to Prohibition, not capitalist exploitation.[79] White collar and blue are shown working together, each with a vital role to play in making machinery work for the improvement of humankind. Rivera avoided the champagne-sipping capitalists he had depicted just four years earlier in "Wall Street Banquet," a mural in the Ministry of Education in Mexico City. His insistence that Lenin be included in a mural prepared for Rockefeller Center (after Detroit) resulted in its destruction. Indeed, if fomenting the proletariat revolution were the only thing on Rivera's mind in Detroit, he passed up many strategic opportunities to beat that drum.

Why? Perhaps it was Rivera's genuine admiration for the man Henry Ford, and for the historic role that Ford's assembly

line would play in the improvement of the human condition—
however it might all turn out in the end. Perhaps it was his
preference for allegory over brutal realism, attaching cosmic significance to the ability of technology to free humankind from
drudgery, starting with the simple agricultural tools of his native
Mexico and culminating in Rouge. Or perhaps he thought that
by painting a polysemic and poetic portrait of "Detroit Industry,"
"opposite ends of the political spectrum were able to see their own
reality."[80] Even if the immiseration of workers at Rouge was disguised or obscured, his comrades on the line could still imagine in
the murals the eventual overthrow of private productive property,
while his capitalist patrons might convince themselves that the
murals celebrate the spirit of their own ingenuity and entrepreneurship. Rivera could not afford to lose the Detroit commission
by painting a more strident attack on capitalist oppression. He
needed that pulpit, as much as Ford needed Greenfield Village.

———•———

It is simply that reality really is something in which one has to believe.
«SIMON KNELL[81]»

Some places make assertions about the conditions of society,
past, present, or future—more or less credibly, more or less persuasively. Neither Greenfield Village nor "Detroit Industry" is a
papier-mâché and cardboard cutout, but to call them accurate
representations of emerging industrial capitalism exaggerates
their honesty. Both truth-spots—Village and Garden Court—
make us believe in their own integrity more powerfully than the
real places and conditions they imperfectly represent. Both places
exploit the gray space between authenticity and artificiality—
using contrivance to accomplish the appearance of reality. Authenticity is more about authority than fidelity.[82] Whatever Potemkin
had done to those villages along the Dnieper River, they became real when Catherine decided that they provided sufficient
credible evidence to indicate that the campaign to colonize and

develop Russia's southern provinces was a success. The reality of industrial society gets settled as visitors stroll down Main Street in Greenfield Village or gaze up at the Rouge plant in the Detroit Institute of Arts, as they decide to believe as true (or not) the visions of the past and future that Ford and Rivera had built for them.

5

Trapdoor to the Transcendent

"I, for my part," replies Piers, "will dress myself in pilgrim's clothes and travel with you until we find Truth."
«WILLIAM LANGLAND, *Piers Plowman*, ca. 1380[1]»

The very principle of religious architecture has its origins in the notion that where we are critically determines what we are able to believe in.
«ALAIN DE BOTTON[2]»

On the ninety-minute flight from Barcelona to Santiago de Compostela, I took forty-six steps from my seat to the toilet, round-trip. That is only about one million steps fewer than those taken by pilgrims 30,000 feet below me, on the ground, walking the Way of St. James. I flew over more than 10,000 people with floppy hats, heavy packs, walking sticks, sturdy boots, blisters on blisters, scallop shells, and some kind of purpose, covering 482 miles in about a month—roughly 600 arrive at the remains of Saint James each day, many encouraged by popular accounts of the ordeal by the actress and otherworldly Shirley MacLaine[3] or *The Way* (a 2010 film by Emilio Estevez, with his father, Martin Sheen, playing the role of a man in search of something). At the peak of the pilgrimage in the twelfth and thirteenth centuries, those numbers of pilgrims were doubled. A millennium of feet beating a common path through the countryside of northern Spain, like wildebeests on the Serengeti.

But not exactly: no single goal moves these pilgrims to walk, like the need for fresh grass. In medieval days, their motives were tied closely to the institutionalized necessities of the Catholic Church: piety, devotion, penance, forgiveness, miracle cure, indulgence, purification, gratitude, exorcism of demons, test of faith.[4] Now, reasons for doing the Camino are often more personal and diverse: overcome a loss, reawaken (or forget) something inside, self-discovery, endurance test, escape, hopeful insecurity, wonders of nature, because it's there, because so many others have done it, so you can tell others that you did it.[5] What connects pilgrims across the centuries and along the Way is a sense that this pilgrimage is not a mere hike, ramble, stroll, or even just a very long and hard walk. Few people would voluntarily expose themselves to the hellish obstacles waiting for them on the road to Santiago—if not for a heavenly prize enjoyed only by those who make it. Maybe a better parallel than migrating wildebeests is the imagery that drives Spike Jones and Charlie Kaufman's 1999 debut film *Being John Malkovich*. The small trapdoor behind a filing cabinet in a nondescript New York office becomes a portal to the transcendent, in this instance, a trip into the mind of the title actor. The pilgrimage road to Santiago de Compostela has always been a little like that: a "thin place"[6] where the gap shrinks between quotidian here and now and something . . . more (extraordinary, ecstatic, mystical, beyond the immediate). Successful pilgrims return from Santiago to their normal lives with something astonishing that they believe in *more* than when they started off from St. Jean Pied de Port, in the French Pyrenees, just across the border with Spain. The place has made their walk a transformative journey, and most pilgrims are certain of that. But what are the grounds (literally) of their certainty?

It only seems like every single pilgrim who has walked the Camino since the ninth century has written a book about it (or made a film, blogged, put albums of pics on Facebook, etc.).

The narratives range widely in kind: how-to survival manuals, weighty historical tomes (the pilgrimage is explained by prosperity sought by towns along the trail or as a buttress against infidel Muslims encroaching from the south), architectural fieldguides, religious justifications, and deeply personal testimonials. The Camino may be the most inscribed trail in the world, and my own story (I flew, remember) draws on a tiny subset of *others'* tales in order to attack the question that animates *my* book: how does this place, both path and destination, affirm or change a pilgrim's beliefs—whether those beliefs are medieval or modern, official church dogma or free-form fantasies, previously held or just awakened, private or shared with everybody, mystical or introspective?

By the way, there is precedence for my miraculous one and one-half hour airborne nonpilgrimage to Santiago de Compostela. The story goes that the apostle Saint James the Greater, son of Zebedee and Salome, brother of Saint John the Evangelist, did some evangelizing of his own on the Iberian Peninsula (clinching evidence is wanting). But having little success among the pagans there, he returned to Jerusalem, where Herod Agrippa summarily beheaded him. James's buddies took his body to the Mediterranean shore and sailed all the way round to the northwest coast of Spain in a mere six days (blown along at jet-like speed on puffs of angels). After landfall, his mortal remains were buried in a Galician field to be found nine centuries later by a shepherd guided by still more angels and some special stars in the sky—and after proper certification by a bishop and pope that those were genuine apostolic bones, King Alfonso II began work on a proper church, and Santiago soon became a Christian destination to rival Rome or Jerusalem. Sometime during all of this, it is written, a virtuous man was thrown into the Atlantic by his startled horse and surely would have drowned had it not been for Saint James's (Santiago in Spanish) timely intercession. The lucky guy emerged from the deep covered in scallop shells. The faithful and the seekers have been walking to Santiago de Compostela, with their coquilles proudly displayed, ever since

("Compostela" is taken by many to mean "field of stars," but scholars[7] aren't sure about that either).

———•———

Before Baedeker and Rick Steves there was **Aimery Picaud**,[8] a twelfth-century Cluniac monk from Parthenay, a town along a French portion of the Jacobean pilgrimage route 200 miles or so southwest of Paris, who probably wrote Book 5 of the *Liber Sancti Jacobi*, a Francophilic account of the Way also known as *Codex Calixtinus* (after Pope Calixtus II [1119–24], who almost surely did not write it) and translated as *The Pilgrim's Guide to Santiago de Compostela.*

Contemporary medieval historian Katherine Lack created a fictional pilgrim's tale (set in 1423) inspired by the 1986 discovery of the bones of wealthy dyer **Robert Sutton**[9] in Worcester Cathedral, who was buried with a "stout staff" and a telltale scallop shell.

The devout priest from Devon and fellow of Exeter College, Oxford, **William Wey**[10] made a pilgrimage to Santiago in 1456 by boat from Plymouth to Corunna and then the last forty-five miles over land, but made up for the maritime shortcut by taking two subsequent trips to Rome and Jerusalem.

A priest from Bologna, **Domenico Laffi**,[11] walked the 1,330 miles to Santiago three times (1666, 1670, and 1673), and wrote a travel book that draws on his rich familiarity with early modern Italian and Spanish architecture, art, literature, and history.

Irish historian and musician **Walter Starkie** (1894–1976)[12] also walked the Way of St. James three times, but nearly three centuries after Laffi (between 1924 and 1954), and focused his monograph on the history, architecture, and especially the folk music he heard and played during the long walk.

The best-selling Brazilian writer **Paulo Coelho**[13] walked to Santiago in 1986 as part of a Catholic reawakening, and his search along the Way for a talismanic sword became a transformative voyage of self-discovery.

The American writer **Jack Hitt**[14] titled his pilgrim's tale *Off the Road*, with a nod to Kerouac and full of agnostic cynicism—leaving readers with a hilarious story of unforgettable fellow travelers that became the foundation for Estevez and Sheen's movie.

Actress **Shirley MacLaine**[15] needed no encouragement from the Camino to conjure those she met in a previous life, but her pilgrimage to Santiago made them all so much more real.

Conrad Rudolph[16] left for his early 2000s pilgrimage as an academic historian of medieval art, but, after an encounter with a fingerless beggar, returned as someone richer.

Hape Kerkeling[17] rivals Hitt in hilarity: no surprise—he is a popular comedian and actor in Germany who was not above hopping on a bus along the Way in 2001 (his best-selling story has been translated into seven languages).

With her tagline "Your sixth sense should be your first sense," Chicago-based intuition guide **Sonia Choquette**[18] needed every one of her senses to survive the pilgrimage walk, written up in 2014.

Like scallop shells plastered into sidewalks marking the path of the Camino through cities and villages, here are my own yellow arrows (another way the trail is blazed)—to guide you through the discussion ahead. These eleven pilgrims, and millions like them, are made to believe something—usually something new about themselves, or something reassuring about the meaning or purpose of life—by the geographic location, material surrounds, and interpretive layers that comprise the place known as the Way of St. James. How? (1) Pilgrimage removes people from the comfortably familiar world of home, and by submerging them in an often radically different location for an extended time, it enhances their vulnerability to belief-changing signals by making the once taken-for-granted less secure. (2) The struggles and sacrifices, the pain and risks, endured on the Camino boost the perceived value of whatever lesson one gets at the end, attaching to those new understandings a measure of hard-won certainty and reliability. (3) The *sacred* quality of the road to Santiago is perpetually reasserted by ever-present juxtapositions of the *profane* along its sides, forcing on pilgrims a sense of transcendence even among those who start out as skeptics. (4) Countless ghosts of antecedent pilgrims (materialized in the worn path itself or in statuary and lore) create an obligation for each new pilgrim to sustain the transformative, truth-affirming capacity of the Camino—one cannot fail the predecessors who made it all possible. As a charismatic place, both extraordinary and authoritative, the road to Santiago makes pilgrims believe. "Ultreya!"

———•———

The mere fact of spatial separation from the familiar and habitual . . . represents at once a negation of many, though not all, of the features of preliminal social structure and an affirmation of another order of things and relations.
«VICTOR TURNER[19]»

Santiago de Compostela is far away from almost everything. Just fifty miles to the west, on the coast, is Finisterre, a place still thought of as "the end of the earth." The very idea of pilgrimage insists upon a journey to a distant and thus different place, a journey of sufficient duration that it interrupts routines and ordinary plausibility structures: you cannot be a pilgrim at home. Anthropologist Victor Turner suggests that the "peripherality of pilgrimage shrines" is a precondition for the sequence of stages that defines the process: "beginning in a familiar place, going to a Far Place, and returning to a Familiar Place, theoretically changed."[20] He refers to that transitional middle—the pilgrimage experience—as "liminal," an interlude between the formerly familiar ("preliminal") and the not yet fully grasped. Paulo Coelho consistently refers to the Strange Road to Santiago, perhaps because it was for him not unlike what it was for medieval pilgrims as described by religious historian Horton Davies: "It offered the chance to travel through strange lands, where foreign tongues were spoken . . . and where landscape, flora, and fauna differed from the homeland."[21]

Scholars have described pilgrimage as a "displacement," a "destructuring of routine," and "in sharp contrast to normal life, which is programmed by work, societal norms, and the daily planner."[22] Coelho walked "with my connection to civilization severed."[23] Conrad Rudolph felt "very much apart from the rest of the world, a world with which you are familiar."[24] For Sonia Choquette, "life as I knew it had disappeared."[25] Robert Sutton ceased to be a wealthy dyer from Worcester, "having shed his familiar position in the city hierarchy. Instead of his money and rank, his pilgrimage had become his key to society. He quickly discovered he had exchanged respect for his wealth for respect for his calling."[26] The first step in discovering something new about oneself or about the meaning of something is to let go of the ways of thinking and acting back home. The idea of pilgrimage as a kind of cleansing or purifying begun by emptying body and soul of habitual practices seems to resonate with medieval and modern pilgrim alike.

For Jack Hitt, it is not simply the Far Away geographic location of the road to Santiago that compels separation from life back home, but also the means by which one traverses the path: walking slowly. Like Sutton, so much of Hitt's old self is left behind: "subletting my New York apartment, quitting my job, and resigning from my generous health plan. . . . My long-set routines would be shattered, and my daily responsibilities would evaporate. I'd walk out of the pop-culture waters in which I had spent a lifetime treading and onto a strange dry land." But unlike Sutton, accustomed to walking everywhere because there were fewer faster alternatives in the fifteenth century, Hitt gives up speed (and gains insight): "What the modern pilgrim is exiled from is not a place but velocity. . . . I have left the realm of the car. What distinguishes me is not that I am out of town but that I am on foot." Although some pilgrims to Santiago have used other means to get from here to there—William Wey on a boat from England, Hape Kerkeling on a bus (for short stretches), and many modern pilgrims on bicycles—there is something more authentic about doing it all on foot. Evidently, walking gives more than blisters: the slow pace allows for a thicker apprehension of what the pilgrim sees or imagines. For Hitt, "the idea was to slacken that pace to the natural rhythm of walking. The pilgrim would be exiled from numbing familiarity and plunged into continual change. The splendid anarchy of the walk was said to create a sense of being erased, a dusting of the tabula rasa, so that the pilgrim could consider a variety of incoming ideas with a clean slate."[27]

Others report the same experience: "My ingrained habits are loosening," writes Kerkeling (as he vows never again to read the *Süddeutsche Zeitung* on the Camino), and Rudolph finds himself in a "mental sauna, sweating out the stress of daily life."[28] What comes next along the pilgrim's way is a heightened "psychic receptivity"[29] to new understandings, a growing reluctance to cram experiences into formerly reliable interpretive boxes, and a kind of freedom or escape—at once exhilarating and scary. Sutton admits that the street-level intermingling of Jews, Muslims, and Christians in Pamplona "was a radical, new and deeply unsettling concept" (in his day, the first two groups were either banished from Christian towns or segregated).[30] Shirley MacLaine's pilgrimage is a kind of "surrender," an encouragement to be "open to the reality of other dimensional truth"—and Choquette is "so grateful for my total freedom. It was a gift."[31] Rudolph becomes more "susceptible" to the differences and novelties forced upon him by the road, and feels a "general loss of . . . all that's familiar." Gradually, life along the road becomes a pilgrim's new normal, a provisional system of beliefs that restores a sense of plausibility to whomever he or she is becoming. Rudolph asks: "How long is two and a half months? Long enough to trick you into the strange feeling that the even stranger journey you're on is normal, everyday life."[32]

Interactions along the Camino are not, Turner writes, "governed by the old rules,"[33] and some pilgrims find themselves engaging in behavior or entertaining thoughts that simply surprise them. Sociologist Neil Smelser describes a "regenerated person" who lives life "on new and altered terms," following what Thomas

DeGloma calls "cognitive and epistemic metamorphoses."[34] In a Spanish field surrounded by cows, MacLaine "pulled down my shorts and urinated. Yes, that was still real."[35] The rigors of the road ask for accommodation and acquiescence, however strange those attitudes and behaviors might appear back home: "The longer I continue along this path, the more I feel at ease. This is not home to me, but it's no longer so very alien." Kerkeling could have had MacLaine in mind when he wrote: "She thinks it's absolutely normal to experience something extraordinary." He finds himself "up for a bit of experimentation," and being a city boy, finds it odd that he would choose a "secluded nature trail" over a path beside a highway: "This is another thing I wouldn't have done of my own accord two weeks ago."[36] Sonia Choquette submits to the linear unidirectional flow of the road as an "itinerary" ("a structured sequence of time and space"),[37] allowing the places walked through to give a new orderliness to her emerging self: "I was simply to follow the signs—which I'd been told were yellow arrows and occasionally the famous scallop shells . . . marking the Camino. . . . The only thing I could do from here to the end was put one foot in front of the other." Pilgrimage is not an escape from all convention into anarchy but the substitution of a different set of life-ordering principles, to be discovered and heeded. Choquette might once have measured achievement by the number of her books, online courses, and CDs sold from her inspirational website; on the road, "I loved my daily pilgrim's stamps. They were victory badges, each one saying, 'Yes, I made it!' . . . Having them in my passport recognized me as a true pilgrim. And I liked that."[38] "Passports" were originally a means to distinguish honest pilgrims from fakes (the latter are not worthy of alms, free lodging, or safe passage through hostile territories), and a stamp is given by innkeepers or religious functionaries to mark completion of each stage of the Camino (at Santiago, passports are presented to officials as evidence warranting a Compostela, the fancy certificate attesting to successful completion of the Way). Coelho was "completely absorbed by the Road to Santiago [and] most other things had lost their importance."[39]

For Coehlo, "after so much time walking the Road to Santiago, the Road to Santiago began to 'walk me.'"[40]

Almost every pilgrim returns home a different person for having walked the walk. Most pilgrim stories readily admit to the transformation, and how firmly a pilgrim believes in it. Robert Sutton started as a dyer, but "when his journey was finally over, and they laid him to rest, he was remembered as he most wanted to be—as a pilgrim."[41] Anthropologist Nancy Frey continued her interviews with Santiago pilgrims even after they completed the walk and returned to ordinary society. For some, reentry is itself "destabilizing," a kind of "reverse culture shock." In the absence of the demanding structures imposed by life on the Camino, Frey reports that "extremes in behavior are common, such as drinking, eating, talking and even continuing to move." Many pilgrims were certain that they had been changed, including one who decided that he really needed to go the distance, on to Finisterre: "He cried for something more . . . knowing in this moment that his vision of life had changed. He knew that he was different." An American scholar told Frey: "My old body has died; in many ways I have also died to my old self. . . . My life, my work, my family will never quite be the same."[42] Shirley MacLaine predictably experiences "truth-shock," but "underneath all my thoughts about my life in the world back home was the new world inside myself."[43] Choquette writes that walking the road was like "peeling away more and more of the old pain from my body, revealing a fresh new me underneath . . . I knew it was the Camino itself that was causing this. The energy of the path was transforming me."[44] The notion that a place can have forceful effects on human practices and beliefs has never been so clearly stated.

But then there is Jack Hitt, who even wonders just how Far Away the Camino really is. In Uterga, a tiny village, his hosts offer him a drink—possibly of "some local confection or an authentic Basque libation." "Oh, no, they tell me," producing "an enormous bottle of Jack Daniel's Tennessee mash." Hitt can admit only to the "pilgrim neurosis": "While I become less and less confident about being here, the others grow increasingly assured of their enterprise." He sets himself apart from many fellow travelers: "Every pilgrim's temptation is the need to encounter a brand new truth, preferably one that's panoramic, cinematic and ecstatic." If Hitt found truths on the Road to Santiago, they were little ones: "Pilgrimages are all about finding a good chunk of chorizo, cool water, a café con leche, some manchego, and fresh bread and . . . toilet paper that doesn't qualify as grade C sandpaper."[45]

———•———

No pain, no gain.
«JANE FONDA»

My grandma always said: "If it costs nothing, it is nothing."
«HAPE KERKELING[46]»

The Way of St. James is one tough place. According to medieval law, "when a year and a day had passed since news had last been had of him," a pilgrim "should be considered dead."[47] The law made it possible to reconcile debts and marriages, and it was comforting to family and friends of the deceased to know that their pilgrim went straight to heaven, whatever sins they bore. To judge from the frequency of more recent trailside memorials to those who have died along the Way, pilgrims continue to face the risk of death in their pursuit of Santiago and enlightenment. Medieval pilgrims heard "tales of gruesome murders of pilgrims in lonely inns,"[48] and in 2015 near Astorga, an American woman was probably lured off the road by phony yellow arrows painted by her assailant. A "fallen pilgrims" website lists those who have died along the Way since 1986: murder is extremely rare, and the more common causes of death are heart attacks and getting hit by vehicles on highways. Besides the murder victim, twelve other pilgrims died on the Santiago pilgrimage in 2015.[49] Sonia Choquette "overheard in the café last night that a woman from Canada got lost in the Pyrenees that day after I had left St. Jean and was found dead."[50]

Happily, most pilgrims make it to their destination (80 percent of them finish, since the road's revival in the 1980s[51]), but not without the struggle of a lifetime. Few hazards along the Way are life-threatening, but they are sufficiently taxing that the experience becomes valuable and memorable—and for the many transformed pilgrims who touch the transcendent (or reach some other kind of wisdom), the travails en route intensify the credibility of new beliefs and understandings. The preferred Jacobean route (there is more than one road to Santiago) starts out in the Pyrenees Mountains through Navarra and La Rioja, then settles into the high plateau Meseta of Castilla y León (hot, dry, treeless, endless vistas of wheat), ending up with a steep climb into the mountains of Galicia. This is no walk in the park, especially for the many pilgrims who are not veteran trekkers. The elements pose problems: rain soaks clothes and shoes; cold temperatures at higher elevations require pilgrims to carry extra covering layers; heat can be exhausting (made worse by a scarcity of water); wind and sun burn the skin. Kerkeling felt them all: "It would be impossible to overstate how much your feet hurt when you walk the Camino de Santiago."[52] Blisters from poorly fitting shoes and/or wet socks are endemic to this road, but for Choquette, that was just the beginning: "I don't know what was worse: going up, which just about killed my back and butt; or going down, which equally killed my knees, thighs and toes. In fact, I banged my toes so much that as I moved along, every step sent a sharp pang that at times made me cry out."[53] Various maladies (colds, flu, fever) spread quickly among pilgrims who spend nights in close quarters and share food and drink from common utensils. The sheer exhaustion of walking every day for a month lowers bodily resistance to illnesses and increases the odds of a misstep on a gravelly slope. Rudolph sums it up: "The average day on the pilgrimage is physically harder than the hardest day in the average person's life."[54]

Ordinary creature comforts could never be presumed. Both medieval and modern pilgrims occasionally "camped out" for the night, but usually they found lodging either in commercial inns or in a variety of cheaper albergues, refugios, hostels, monasteries, priories—many of them run by religious orders, municipal associations, or confraternities (brotherhoods of veteran pilgrims, usually from a specific nation or region). Actually getting a bed at the end of a tiring day has never been a guarantee, and privacy is always in short supply. At Puente la Reina, Laffi "looked for an inn," "but the place was already full of people" (eventually he was permitted to sleep in a nearby chapel, one of those little miracles that makes the challenges of the Camino survivable).[55] Things weren't much better in the 1990s, when Jack Hitt found the search for an available bed just as intense: "anarchic competitions among the tribes of pilgrims when we enter a town in the late afternoon."[56] Some pilgrims would begin their daily walk well before dawn, sometimes to avoid midday heat, but also to beat others to the best bed at the next resting place. Once inside, pilgrims today might find better hospitality than in the twelfth century. Historian Jonathan Sumption notes: "Medieval innkeepers were not much loved. . . . They displayed fine wines and served cheap ones. Their fish was bad and their meat putrid. Their candles did not burn. Their beds were filthy. They gave change in bad coin. The inns were often brothels and always dens of drunkenness. . . . 'Truly, Judas lives in every one of them.'"[57] Kerkeling avoided the cheaper and chummier albergues, and remembering his grandma's words, preferred hotels with stars: "I don't need to wade through other people's athlete's foot to find illumination!" Still, he found it impossible to avoid an occasional "greasy flowered plate holding undefinable bits of meat."[58] Laundry facilities are sporadic: after smelling the accumulated sweat in her clothes, MacLaine vowed that she "would burn them at the end of the journey."[59]

And then came the acute dangers. Once when Shirley MacLaine went to pee en plein air, she "sat in an anthill" and got royally stung.[60] Medieval pilgrims could expect to face vicious animals large and small. Domenico Laffi was warned not to leave the refugio too early in the morning "because the wolves would kill us." He came upon a French pilgrim dying on the road, "covered with locusts": "Those cruel little creatures had begun to devour him, and while we stayed with him we had great difficulty in protecting ourselves from their voracious appetites."[61] Robert Sutton would have picked fleas and lice from his clothes "repeatedly"[62]—for modern travelers, bedbugs. There may be fewer wolves near the Camino these days, but nasty dogs remain: "A monstrous black dog leapt at me from inside a tin barn. He went for my throat."[63] MacLaine was saved by an unyielding leash. For the Chicagoan Choquette, "the air smelled so strongly of acrid cow dung it almost knocked me out,"[64] but Hitt found a silver lining in manure piles, calling them an "olfactory signal of pending rest. It means animals, which means people, which means shelter, which means coffee and water and food."[65] At least medieval pilgrims did not need to worry about menacing vehicles speeding along highways that, at times, serve as the pilgrimage Way. In the mountains of El Bierzo, Kerkeling walked the "highway of horrors": "The space between me and the many big trucks amounts to a scant eight inches, and I squeeze my thighs against the waist-high metal guardrail and stare petrified into the roaring water" of a "rushing river" below.[66]

As if all that were not enough, pilgrims must put up with other pilgrims, whose contribution to the experience could be just annoying or far worse. To be sure, companionship for a long and arduous walk is often welcome, and friends can steer a lost pilgrim back on track (another risk). There is safety in numbers, from wolves or human predators.[67] But the benefits of companionship sometimes come with unwanted baggage. Kerkeling stayed in private hotel rooms to avoid "snoring Americans and belching Frenchmen."[68] Those who try to walk together find themselves moving at different speeds: "It never works out. The pace and timbre of one's step on a long haul has a unique quality, like a fingerprint."[69] Choquette realized that "Camino time is special" and "understood not wanting to waste it in bad company."[70] Most modern pilgrims thus seek solitude (like Thoreau), an "intensely private encounter,"[71] even as they are always surrounded by multitudes pursuing the same thing. Jack Hitt found that "companionship, while comforting, is fouling my intent.

Instead of freedom of thought and movement, the road has quickly become bogged down in a crude version of the world I left behind."[72] Other people along the road, not necessarily pilgrims, are more than a nuisance. French monk Aimery Picaud warned medieval pilgrims about unscrupulous Navarrese who would lay in wait along the Río Salado with their knives sharpened, ready to tell any passing pilgrim that the water was safe for horse and man to drink: "Accordingly, we watered our horses in the stream, and had no sooner done so, than two of them died: these the men skinned on the spot."[73]

All this torture comes at a price. My plane ticket to Spain was $2,000. Sonia Choquette spent $869.42 on equipment and $1,000 on travel and medical insurance. The pilgrimage route has always had its rip-off artists. Hitt was shocked to receive the bill "for several rounds of coffee and a couple of plates of food. It's for eighty-six dollars."[74] Being away from home for a month or more comes with its own costs, even if cheap lodging is endured. But the material costs of the pilgrimage—and even the abundance of harrowing experiences on the road—are quite beside the point: long ago and now, risks and dangers are expected and welcomed as portals to revelation or deeper self-understanding. Medieval pilgrims to Santiago assumed suffering and struggle as part of the package, believing that "a pilgrimage should be accomplished in poverty," and thus pilgrims become "holy figures entitled to alms and good treatment from those they met."[75] Miracles are born out of misery and affliction, affirming the medieval pilgrim's faith that Saint James is ever present along the Way and ready to assist. Starkie recounts an old tale about a sick pilgrim in the eleventh century who was picked up by Saint James "on his flying horse" and carried "in the twinkling of an eye to Compostella, because he had stayed behind like a good Samaritan to tend his dying companion."[76] (Santiago and I both flew!) William Wey believes that a pilgrim's scrip was recovered from a thief via the intercession of Saint James.[77] These days, such miracles are often dismissed as mere coincidence or serendipity, but they happen so regularly that modern pilgrims take them as evidence of having slipped into another dimension. Kerkeling happens upon his friend Seppi, whose foot is bandaged from an earlier fall. Seppi tells him that a mere five minutes behind him on the road was a German nurse who had skills and supplies to patch him up: "This coincidence doesn't surprise me in the least. That's the way things work on the Camino! I would have been surprised if he *hadn't* been helped. God seems to have sent forth countless numbers of nurses with bandages and ointments."[78] Out of pain and suffering—miracles, to affirm new beliefs. Even blisters teach lessons. A Spanish student told Frey that "suffering makes us more human. . . . Blisters of the Camino are the problems of life. To continue walking despite blisters produces both pain and joy."[79]

———•———

One of the oldest sayings of the road—*Ir romero y volver ramera*—translates "Start out a pilgrim, return a whore."
«JACK HITT[80]»

Within the sacred precincts, the profane world is transcended.
«MIRCEA ELIADE[81]»

Some places on earth are more sacred than others.[82] Trapdoors to the transcendent cannot be everywhere (although they might be found or made just about anywhere in particular). This leaves a lot of territory that must be something other than sacred, and French sociologist Émile Durkheim more than a century ago focused attention on that other territory: profane. The distinction between sacred and profane is among the foundational dichotomies we live by, however leaky it sometimes gets in practice. For Durkheim, the distinction is at the heart of all "religion" in its most elementary forms, but persists as an interpretive tool even in fully secularized situations and among agnostic people. The quality of being sacred does not inhere in the object itself (in secular times, "society" itself could be considered sacred) but in the practices and rituals of believers who define the realm as "set apart and forbidden." The sacred is forbidden not in the sense of being inaccessible but rather explicitly in the sense of being unavailable for mundane, ordinary, or instrumental use. The bread we eat to satisfy hunger is profane by contrast to, in Christian traditions, the wafer taken at Holy Communion and said to be the body of Christ. The sacred is a realm set apart absolutely and governed by behavioral prohibitions and prescriptions, and Durkheim suggests that "the sacred is thrown into an ideal and transcendent reality, while the residuum is abandoned as the property of the material world."[83]

The idea that *places* like the Camino (or Delphi) could be physically marked off as sacred was developed by the historian and philosopher of religion Mircea Eliade: a "holy place" is where one could expect "the revelation of a reality *other* than that in which he participates through his ordinary daily life," "places of passage between heaven and earth," a "different space from the buildings that surround it."[84] The Way of St. James has been endowed from the beginning with extraordinary capacities set apart from mundane and instrumental utilities—a "hot line to the divine."[85] It is not just a road for moving people and goods from the Pyrenees to Santiago de Compostela; it must become something more than a path for transportation, commerce, exercise, or bird-watching. And yet the Camino's status as a sacred place, especially for modern pilgrims, depends fundamentally on its constant juxtaposition to the mundane and temporal objects and practices that hedge it for almost 500 miles. The Way is made sacred in and through omnipresent visual contrasts to its profane surrounds. This dirt and gravel path—and the buildings and settings immediately alongside it—becomes a linear scaffolding for the transcendent, rendering visible and thus more compelling the grounds for accepting new truths that might otherwise remain merely abstractions.

When Robert Sutton walked the Camino in 1423, he came upon "so many hospitals, so many shrines, each memorable in some way, but mostly fading and blending into each other like the shimmering heat haze on the crest of every hill."[86] Sonia

Choquette, six centuries later, vowed that she would go into at least one church a day—and indeed that is possible, if one includes other religious buildings (monasteries, chapels, priories, abbeys) and those that might be disused today or in ruins. The road to Santiago is one long and dense string of sanctuaries—places set apart from the profane inns, albergues, cafés, shops, and highways that also line the Way, places that ostensibly have no purpose other than veneration, devotion, or mind-clearing respite. These "holy places," writes Turner, constitute a "sacred topography" where "the landscape itself is coded into symbolic units packed with cosmological and theological meaning"—"charging up with sacredness many of its geographical features and attributes."[87]

When Walter Starkie walked inside the Cathedral of St. Isidore in León, he felt "that eerie sensation of the supernatural which a humble pilgrim feels even today in the church . . . bearing us all aloft into another world."[88] Some sacred spots are palpable reminders of where miracles happened and relics are stored, with evidence on hand to persuade the skeptical. The Royal Monastery at Carrión de los Condes houses the remains of the martyr Zoilo (Saint Zoilus), and although the place is a World Heritage Site, Kerkeling believes that "actually it is *other*worldly."[89] At Santo Domingo de la Calzada, pilgrims feed crumbs to a cock and hen, who then begin to "crow with joy and make a great to-do," Laffi reports.[90] Starkie adds that many pilgrims hold the "superstitious belief" that "if the fowls did not eat them [they] would die on the Road of St. James."[91] This ongoing ritual perpetuates the memory of a miracle performed, of course, by Saint James. A pretty daughter of the local innkeeper tried to seduce a young pilgrim, and when he spurned her advances, the girl hid a silver goblet in his pack—and declared, the next day, that he was a thief. He was quickly sentenced to be hanged. The boy's distraught parents went on to Santiago anyway (where they prayed to the apostle), and upon their return trip through Santo Domingo, they found their son still strung up but alive! They went immediately to the sheriff, who told them that the boy was no more alive than the chickens he was about to eat for dinner—on cue, the cock rose up from his plate and crowed. The boy was pardoned.[92] Conrad Rudolph witnessed "the boy's tunic and chains still hang[ing] on the wall next to the cage [with descendant birds inside] as proof."[93]

Even when a pilgrim is not inside a special sanctuary, the sacredness of the road itself is cast into high relief by the profane stuff all around it. Souvenir shops selling scallop shells and other trinkets began to surround the Cathedral at Santiago as soon as there were enough pilgrims to support the business: "In the thirteenth century there were a hundred stalls,"[94] and "the archbishop of Santiago took a percentage from licensed badge-sellers after 1200 and it was for many years a major source of revenue."[95] The Catholic Church itself blurs the line between sacred and profane by engaging in "commercial" activities of its own. A mascot was created for the Jubilee Year 2010 to stimulate pilgrim traffic—"Xubi," who looks like a blue-green Teletubby with a curl and a Twitter account.[96] After a part-time priest tried to "cadg[e] a few pesetas," Hitt's companions were "furious that the sacred moment of the pilgrim's meal was defiled with fund raising."[97] Commonplace features of modernity clash with the ancient way, becoming profane intrusions into the pilgrim's other world. Perhaps trying to assuage his guilt about hopping a bus for twenty miles into Burgos (pop. 200,000), Hape Kerkeling complains: "Several centuries ago, there were sheep pastures on the horizon; today you ride through a major industrial area."[98] Hitt resents the Franco-built public-housing complexes surrounding Ponferrada: "Towers of colorless concrete with blocky balconies soar at the edges of four-land frontage roads."[99] Coelho was depressed at the thought of "a new, paved expressway, . . . automobiles with scallop shells painted on their hoods, and souvenir shops at the gates of the monasteries."[100] As intrusions into the pilgrimage experience—or distractions from it—the very presence of these profane souvenir shops, mascots, factories, and highways astride the Camino *set up* the road as sacred ground by vivid contrast.

Pilgrims themselves can profane the transcendence of the Way. Shirley MacLaine found "so many discarded cigarettes along with plastic bags, papers, cartons, and condoms. How could people trash such a sacred land?"[101] Kerkeling "can't tell whether many pilgrims find the illumination they were seeking here, but they sure do leave quite a lot of garbage along the way."[102] Those who do not *walk* every step of the Camino from France, those who join the road for only the last 100 kilometers (but enough to earn their Compostela at the end), those who ride bikes ("for them it was purely sport")[103] or take buses or taxis, those who have their bags transported by car from hotel to hotel, those who stay in paradores (fancy hotels in historical buildings) and not in albergues—all of them, for other pilgrims, *defile* the sacred journey. And those who make too many compromises risk being defined as a "tourist," "among our chief insults on the road," writes Hitt (who was himself chided for not being a real pilgrim after he stayed one night in a parador).[104] Choquette took two packs to Spain: she carried the smaller one every day but had the larger one moved along for her by cars—she named it the "Cheater" bag. Hitt is ever the reluctant pilgrim, and even at the end of his journey "an air of fraudulence lingers": "Tourists unsheathe their cameras and illuminate my already soiled epiphany with the strobe of flashes."[105] Coelho was "shocked to find [at the Peak of Forgiveness] a group of tourists sunbathing and drinking beer; their car radios blasted music at top volume. They had driven up a nearby road to get to the top of the mountain."[106] Other pilgrims desecrate the road by acting in ways that they believe are morally inconsistent with expectations of pilgrimage. A sixty-year-old German man, traveling without his wife, told Frey that he yielded to temptation by "getting drunk with a woman, crossing lines he felt were questionable."[107]

What matters is not that the line between sacred and profane occasionally gets transgressed or obscured, but that counter-measures then emerge to reassert the symbolic distance between them—to plug the leak. The Camino is full of tangible evidence of resacralization. The wages of adultery are inscribed in stone: "At Santiago, the figuration of lust is . . . portrayed by both a man and a woman bitten in their genitals. The woman, for good measure, has her tongue dragged out and bitten by demons."[108] On the south portal of the Cathedral, Aimery Picaud found that "there is a woman next to the Temptation of the Lord, who holds in her hands the filthy head of her lover beheaded by her own husband, and this one forces her to kiss it twice a day. Oh, what a great and admirable punishment meted out to the adulterous woman, to be recounted by everyone."[109] Warning to pilgrims: don't even think about it! In medieval days, "there were so many stabbings of pilgrims by pilgrims in the cathedral of Santiago (probably brought on by heavy drinking during feast days) that normal church functions were regularly interrupted because of the constant need to reconsecrate the church each time blood was shed within it."[110] Jack Hitt is not worried that commercial hype will sully the road: "No one who endures months of walking through northern Spain will mistake the trip for a visit to Euro Disney. The road can take care of itself."[111] The power of the Camino to make pilgrims believe depends upon its (re)consecration as sacred ground. In the end, Rudolph found that the road "convey[ed] a spiritual intensity so extreme that it's completely irreconcilable with the world that surrounds it, in which it exists."[112] Kerkeling saw swarms of colorful butterflies along the Way, but "every time I deviate in the slightest from the path, the butterflies disappear."[113]

————•————

And not some secular skip up the Appalachian Trail, but an ancient and traditional one
«JACK HITT[114]»

Had to marvel at how beautiful this old monastery was, even if it did feel a little haunted by the heavy spirits of the past.
«SONIA CHOQUETTE[115]»

I have tried to imagine what it would have been like for the Very First pilgrim who walked to Santiago de Compostela as part of some extraordinary quest. A well-marked path did not exist: no scallop shells or yellow arrows to show the way, only a multiplicity of tracks linking cities and villages in northern Spain, some of them eventually ending up in Santiago. The Very First pilgrim would have found only sporadic indications that this was a sacred way: a church here or a monastery there or possibly relics at Oviedo (which today is not even on the most traveled route). Food and lodging would have been hit or miss (no chain of hostels at regular intervals), and there were surely long stretches in the Meseta where even potable water was scarce. Still, somebody had to be First, and it might have been Gottschalk, the bishop of Le Puy, who walked to Santiago in 950 and perhaps spurred others to make the trek (or was it "shrewd promotion"?).[116]

The idea of a marked sacred path as we know it today evolved slowly by accretion and through a symbiotic relationship between pilgrims and those along the Way offering services, protection, and transcendent moments. The cock-and-hen legend at Santo Domingo de la Calzada suggests that pilgrims were lured to certain towns and routes by the presence of miracle sites, albergues, sources of food, and protection (provided by the Knights Templar, for instance, whose castle at Ponferrada would have comforted medieval pilgrims fearing bandits or Moors). In turn, as pilgrims over the centuries voted with their feet for one road over another, religious orders (like the ambitious monks at Cluny in Paris), innkeepers, and (much later) tourist development offices all had reasons to give a sharper definition to the chosen path. The Very First pilgrim did not create the Way of St. James, but the several hundred thousand pilgrims who then followed his or her footsteps beat a path that eventually got well marked with scallops, yellow arrows, dedicated services, and sacred sites.

Pilgrims made the pilgrimage way.[117] The Camino is an ambulatory palimpsest. Layers upon layers of meanings and revelations are rendered materially visible for subsequent pilgrims, in effect, shaping their experience and creating expectations of what the walk will do for them. More than that, preceding pilgrims create obligations for those who follow: failure to discover something "bigger than ourselves"[118] is to let down the beneficent ghosts who haunt every step. If *they* touched the transcendent, well, so must I! Heather Blair's study of Japanese pilgrims who climbed the Peak of Gold at roughly the same time that the road to St. James gained initial popularity in Europe introduces the useful idea of "compelling precedent"[119] to capture the effect of earlier pilgrims on later ones—stimulating hesitant pilgrims to take the plunge and defining for them what a successful and authentic experience would entail.

Pilgrims today cannot escape the immanent "traces"[120] embedded in the path created for them by their forewalkers. Starkie believes that "every step the pilgrim makes today . . . evokes memories of those who passed that way century after century ever since the discovery of the sarcophagus of the Apostle in the ninth century."[121] Choquette "was alone but walking with millions" and could "almost hear their footsteps and sense their breathing."[122] Connections to pilgrims of yore are made visible and even palpable via material reminders inscribed along the road. At Puente la Reina, Coelho encountered "a statue of a pilgrim in medieval garb: three-cornered hat, cape, scallop shells, and in his hand a shepherd's crook with a gourd—a memorial to the epic journey . . . that Petrus [his guide] and I were reliving."[123] Hitt had the same experience: "No church on the road neglects to honor the pilgrim in the presumed eternity of stone. We are cut into the walls, carved atop the capitals, painted onto panels, and sculpted in wood. . . . After a brutal day's walk, sitting in the cool of thick stone, it's hard not to feel a little flattered." He also felt "a warm intimacy with the hundreds of millions of pilgrims who have walked this road in the last millennium or so" each time he came upon a yellow arrow.[124] "Little cairns" made by pilgrims from rocks along the Way made Kerkeling feel the same emotion: "Every pilgrim takes the time to leave his signature in this dusty heat. . . . Suddenly I feel a bond with all the people who have traveled this path, with their wishes, yearnings, dreams, and fears, and I am keenly conscious that I'm not, in fact, traveling alone. . . . And each little structure seems to be saying 'I made it, and you'll make it too.'"[125] The "spirits of the past" are "heavy" precisely because they create an obligation for modern pilgrims to go and do the same: enter the beyond, one step at a time.

Modern pilgrims secure that bond to the ancestors as they participate in rituals specific to the Camino that have persisted for centuries. Near the highest altitude on the Way, pilgrims find an iron cross on top of a thirty-foot pole. Coelho writes that the cross was left there during Caesar's invasion of the Iberian Peninsula, and that pagans first started to leave pebbles from elsewhere at its base.[126] As the Estevez/Sheen movie version pictures the site today, the accumulated stones make for a climbable cone that reaches at least one-third of the way up the wooden pole, each one symbolizing some burden or encumbrance now unloaded (making the journey forward that much lighter, a little drama of self-transformation). Farther along, pilgrims are expected to pick up a piece of limestone from Triacastela and carry it to Castañeda—where once there were furnaces for firing the stone to make lime used in the construction of the Cathedral at Santiago. Upon reaching that Cathedral, grateful pilgrims line up at the statue of Saint James in the High Altar and give him an embrace from behind (and maybe leave their pilgrim's hat or other offering). At one entrance to the Cathedral, Saint James's foot "has been kissed so many times over the course of the centuries that it has shrunk by several sizes," according to Kerkeling.[127] There may be some truth to that: so many pilgrims have put their five fingers into the five hollows carved out on the Cathedral's Tree of Jesse (in effect, holy genealogy in stone) that it has been roped off to prevent fragmentation of the granite.

It will come as no surprise that Shirley MacLaine in particular discovered some deeply personal connections with long-ago pilgrims: "Was this why people over the ages made the pilgrimage? Had any of them experienced the same thing that was happening to me?" The answer is yes, of course: "Was I, in effect, walking backward in a time that already existed in me? Yes, I thought. I have been here." Pilgrims walking the Camino "created footmarks of past truth . . . lurking within each one of us as foreshadowings."[128] MacLaine found *present* truth there as well. But even for modern pilgrims not inclined toward reincarnation, "the awareness that you are doing what so many before you have done" becomes, for Conrad Rudolph, "like some mystical sign indicating the way."[129] Frey suggests that modern pilgrims "want to travel the same routes as the medieval pilgrims who first ventured to Santiago, and to experience them in the same way." Through such emulation, "the hope is that the pilgrim will better understand himself or herself, God, the way, and the past."[130] Demurral comes from Jack Hitt: "No pilgrim can make sense of the road if he reduces it to mere reenactment. I can't be a medieval pilgrim." That may be so, but by the end of his own pilgrimage, Hitt ponders not the Very First pilgrim but the Most Recent one: "With each step, we are precisely the last person to cover that patch of ground. And a few minutes later even that lame distinction will vanish, our footprint trampled by a crowd of schoolchildren, or a mule, or robust senior citizens from Holland."[131] If pilgrims on the Camino today are obliged to appreciate (if not always emulate) those who walked before them, they incur equally powerful debts to those who walk after. The road cannot end.

——·——

One's destination is never a place, but rather a new way of looking at things.
«HENRY MILLER[132]»

I end this journey where I began, like a pilgrimage—and there is irony in my epigraph from *Piers Plowman*. Piers makes his first appearance in the allegory when he faces a crowd of folk, each of whom seems guilty of one or another sin (with names like Lust, Envy, and Greed). The crowd has already been told by Reason, "You pilgrims who search for St. James or the martyr-saints of Rome, go and look for St. Truth," giving a strong hint that penance may not come from a literal walk to a pilgrimage destination. Setting out on a supposed pilgrimage anyway, but only getting lost, they meet a professional pilgrim who sports all the symbols of having walked many sacred roads—including "shells from Galicia" for his journey to Santiago de Compostela. The sinners ask the pilgrim if he knows the whereabouts of a shrine to St. Truth: "Never, I can tell you, and nowhere." A plowman now speaks up and tells the crowd that they are welcome to help him plow his field, where they will find Truth and grace not in a Holy Site at the end of a long walk but through a virtuous and moral life of good works. Just after Piers tells a Knight that he will travel with him "until we find Truth," the "Pilgrim clothes" he dons are those of a plowman—a "seed-basket" instead of a scrip (or backpack), and no floppy hat, staff, or scallop shell.[133]

Historically, there is a long and deep trough in the number of pilgrims walking to Santiago, starting just about the time *Piers Plowman* was written in the fourteenth century, and accelerating downward during the Reformation. The decline had several causes: with the fall of once-Islamic Córdoba around 1380, the need for multitudinous Christian presence in northern Spain became less urgent; warnings about dangers and risks may have been heeded; excesses in the growing market for easy indulgences (wealthy people seeking penance could hire a surrogate pilgrim) profaned the very exercise; and Luther offers the capper: "The true Christian pilgrimage is not to Rome, or Compostela, but to the prophets, the Psalms, and the Gospels."[134] From the early modern period well into postmodernity, relatively scant numbers of pilgrims walked the Way of St. James—maybe fewer than 500 a year in the early 1980s. Then, the steep uptick: about 2,000 pilgrims received the Compostela in 1986, more than 250,000 in 2016. How odd that in a secularized, rationalized, and disenchanted world, a certain kind of truth—transcendental, spiritual, mystical, otherworldly—is once again found by hordes in an all-too-real place: on the road, and at the journey's sacred end.

6

The Whole Truth and Nothing But

Justice is but truth in action.
«JUSTICE LOUIS D. BRANDEIS[1]»

Maybe it is only coincidence that St. Louis is the site of two conspicuous legal cases, separated by 168 years, each a defining moment in protracted struggles over civil rights for African Americans. Dred Scott and his wife, Harriet, filed suit in 1846 at the Old Courthouse against their owner, Irene Emerson, claiming that she treated them in a manner that would be unlawful if they were free citizens—confinement, beatings, work without wages—but commonplace and legitimate for the treatment of slaves.[2] The Scotts, now returned to St. Louis, asserted that they were free citizens on grounds that they had lived for six years with their owner in the free state of Illinois and indeed had been married in the territory of Wisconsin, also designated free by the Missouri Compromise of 1820 (which made slavery legal in its namesake state). They presented their case in the lower courtroom of the west wing of the Old Courthouse, with Judge Alexander Hamilton (not that one) presiding—and lost, but won the right to appeal. Thus began litigation that went on for eleven years, starting in the Missouri state court system, and moving on in 1854 to the US district court for Missouri, which at the time convened at the Papin Building, upstairs in a "small back room over a Main Street store."[3] Though Dred and Harriet Scott stayed back in St. Louis as slaves, the case went on to Washington and the US Supreme Court in 1857. Chief Justice Roger B. Taney, speaking for the majority in a 7–2 decision, ruled that Dred and Harriet Scott (and their two daughters) remained slaves despite their time on free soil and despite the fact that ninety former slaves had earlier won their freedom on the same grounds in Missouri courts. Without benefit of citizenship, the Scotts had no right even to file suit in the federal courts. Moreover, the court found the Missouri Compromise itself unconstitutional, suggesting that the federal government had no right to forbid slavery in the new territories. Most historians agree that the Dred Scott decision inched the country closer to Civil War.

In August 2014, the Civil Rights Division of the US Department of Justice began an investigation of events surrounding the shooting of Michael Brown, an African American teenager, by Officer Darren Wilson on Canfield Drive in Ferguson, Missouri, just outside of St. Louis. The federal investigation eventually echoed the prior and independent conclusion of a St. Louis County grand jury: the evidence failed to justify an indictment against Officer Wilson for violating the civil rights of Mr. Brown (i.e., the policeman's use of lethal force was warranted by an immediate threat posed by Mr. Brown). However, following a more encompassing investigation, the Justice Department issued a report in March 2015 criticizing the City of Ferguson—its police department and its local courts—for systematically discriminating against African Americans by arresting, ticketing, and collecting fines from blacks at rates higher than those for whites. Attorney General Eric Holder sued the City of Ferguson for "routinely violating the constitutional rights of its black residents,"[4] and in January 2016 the two parties settled the case without a trial. They agreed to a consent decree that identified the changes that Ferguson would need to make in order to bring its practices and culture into compliance with the Constitutional rights of all citizens. At the first anniversary of the shooting of Michael Brown, civil unrest in Ferguson and St. Louis propelled the Black Lives Matter movement, "the 21st Century's first civil rights movement,"[5] to national significance. On April 19, 2016, District Judge Catherine D. Perry held a public hearing on the consent decree in Courtroom 3 North of the Thomas F. Eagleton US Courthouse at 111 S. Tenth Street, St. Louis: thirty-two members of the public spoke up, and twenty-three written responses previously received were also considered.

Dred Scott to Ferguson measures a sea change in our national understanding of race and civil rights. Federal judges once chose to value the property rights of slave owners over the supposedly "unalienable rights" of "life, liberty and the pursuit of happiness" asserted by the Declaration of Independence. Much later, the attorney general and a federal judge pursued the prosecution of a tiny municipality in Missouri precisely for its failure to extend those rights to all. Progress. But my interest here is in the venues: *where* did justice get settled, and how did those places matter?

When Dred and Harriet Scott decided to sue for their freedom, they went to the Old Courthouse in downtown St. Louis, perhaps choosing to enter the building from steps on its east wing. Slaves were routinely auctioned on those very steps if their owners were bankrupt or if a will was contested, because that entrance was closest to the probate court. When Harvard professor Cornel West and other activists associated with Black Lives Matter such as DeRay McKesson and Johnetta Elzie chose to mark the first anniversary of Michael Brown's death with protest and civil disobedience, they chose to gather on the east-facing steps of the public entrance to the Eagleton US Courthouse just blocks away from the Old Courthouse, where forty of them were arrested for trespassing. Even if the outcome of Dred Scott's failed legal challenge forces the conclusion that courts sometimes reach judgments that appear in different times to be a retreat from the fair and just, and even if the court-ordered

rehabilitation of Ferguson's policing practices did little immediately to stanch the bleeding of black men killed by cops na-
tionwide, those who pursue justice keep heading to courthouses
and to courtrooms as authoritative sites for adjudicating facts
and settling disputes over the weightiest matters of guilt or in-
nocence under the law.

———•———

The Place of Justice is a Hallowed Place.
«FRANCIS BACON[6]»

Courts are places and undeniably places of power. Here, the state
legitimately metes out violent punishment, restricts freedom, and
imposes material penalties on citizens found guilty of wrongdo-
ing.[7] And yet, beginning with the earliest American courthouses
and courtrooms from the eighteenth century,[8] the architecture
of these buildings and their functional arrangement of physical spaces have sought to dilute the appearance and exercise of
unwarranted power. The US Constitution says nothing explicit
about the design of federal courthouses and courtrooms, but
the Sixth Amendment describes the rights possessed by those
accused of crimes—a description that can in effect be translated
into blueprints, floor plans, and interior order. Because the accused has the right to a "public trial," courthouses must welcome
those who wish to witness judicial proceedings and provide designated space for them inside the courtroom proper. Because the
accused has the right to an "impartial jury," courthouses must
have spaces and passages that permit the conversion of ordinary
citizens into jurors who are protected from compromising contacts and unjustified influence. Because the accused has the right
"to be confronted with the witnesses against him," judicial buildings must architecturally manage the flows of the accused (even
if in custody) and the witnesses (for both parties) through the
courthouse in a way that prevents the possibility of intimidation or contaminating interactions while ensuring their direct

confrontation before a judge and, sometimes, a jury. Finally, because the Sixth Amendment grants the accused the right "to have the Assistance of Counsel," spaces must be provided for attorneys to defend their clients.

Visual comparison of the Old Courthouse in St. Louis (1839) to the Eagleton US Courthouse (2000) suggests that the Constitutional rights of the accused can be rendered architecturally in profoundly different buildings. Or so it seems: one has two working floors; the other rises twenty-nine stories. But in so many other ways—in the values symbolically represented, in the flows of people enforced by walls and doors, in the arrangement of role-specific work spaces in each courtroom—my tale of two courthouses is really about the manifold similarities and continuities between them. Despite huge changes in building technologies and massive growth in the scale of the judicial enterprise since the mid-nineteenth century, the Sixth Amendment shines through as a template shaping special places where rights of the accused are consistently built-in.

By the time the Old Courthouse was fully built out in 1861, it was the tallest structure in the city. Today, it squats underneath Eero Saarinen's 630-foot Gateway Arch—but majestically so, with its copper roof oxidized blue-green. The original plans, more or less realized through decades of construction and renovation, called for a Greek Revival style building made of brick and stone, "consisting of four wings, with two large porticos, stone columns 32 feet tall, and a low dome rising 130 feet above the yard."[9] Each wing originally held two courtrooms, upper floor and lower, and in the middle was a rotunda ringed with more columns and an oculus at the top—to "let in light from above."[10] The original "Dred Scott Courtroom" has been substantially renovated and is now bisected by a new wall needed to hold up the courtroom above, which has been restored to look something like the space where the Scotts faced Judge Hamilton in 1846. It is instantly legible for any visitor today who has ever tuned in to *Perry Mason*, *Matlock*, *Law & Order*, *The Practice*, or *Boston Legal*. The public, the attorneys, their clients (except defendants in custody), and the witnesses enter from the rear, facing the judge's bench straight ahead, which is elevated by several steps and fronted by a lower desk for the court reporter. The "bar" (a curved wooden railing with carved balusters) separates the space for spectators to sit from the "well," which has two sets of tables and chairs (one for the prosecution, the other for the defense). To the right of the well, farthest from the defense table, are twelve chairs for the jurors, and to the left beside the judge (but a step below) is the witness stand. Terrazzo floors, deep mahogany-colored wood finishes throughout, and a domed ceiling held up by still more Greek columns convey dignity. It all speaks "courtroom."

When this elliptical room is fitted into the rectangle defined by the west wing's exterior walls, it creates four small niches at the corners—and each has a door from the courtroom. In one corner are the judge's chambers, where Hamilton could robe, compose himself, and perhaps meet with attorneys in sidebar conversations beyond earshot of the jury—and from which he would emerge only after everybody else was assembled and there was order in court. If the case involved a defendant in custody, the bailiff or marshal would bring the accused into the courtroom from a second door before the jury was seated, so that shackles (if any) would be less apparent: innocent until proven guilty. The third door leads to the jury deliberation room, a physical retreat from all other people involved in the trial, including the public audience, where jurors can decide in patient reflection the facts of the case. But not too patiently. My tour guide (the Old Courthouse in St. Louis is now managed by the National Park Service) explained that the jury deliberation niche had high windows and became unbearably hot in the summer and freezing cold in the winter, which is just what the judges wanted: faster verdicts make for speedy trials. The fourth niche may have housed a law library. Other courtrooms in the building follow the same design, including one on the upper floor of the east wing, where Dred and Harriet Scott and their two children (now chattel of a more sympathetic owner) were finally manumitted in 1857, in effect reversing Judge Taney's historic decision (Dred Scott died a free man just one year later).

If Judge Hamilton could be teleported across time and space to Judge Perry's courtroom in the Eagleton US Courthouse, he would probably feel deeply ambivalent—so much is familiar, so much unrecognizable. Computer screens on the judge's bench and in front of the recorder would puzzle him, as would the floor microphone in the well, the security cameras high up on the walls, and, indeed, electric lights. He would be delighted by climate control provided by modern HVAC systems, and would feel right at home with the dignified wood finishes and the natural light streaming through floor-to-ceiling windows. Hamilton would need no help understanding who sits where: his bench, attorneys' tables, jury box, witness stand, and public gallery are located here as they were in the Old Courthouse. He would understand the multiple doors for entering and exiting the courtroom—their distinctive purposes have changed little. But if Judge Hamilton were to peek behind any of those doors, he would find not a cramped niche but a bewildering array of hallways and rooms—attesting to the enlarged role played by auxiliary activities and the sizable increases in personnel needed to dispense justice these days.

In a way, the Eagleton US Courthouse is the culmination of more than two centuries of tinkering with the best architecture and building design for protecting Constitutional rights to a fair trial. There was much room for improvement. The Old Courthouse was a less than hospitable place for Dred and Harriet Scott to seek their freedom: "The rumbling of carts and wagons, the grinding of streetcar wheels, the clip-clopping of horses' hooves (and the stench of their waste in the street) and the calls of street vendors would all come wafting in through the open windows in the summertime."[11] When their case shifted to the federal judicial system in 1854, there was no purpose-built courthouse at all—only a storefront with blank space upstairs where loose furniture could be arranged for a proper hearing. By the 1890s, the US District Court for the Eastern District of

Missouri and US Court of Appeals for the Eighth District took up residence in the US Custom House and Post Office, done up in Second Empire style with a prominent iron mansard dome. Tailor-made courtrooms were located on the third floor, but in a building shared with diverse federal offices whose activities and clientele varied from those of the judiciary (lighthouse and steamboat inspectors, for example, and the US Army Corps of Engineers). In 1935, the federal courts at St. Louis moved to a building largely designed just for them (some customs activities also migrated there), a typical Works Progress Administration art deco structure at Twelfth and Market Streets (today, the Carnahan Courthouse for the St. Louis City Circuit Court).

By the 1980s, those judicial digs had become inadequate for the volume of proceedings and for the staff needed to keep the wheels of justice turning smoothly—not just in St. Louis, but in almost every American city with a federal courthouse. Construction of the Eagleton US Courthouse at the end of the twentieth century became part of the "largest (federal government) building program since the New Deal for the renovation and construction of new courthouses." Chief Justice William Rehnquist wangled preliminary commitments from Congress for up to $8–10 billion "to build more than 50 new Federal courthouses and significantly to alter or add to more than 60 others." The General Services Administration (GSA, which owns federal property like courthouses and post offices) proudly reported that between 1996 and 2006, it had "delivered 46 new courthouses or annexes" for a mere $3.4 billion—including Eagleton, which by itself came in at about $200 million.[12]

The building boom in federal courthouses was justified not only by the need for more space, but by the need for *better* space. The Judicial Conference of the United States (made up of the chief justice of the Supreme Court and the chief judges in all federal district and appellate courts) worked hard to define the architectural contours of courthouses and courtrooms so that they would more effectively serve the needs of justice in a new millennium, at a moment of rapid technological change (computers), growing security concerns, and rising numbers of specialized cases dealing with new issues such as civil rights. The judges saw little need to start from scratch: their ambition was to create new courthouses that perpetuated displays of the core symbolic values of the judiciary (openness, for example) and that arranged passages and rooms to improve the odds that the Constitutional rights of the accused would be materialized. The result is the *U.S. Courts Design Guide* (originally published in 1991 and subsequently revised), prepared by the Administrative Office of the United States Courts (an arm of the Judicial Conference) in collaboration with the GSA. The *Design Guide* codifies the architectural preconditions of justice and, to a degree, standardizes the design of all new and renovated federal courthouses. It is, for me, a treasure trove of detailed injunctions setting down the rules for judicial spaces that can become truth-spots, for buildings that protect the Constitutional rights of the accused against arbitrary state power and thus achieve a measure of legitimacy for processes of deciding justice. But how?

———•———

The most important thing about a courthouse is that it must . . . speak about the meaning of the system of justice and the idea of accessibility, the idea that every citizen will have equal access to the administration of justice.
«HENRY N. COBB, *architect, US Courthouse, Hammond, Indiana*[13]»

It had to look like a courthouse, a St. Louis courthouse.
«BOB SCHWARTZ, *architect on the Eagleton project*[14]»

Appearances. When protesters gathered in August 2015 on the steps of the Eagleton US Courthouse to mark the first anniversary of Michael Brown's shooting, how did they feel when they looked up . . . and up, and up? A skyscraper of twenty-nine floors can be imposing, maybe even intimidating, and not necessarily inviting.[15] Among the new federal courthouses built around the turn of the twenty-first century, Eagleton is the tallest and largest: 567 feet high (just 63 feet shorter than the Arch), one million square feet, twenty-five courtrooms, "seven hundred judicial employees,"[16] taking up an entire city block— simply massive. The building is frosty even on a hot summer's day. If protesters had been allowed to enter Eagleton that day, they would have faced a phalanx of uniformed federal marshals routinely on duty in the atrium, and a screening operation that would make the Transportation Security Administration envious. Steve Brubaker, design architect on Eagleton, told me that the St. Louis federal judges wanted their new workplace to make a statement: "The judges wanted something that was obviously important. You just don't want to come here wearing shorts."[17] Mission accomplished.

But Eagleton is a public government building—civic space— and its gargantuan scale must somehow be reconciled with the idea that it is a place of the people, for the people, and by the people, especially for those accused of crimes, who are promised a "speedy and public trial" by the Sixth Amendment. It is not easy to make a monumental colossus seem welcoming—or accessible, open, and transparent (values the judiciary would like to convey). The *U.S. Courts Design Guide* stipulates that new federal courthouses "must be planned and designed to frame, facilitate and mediate the encounter between the citizen and the justice system."[18] How, then, to bring this behemoth down to human scale, to project the ideal that each case heard inside is uniquely vital? For security reasons, the front entrance to Eagleton is set back from the street. But instead of filling the apron with endless concrete or stone bollards like those used at airports, designers put "trees and planters," "intimate gardens," and other "unobtrusive perimeter controls" along the walkways to "give this expansive plaza a human scale" and to make the place "approachable." Add "sweeping stairs and landscaped terraces," and you get solid barriers likely to deter somebody wishing to drive a bomb-filled truck into the courthouse—but humanely rendered.[19] The security screening area inside the voluminous public atrium is tucked inside a smaller structure within the dome, which Brubaker compared to Bernini's Baldachin at St. Peter's in Rome—both designed to make the arrival just a bit more intimate.

The ratio of glass to stone on the façade is greater in Eagleton than in the 1930s art deco building it replaced, and not just because of shifting architectural fashion or new construction technologies. Architects and maybe judges seem to believe that abundant windows in a courthouse put the judicial proceedings inside on display, conveying a sense of their transparency and accountability—nothing to hide in these obvious exercises of state power. Glass reveals but also exposes, and the *Design Guide* notes that "glazing costs are higher in judicial facilities in order to address blast, seismic, and ballistic threats."[20] Still, the GSA praises Eagleton for its "expansive use of glass for floor-to-ceiling windows that run from the entry plaza to the building's dome," and adds, "Thoughtful security makes this openness possible. Courtrooms and chambers are several floors above ground level."[21] William Bain designed the new federal courthouse in Seattle, and describes its top-to-bottom glass wall as "a metaphor for the transparency of the judicial system." "This special building comprises both strength and transparency. It represents our Federal government, and as such, has a great responsibility to express not only the government's strength and power but also our nation's commitment to an open and impartial judicial system."[22] Bain asks a lot from a pane of glass. The US Courthouse in Orlando creates "sunlight-filled courtrooms, jury rooms, offices, and public spaces [that] both symbolize the clear light of reason represented by our laws and humanize the setting for visitors, judges, and staff."[23] No surprise that the designers of Eagleton put an oculus at the top of the dome in the entry rotunda, an echo of the one at the Old Courthouse, "open to the sun and sky"[24]—and, Brubaker adds, also open to a distinctively midwestern sky that is impressively moody, as changeable as verdicts are unpredictable and as justice itself is ambiguous. For people who come to witness a trial at Eagleton, it is easy to find an exterior window enabling a gaze onto familiar and orienting surrounds—for many of them, home.

Eagleton must be recognizable as a public courthouse, distinctively "ours" among the forest of business skyscrapers in downtown St. Louis. Ferguson protesters surely had no trouble finding the place, especially if they used the diminutive and beloved Old Courthouse as a touchstone for what a judicial building should look like. Gyo Obata, founding partner of the global architectural firm HOK and lead designer on Eagleton, suggests: "In St. Louis, domes and columns are the icons of civic architecture. Looking back over more than two centuries of history, . . . Federal buildings have all used domes and columns to announce their stature and create a dignified public presence. In the Eagleton courthouse, we wanted to be contemporary, but we also believed it was important to carry forward the symbols and traditions of St. Louis civic design." Exterior columns ring the domed portico at the main public entrance, and then there is a second, larger dome 500 feet or so above, also held up by columns, and prominent from the Arch or almost anywhere else in St. Louis. The domes on the local horizon make this civic building stand out, says Obata, from the "architecture of industry and commerce"—storefronts, warehouses, and skyscrapers that "express their efficiency and order in the grid and crisp horizontal cornices that separate building from sky." How different are the columns and domes at Eagleton from an earlier generation of judicial buildings, like the Dirksen US Courthouse in the Chicago Loop, a 1964 Mies van der Rohe masterpiece that "does not present itself as a courthouse, although there are over twenty courtrooms filed inside." It is a placeless piece of Bauhaus, a flat-topped black box sometimes referred to as a "filing cabinet,"[25] a huge "faceless office building."[26]

Public accessibility, however, has its limits. Ferguson protesters were restrained from entering Eagleton by temporary steel barricades and yellow crime-scene tape. The public eventually did get their day in court, when invited by Judge Perry to an open comment session inside an Eagleton courtroom eight months later (five minutes for each speaker, no placards allowed). Courthouses architecturally protect the integrity of the judicial process by being "public" in a selective and filtering way. Any citizen has the right to attend any judicial proceeding on the docket: a marshal in the rotunda, just beyond the screening machines, will tell you how to get to the courtroom of your choice. But when visitors cross the threshold from city to courthouse, they enter a space where rules of conduct change, in the interest of a fair trial. Entering a courthouse "can be conceived as the movement from the disordered world of the street to the highly ordered precinct of the courtroom."[27] Sandra Day O'Connor, associate justice of the United States Supreme Court, describes the new Phoenix courthouse named for her as giving "the visitor the impression of openness, of access to justice"—but at the same time, it is a "tranquil space in which to resolve the sometimes very difficult issues in our courts."[28] Justice depends upon a place apart, a sanctuary of sorts—which is why judges no longer conduct business in taverns, as they did in the earliest days of the republic. Judith Resnik and Dennis Curtis write: "Buildings served not only as stages but also as constraints. Bringing rituals . . . indoors undercut the opportunities for subversive eruptions of large audiences gathering in outdoor spaces," but when restraint is carried to excess, courts become "exclusionary sites of privilege to which all were not welcome."[29] Courthouses work as truth-spots by not being completely public or open.

——·——

The choreography of movement in and out of a courtroom is complex. There are individuals and groups that should be kept separate from one another, and courtrooms therefore usually are designed with several doors for entry and exit. Think of a French bedroom farce played very quietly and very slowly.
«GEORGE A. DAVIDSON[30]»

Passages. There are a lot of elevators in the Eagleton US Courthouse. Those who decided to comment on the Ferguson consent decree in April 2016 were ushered from the entry rotunda through security screening, passing by the docket monitors, and into an alcove with twelve elevators available for the public, only some of which go to the floor where Judge Perry set up shop (some go to district courtrooms, others to appellate or circuit or special courtrooms). But these public elevators are only part of the story. There are two elevators just for the judges; one elevator for exclusive use by defendants or witnesses in custody; two elevators for the staff (recorders, receptionists, file clerks, librarians, and so forth), and two additional elevators to get the staff down to the parking areas; two service elevators for shipping/receiving and custodians. That adds up to twenty-one elevators for twenty-five courtrooms on twenty-nine floors—an abundance, compared to the typical office building of comparable scale—and none of these elevators is redundant. When the elevators arrive at a courtroom floor, they open out to an extensive labyrinth of hallways leading to waiting areas, conference rooms, suites of offices, toilets, and storage areas—eventually terminating at the courtroom itself. The *Design Guide* says: "Although building users are frequently unaware of the quantity of square footage allocated to building corridors and aisles, this circulation space often accounts for 30 to 50 percent of the usable space in a building."[31] This figure also far surpasses the equivalent proportion in a typical office tower. Not surprisingly, there are four "distinct" entrances from outside, "for the public and staff, judges, prisoners, and deliveries."[32] Eagleton dedicates a *lot* of space to the task of moving people *very carefully* from the outside of the building to the courtroom—a kind of "processional."[33]

Why? The interior design of Eagleton follows stringent rules set down in the *Design Guide* for segregating discrete categories of people as they move to and from the courtrooms—in the interest of a fair and impartial trial. Federal courthouses have three separate circulation systems leading to the courtroom, and they must never intersect (except at spots well insulated by security doors, locks, cameras, guards, and signage). Arranging passages on a courtroom floor at Eagleton was something like designing an electrical circuit where the wires must never cross—lest the system of justice short out. The *Design Guide* spells this out: "(1) *public* circulation and access for spectators, news media representatives, attorneys, litigants, and witnesses; (2) *restricted* circulation and access for judges, law clerks, courtroom deputy clerks, court reporters/recorders, and jurors; and (3) *secure* circulation and access for prisoners and U.S. Marshal Services personnel."[34] The three discrete circulation systems are not optional but imperative: "Any uncontrolled intersection of differing circulation patterns constitutes a breach of security and must be avoided."[35]

The same principle of absolute segregation applies to the functionally specific spaces that surround every courtroom at Eagleton—"like petals around the center of a flower," Brubaker told me. At the Old Courthouse, four tiny niches just off the corners of the courtroom sufficed as support space; now, auxiliary activities require more square footage per floor than the courtroom itself. Architects spend a lot of time plotting out "adjacencies"—deciding which activities (and rooms for those activities) need to be next to each other, and which must be kept apart. For federal courthouses, the *Design Guide* leaves little to their discretion: "The district and magistrate judge courtrooms require direct access from public, restricted, and secure circulation. Associated spaces located near the district courtroom include attorney/witness conference rooms, accessed from public circulation; the judges' conference/robing room (provided only if the judges' chambers are not located close to the courtroom), accessed from restricted circulation; the trial jury suite, accessed directly from the courtroom or restricted circulation; and prisoner holding cells, accessed from secure circulation."[36] Judges' chambers (not a niche now but a capacious suite of rooms) are surrounded by a library, offices for law clerks, secretarial and reception areas, storage, and a toilet, all of which must be kept away from the public, defendants, witnesses, and jurors—requiring "total enclosure . . . for acoustic and visual privacy, to protect confidentiality, and to prevent distraction."[37] Isolation of these chambers also prevents the possibility that a judge could form premature but prejudicial impressions of an accused person or a witness or a juror—based on contacts outside the exquisitely composed normative order of the courtroom itself.

The spatial handling of jurors, their managed passage to and through the courtroom, is designed to achieve an architecture of impartiality (as required by the Sixth Amendment). All potential jurors begin as ordinary citizens called to the jury assembly room at Eagleton, located off the public circulation system just behind the elevators. It is a huge space, mainly a holding pen, with video-projected instructions of the duties and demeanor expected of jurors, and a display case with archaeological artifacts dug up when the Courthouse was built (a local St. Louis touch, designed, I suppose, to make prospective jurors feel more at home): "Jury assembly facilities should be located on a main public entry floor, preferably close to the district court clerk's office. The facilities must have controlled entry and should provide for the convenient movement of jurors to and from courtrooms."[38] A panel of potential jurors is then moved upstairs to a courtroom, where voir dire questioning results in a subset selected to serve on a trial. From the moment of their "transubstantiation"[39] from citizen to juror, impartiality requires that all contacts with ordinary citizens, the judge, both parties to the trial, attorneys, and witnesses take place only in the courtroom itself until a verdict is reached. When both sides have completed the presentation of their cases, and the judge has given instructions, the jury retreats by themselves to a deliberation room, via a secure passageway that prevents mingling with all other players in the courtroom drama (including the audience). The *Design Guide* insists on this: "The deliberations of a trial jury must be strictly confidential. . . . Jurors must access the trial jury suite from public circulation through a controlled access point into a restricted corridor. The jury must not pass through the public seating area of the courtroom when moving to or from the trial jury suite; instead, jurors must access the courtroom directly from the trial jury suite or through a restricted corridor. Trial jury suites must not be located where the public, attorneys, and litigants can see, hear, or gain access to jurors. During deliberations, access to the suite is strictly controlled by the sworn-jury custodian."[40] Jurors are expected to base their verdict only on material that is presented for all to hear in court: if members of the jury have any contact with anybody else outside the courtroom, the integrity of the process is compromised. Impartiality also requires that individual jurors retain the right to speak freely with their peers, knowing that what they say will never be attributed to them personally (no reprisal)—and so the room is soundproofed, with a guard outside the door.

Segregated passages and isolated functional spaces for different players in the justice process are defining elements of floor plans at Eagleton. These design features materialize the rights of the accused to a fair trial, an impartial jury (and judge), a courtroom confrontation with witnesses and plaintiffs (but not before), and representation by counsel. Linda Mulcahy writes: "Segregated circulation routes can be seen as a way of increasing the legitimacy of the trial by protecting the vulnerable from unsuitable encounters."[41] Hardly a "French bedroom farce"; more like jurisprudential indispensability.

———•———

The courtroom remains a place of distinctly legal drama and of climax.
«JOHN BRIGHAM [42]»

The built environment clarifies social roles and relations. People know better who they are and how they ought to behave when the arena is humanly designed rather than nature's raw stage.
«YI-FU TUAN [43]»

Lines of site. The gerbil tubes to justice all end at the courtroom. Participants gather in a solemn place where unfolding activities are orchestrated by fastidious arrangements of entrances, exits, chairs, tables, benches, boxes, and bars. Imagine yourself as a citizen who has decided to comment on the Ferguson consent decree. You find your way to Eagleton (no problem spotting it), where a federal marshal points to the elevator that will deliver you to the courtroom on the third floor where Judge Perry will preside. You step out from the elevator into a vestibule with floor-to-ceiling windows—all of St. Louis fans out before you (Busch Stadium just below, the Arch, the Mississippi River). As you go to the courtroom door, you pass by two little rooms on either side labeled "Attorney's Conference Room," with a light (now off) indicating when they are in use. You enter the court from the rear, facing Judge Perry's bench—perched above everything else in the room. You take your seat in the back of the courtroom, the space for the audience, separated from the rest of the action by a wooden railing with a swinging gate. On the other side of the gate, between you and Judge Perry (and the court reporters who sit immediately beneath her at a lower bench) are two sets of tables and chairs, on the left for the City of Ferguson attorneys (defense), on the right for the US Department of Justice (plaintiff). To the right of the attorneys' tables is the jury box, with sixteen seats, now empty because this case was settled without a jury trial (which indeed is the situation for the vast majority of filings in any American court system). Eventually the clerk calls your name, and after you recite the oath (that gives this chapter its title), you take your place on the witness stand. Your role has been predefined by where you entered the courtroom, where you sat, and where you spoke from.[44]

The room would have looked more or less the same if you had been, instead, a witness at Dred and Harriet Scott's trial at the Old Courthouse. Recently built federal courthouses, no matter how much they might vary stylistically on the outside, contain courtrooms that are "something that Thomas Jefferson himself would recognize."[45] The *Design Guide* imposes stringent conformity on a space designed for the needs of jurisprudence and to preserve the rights of the accused. I asked Steve Brubaker if he had any wiggle room at all in drawing up the Eagleton courtrooms. His response, which focused on a rather small detail of the jury box, suggests that latitude is not abundant. In many respects, his jury box comes from a mold enforced by the *Design*

Guide. It is one step or so off the courtroom floor, with risers for each row of chairs, so that jurors can get unobstructed views of the proceedings. At the front of the jury box, facing the attorneys and their clients is a low but solid wooden rail—creating for them a safe and grounded space all their own. Here is where Brubaker goes slightly off on his own, putting short "returns" at the end of the main jury box rail, enveloping jurors even more in a U-shaped frame. He sought "to convey groundedness. They [the jurors] feel rooted in the ground. That allows me to personalize the space—when I sit in that jury box, it is my space, it is my house. This place belongs to me." In the same way, he said, the pronounced definition given to the witness stand makes those testifying under oath "feel embraced." For Brubaker, even though the *Design Guide* does not require returns on jury boxes, it was important to give each role-player a properly bounded and identifiable home turf, from which he or she could be secure in the authority and responsibilities granted distinctively to each of them by virtue of where they happened to be sitting.

In most respects, the *Design Guide* allows for almost zero variation in courtroom design, down to the inch. Here we have the most literal translation of the Sixth Amendment into a set of architectural prescriptions. A fair trial depends on an "infrastructure of visibility,"[46] on the copresence of litigants and their counsel, judge, jury, witnesses, recorder, clerk, the public, marshals, in the only place where they are all allowed to be together, so that everybody can see and hear all grounds for the eventual verdict and sentence. Participants are arrayed about the room so that lines of sight and of hearing enable a communal sharing of the proceedings. Eagleton courtrooms are intimate spaces in a colossal building, not much bigger in volume than the Old courtrooms down the street. This is for jurisprudential reasons: intimacy compels engagement of all involved and at the same time reminds everybody that the goings-on are personal, particular, and immediate to the citizens on trial.

But there are risks in trial participants being too close. A juror could be intimidated by a desperate defendant, passionate witness, or crying spectator who is literally in his or her face, allowing emotional force rather than the merits of argument and evidence to sway the outcome. To preserve intimacy without intimidation (or eavesdropping on privileged conversations), the *Design Guide* specifies just the right distances: "The maximum allowable distance between a juror and a litigant sitting at a counsel table across the courtroom well is 40 feet" (intimacy), but "jurors must be separated 6 feet from attorneys and litigants to prevent the overhearing of private conversations," and "jurors must be separated from the public to avoid interference or intimidation. At least 6 feet of space must separate the jury box and rail dividing the spectator seating area and courtroom well."[47] One attorney reported his experience in a courtroom (not at Eagleton) that evidently did not conform to the *Design Guide*: "The witness box was so close to the jury that jurors felt menaced and the judge himself not terribly secure."[48]

The arrangement of furniture and people in the courtroom must be steadfastly neutral with respect to the interests of the adversarial parties: "No appearance of favoritism may be evident in the layout."[49] In a trial involving the infamous Enron Corporation, "an attorney argued that rather than being confined to the table traditionally set aside for the defendant furthest from the jury box, he and his client should be allowed to sit at the table directly across from the witness stand in order that they could enjoy unobstructed and uncluttered face to face confrontation with the witness." The judge relied on "fairness and common sense": "both the prosecution and the defense" were allowed "use of the table nearest the witness box when presenting their case."[50] Ordinarily, the defense is put on the opposite side of the room from the jury to put a little breathing space between the accused and those who will decide his or her fate.

If any "favoritism" creeps into the design of a courtroom, it favors the authority of the judge, who sits higher than everybody else: "Generally, the judge's bench should be elevated three or four steps (21–24 inches) above the courtroom well." The *Design Guide* suggests that the reason for this pulpit is not so much power as jurisprudential efficiency: "The raised judge's bench and ceiling height contribute to the order and decorum of the proceedings."[51] Somebody must wield the gavel, and only one person can read the law, give instructions to the jury, excuse a witness, and overrule an attorney's objection. Would either party in litigation predictably benefit if such procedural power were *not* accorded to the judge—and materialized in his or her elevated bench at the front of the room? Still, designers of recent federal courtrooms have tinkered with the height and location of the judge's bench—to make its occupant less imperious and to pursue a better balance between state power and the Constitutional rights of the accused. In Boston, the judge's bench is "elevated by only three steps to enable the judge to easily participate in rather than be set apart from the proceedings." In Seattle, "the bench moves into the well to engage spectators as if to signal their enrollment in the judicial process." For much the same reason, architects of the·Jackson, Mississippi, courthouse departed from the traditional rectangular shape of the courtroom in favor of a theater in the round, so that jurors "focus more on participation than their own feelings of intimidation or inconvenience. Instead of places that express the majesty and authority of the law, these are welcoming places in which to search for the truth."[52]

———•———

The law is objective, fair and impersonal.
«JUSTICE STEPHEN C. BREYER[53]»

Courts are also important contributions *to* democracy. Adjudication is one site of democratic practices, redistributing power from government to individual, from one side of a case to another, and from participants to audience.
«JUDITH RESNIK AND DOUGLAS CURTIS[54]»

How *do* courthouses lend support to the beliefs that any citizen has the right to file a complaint, that the adjudication of disputed facts happens fairly here, that verdicts are reached without prejudice or collusion, that the sentences meted out are warranted by what everyone involved had opportunity to consider? Purpose-built courthouses like Eagleton translate ineffable values and principles into legible statements. Planters at the entry plaza, a light-filled glass-walled atrium with an oculus to the sky, panoramic views from vestibules and courtrooms out to the Arch, designated spaces in the courtroom for anybody who wishes to watch (family members, the media, a curious sociologist)—all of that says "Welcome" with as much transparency and openness as could be expected from a twenty-nine-story skyscraper with US Marshals and security screening. Carefully segregated passages for the public, the judiciary, jurors, witnesses, and defendants in custody prevent mingling that could invite suspicions of backstage deals or contaminated testimony—just as those sequestered hallways prevent premature contacts that could bias a juror or even a judge. Courtrooms inside are arranged so that favoritism toward one party or the other is impossible—because everybody inside can see and hear what everybody says and does, down to the sweat on a brow or nervous fidgeting (and without intimidation).

The law is an institution especially fat with words, spoken in court, recorded in endless files and documents, codified in statutes. Through all the verbiage, the Eagleton US Courthouse in St. Louis stands mute, powerfully but silently contributing to the sense that judicial processes inside it are just and fair, grounded in truth.

7

Obama's Three Birthplaces

We, the people, declare today that the most evident of truths—that all of us are created equal—is the star that guides us still; just as it guided our forebears through Seneca Falls, and Selma, and Stonewall. . . . It is now our generation's task to carry on what those pioneers began.

«PRESIDENT BARACK OBAMA[1]»

Inaugural addresses are opportunities for American presidents to say what this nation stands for, as he or she may see it. It is a patriotic moment, designed to rekindle commitments to the enduring values and principles of this country and to inspire the people to work together toward some cherished ambition that remains unfulfilled—but within our grasp. In his second chance, former President Obama's speech held true to form. He rehearsed the crux of the liberal American political ideology: "what makes us exceptional—what makes us American" is our "allegiance" to the "most evident of truths," announced in the Declaration of Independence: equality under God, inalienable rights, "life, liberty and the pursuit of happiness."[2] His premise is that we have not yet made good on this promise, even though at specific moments and in specific places, we have slowly moved (with great struggle) toward a society that fully respects diversity and seeks to grant everybody equal rights. How better to

nail down this particular national narrative about "the most evident of truths" than to place the story in a truth-spot—three of
them, actually, as befits a multicultural society still hard at work
in making the promise of liberty, equality, and justice a reality
for all.

Obama mentions three commemorated birthplaces of identity-
based social movements, each seeking equal rights for its members: Seneca Falls becomes the dawn of the feminist movement,
Selma originates the pursuit of African American civil rights,
and Stonewall is where gay liberation began. His stirring message did not *require* any geographic anchors, but in dropping
the names of these three birthplaces, he bolsters his charge "to
make these words, these rights, these values . . . *real* for every
American." The words "Seneca Falls, and Selma, and Stonewall"
root our national commitment to diversity, inclusion, and equal
rights at three places, and lend a convincing palpability to calls
for their universal enactment—as if the names on their own
could inspire us immediately to take up the old, tough struggles.
Obama says nothing more in his address about the birthplaces—
just their names: no recollection of events, no listing of heroes,
no accounting of losses suffered. To do so, evidently, was unnec-
essary: places have a metonymic power to make us believe (and
compel us to act) even in the absence of explicit details about
what important stuff happened there or what they are famous
for: "Narratives and truths alike can be swiftly 'activated' . . .
through the use of place-names alone."[3]

Places can lend credibility to claims by conveying so much
just with a name—but that is also the source of their vulnerability as truth-spots. Places are precarious affirmations of national
creeds, political ideologies, and identity-based claims to rights.
When abstract ideals and values are grounded in places where
they first animated resistance and liberation, risks arise that have
the potential to subvert their capacity to persuade, affirm, and
inspire. Commemorated birthplaces make us believe—but imperfectly so, with built-in boomerang effects that can turn assur-
ance into doubt, confusion, or contestation. How so?

1. Obama references Seneca Falls to remind us that the pursuit of equal rights for women has a long history in the United States, and that we have an obligation to finish "what those pioneers began"—but what if nobody remembers very well what happened there, and what if it becomes difficult to connect the dots between first-generation suffragettes and the special challenges women face today?

2. Obama points to Selma because it is a moment of triumph that provides a proven model for how African Americans could organize their collective efforts to achieve the same success now—but what if exclusive attention to Selma diminishes important achievements that happened elsewhere before and after, and what if the tactical lessons of Selma for activists today are less useful than those suggested by events at other birthplaces?

3. Obama adds Stonewall to bring gays and lesbians alongside women and African Americans as groups who have suffered the denial of their equal rights and who deserve support from all of us in their struggles to overcome those injustices—but what if the pioneers on-site at the beginning do not comfortably represent the membership of the movement they spawned, and what if recollections of those particular pioneers are less helpful now in securing expanded civil rights for the LGBTQ community?

———•———

Today, the Seneca Falls Convention of July 1848 feels like an obscure event for most Americans. Students of American history probably have some familiarity with it, but most people have never heard of it. Yet this meeting changed the way American society . . . thought about and treated women in the mid-nineteenth century.

«SALLY G. MCMILLEN[4]»

This is the problem with preservation: something is always lost.

«COLIN RAFFERTY[5]»

In a way, the choice of a birthplace designed to celebrate the beginning of a social movement is arbitrary—many possibilities present themselves, and the eventual selection of one birthplace says less about historical events and more about the people making the choice and the present contexts in which they do so. Once chosen, commemorated birthplaces become contested sites and thus slippery truth-spots: is that indeed where it all began, what really started there, and what kind of action should the place inspire in us today? Scholars who have studied commemorative processes, monuments, and memorials seem to agree that recognized birthplaces of social movements help to perpetuate and validate political ideologies, memories, and identities—but they remain permanently fragile and partial, available for challenge on grounds that "something" is always left out or just wrong. Putting up a statue or a plaque in a place where something important began is how "regimes of all stripes take on a material form and attempt to manufacture a popular consciousness conducive to their survival."[6] Those sites are "where groups of people gather to create a common past for themselves, places where they tell the constitutive narratives, their 'shared' stories of the past."[7]

The very act of commemoration itself suggests that in the absence of such efforts, we might altogether forget a birthplace or its enduring significance for sustaining evident truths. I'll wager that in the immediate scramble to figure out what President Obama was alluding to with those three place-names, more people googled "Seneca Falls" than either "Selma" or "Stonewall." To be sure, Seneca Falls is the location of the Women's Rights National Historical Park (established in 1980) and a must-see destination for tourists visiting the Finger Lakes region of upstate New York, but how many people looking at the map can recall much of anything about the supposedly pivotal events that took place on that spot in July 19–20, 1848? This *is* a test. Q: The Seneca Falls Convention brought together about 300 people to discuss hot-button political issues of the day, but who organized the event, and who showed up? Q: Many speeches were given, but what positions were staked out, and what were the points of contention? Q: The Convention wrote up a Declaration of

Sentiments, but what exactly did the document declare, and what were its immediate and longer-term impacts? Tough questions, but I think we can be forgiven for forgetting Seneca Falls.

What makes this birthplace so forgettable? The Seneca Falls Convention happened a long time ago: key players and reliable eyewitness have been dead for at least a century. Nobody today has firsthand memories of Seneca Falls during those two days that put it in the history books. The Convention did not get the media saturation that attends even trivial events today: photography was just barely available in 1848, and audio recording, radio, video recording, television, websites, and Twitter were far-off in the future. If we manage to dredge up visual images or conjure voices from the moment, participants seem so not like us: "The past is a foreign country."[8] Ringleaders gathered *at tea* to plot the event, and in the heat of the summer, they wore bonnets and long dresses (bloomers were revolutionary, no pants or shorts). They prepared broadsides to publicize "a Convention to discuss the social, civil, and religious condition and rights of woman"—print (!), and circulated them only eight days before the gathering was to commence. Participants from afar arrived on the Rochester-Auburn passenger railroad. The Declaration of Sentiments was written by five white, socioeconomically privileged women whose lack of demographic diversity sets them apart from any feminist rally today.[9] It is not easy for women pursuing equal rights now to see themselves in "those pioneers" at Seneca Falls.

Moreover, the two-day affair lacked the kind of drama that make Selma and Stonewall more easily recalled. Participants gathered in the town's Wesleyan Chapel, a sanctuary of sorts, chosen because it was the only building that could accommodate the crowd. Forty men showed up, and the question of whether they should be allowed inside gave rise to an early debate: men could come in, but must remain silent. It was all so polite and peaceful: there were no wolves at the door, no arrests were made, no bloodshed, no deaths. It was brave for those pioneering women to call for universal suffrage, and as they gave speeches and attended rallies in the years after the Seneca Falls Convention, some were jeered and became the target of "rotten fruit."[10] But inside the Wesleyan Chapel, the risks to life and liberty were small—maybe transformative social movements in the pursuit of identity-based rights are remembered better if their birth is marked by struggle, exposure to danger, and sacrifice.

The Seneca Falls Convention was not instantly recognized as a turning point in the drive for women's rights, and its eventual anointment as the movement birthplace and as commemoration-worthy came only after more than a century of strategic memory-work. Participants were united as much by their anti-slavery sentiments as their commitment to women's suffrage, and those two political issues jockeyed for agenda supremacy in the middle decades of the nineteenth century. As the Civil War loomed, abolitionists made more progress in the North than did activists for women's emancipation. Even during Reconstruction, the political and economic conditions of former slaves seemed to be of greater urgency than getting women the vote.[11] President Abraham Lincoln said in 1865: "One question at a time. This hour belongs to the negro."[12] Near the end of the century, at-tention to women's rights got caught up in the temperance movement, where women like Carrie Nation assumed promi-nent roles. Some men opposed suffrage for women because, they believed, women would be more likely to vote for prohibition.[13] Whatever had started at Seneca Falls in 1848 lost momentum in the ensuing decades, beat out or weakened by rival political issues, creating a historical discontinuity between those distant events hinted at by President Obama and signs of real prog-ress that would come much later. It took *seventy-two years* after Seneca Falls before the Nineteenth Amendment became law in 1920, granting women the right to vote. The hypothesis that continuous progress toward women's emancipation began in up-state New York on July 19–20, 1848, lacks evidence.

Recognition of Seneca Falls as the birthplace was slow to gel for another reason: rival feminist organizations with various po-litical agendas and led by different women competed intensely for the authority to write the history of the movement and to give it a particular direction.[14] Among the organizers of the Convention, only Elizabeth Cady Stanton was poised to slingshot her role in writing the Declaration of Sentiments into leadership of an organized women's movement.[15] Lucretia Mott from Philadelphia was the best-known activist to take part in the Seneca Falls Convention, but she preferred giving speeches to organizing a movement, and her relatively advanced age made it impossible during Reconstruction for her to carry the torch. Mary Ann and Elizabeth M'Clintock joined Mott and Stanton at Jane Hunt's house for tea and scheming, but rarely entered the limelight after the 1848 Convention. Only Stanton seemed well equipped temperamentally for the hard work of mobilization, and she found a perfect complement in the organizer Susan B. Anthony—herself not present at Seneca Falls in July 1848, but who would cement her connection to that founding place via her lifelong collaboration with Stanton.

For Anthony and Stanton, Seneca Falls became the right place for the women's movement to have begun because it advanced their particular ambitions in struggles over leadership of the movement, its goals, and its legacy. Their countless books and addresses, produced into the early twentieth century, distilled the Seneca Falls Convention to a single issue—women's suffrage—in order to give it distinctive primacy in the array of struggles alive during that period. Stanton and Anthony opposed the Fifteenth Amendment because it insulted women by extending the right to vote to racial minorities and former slaves—if they were male. Rival feminist and suffragette Lucy Stone, who was not present at "the beginning" in Seneca Falls, believed that Stanton's and Anthony's opposition to the Fifteenth Amendment eroded support among those who otherwise would favor universal suffrage. Stone played down the significance of Seneca Falls as birthplace, recalling earlier achievements as equally pivotal—for example, influential works advocating women's rights by the Grimké sisters written before 1848 and increasing opportunities for women in higher education (Stone attended Oberlin College, which first admitted women in 1837). Stone was a major player at the Worcester Convention in 1850, arguably a better-remembered gathering because its scope and coverage were more national than the relatively local affair at Seneca Falls.

Susan B. Anthony held the reins of the women's movement right through to her death in 1906. Ironically, her framing of the movement whose origin she located at Seneca Falls further distances the agenda of the 1848 Convention from political concerns of women listening to Obama's address in 2013. Commemorated birthplaces "stand for both the continuity and the disjunction between past and present."[16] Anthony filtered manifold issues down to one: women's right to vote. Those gathered in Seneca Falls in fact considered many issues besides the lack of voting rights, including marriage and divorce laws, property rights, educational and economic opportunities for women—and even "fair wages."[17] These were written into the Declaration of Sentiments. But in memory, Seneca Falls was about women's suffrage, and although the right to vote was very slow to come, success eventually was achieved, and the issue was not foremost on President Obama's mind when he named the birthplace of feminism: "For our journey is not complete until our wives, our mothers and our daughters can earn a living equal to their efforts." With women's right to vote secure, can Seneca Falls (as constructed by Anthony) stir the soul of activists in pink hats dealing with eighty-two cents and the loss of reproductive rights?[18]

Memories of Seneca Falls are shaky—maybe a visit to the place could shore them up. My impression formed during a visit there on an unseasonably warm March weekend was that everything had been embalmed, like the Seneca River falls that once "roared" but are now quieted by a dam built in 1915.[19] The Women's Rights National Historical Park has acquired for preservation several homes occupied by women who drafted the Declaration of Sentiments, and built an interpretive center adjacent to a largely reconstructed Wesleyan Chapel. Statues, monuments, and plaques abound. A sculpture entitled *The First Wave* is the centerpiece of the interpretive center (depicting the pursuit of women's rights up to the minute), and freezes in life-size bronze some of those present for the birthing of the movement: Stanton, Martha Coffin Wright, Thomas and Mary Ann M'Clintock, and Frederick Douglass, the abolitionist, who had come down from Rochester to persuade hesitant attendees that the Resolutions should include a demand for universal suffrage.[20] Not far from Stanton's home across the river sits another sculpture, *When Anthony Met Stanton*, with Amelia Bloomer (temperance advocate and transgressive dresser) making the introduction. It gave me pause: even though the two eventual collaborators did indeed meet in Seneca Falls, that did not happen until 1851, although the casual visitor might reasonably conclude from the statue that Anthony was in fact in town for the famous 1848 Convention. In a misleading way, the statue *emplaces* Anthony and her unparalleled role in advancing women's rights back in Seneca Falls, legitimating its status as the birthplace. The Declaration of Sentiments has been etched onto a granite wall at the side of the interpretive center facing the Wesleyan Chapel, with water falling over but not obscuring the sacred text: "In view of this entire disfranchisement of one-half the people of this country, their social and religious degradation— . . . and because women do feel themselves aggrieved, oppressed, and fraudulently deprived of their most sacred rights, we insist that they have immediate admission to all the rights and privileges which belong to them as citizens of these United States." A flat, featureless grassy space sits between the church and the waterfall inscription, ostensibly for reading and contemplation but striking me as simply soulless.

The park ranger who took us inside the Chapel said that "Americans like to see where things happened." But did any of my fellow visitors that day feel much connection to the efforts of the pioneer feminists? Were any of them inspired at that moment, by being in that place, to hit the barricades to demand fair pay for women workers? Scholars disagree about the capacity of places like the preserved Seneca Falls to evoke and sustain memories of pivotal events in "our" past. French philosopher Maurice Halbwachs is optimistic: "Every collective memory unfolds within a spatial framework. . . . Space is a reality that endures: . . . we can understand how we recapture the past only by understanding how it is, in effect, preserved by our physical surroundings."[21] Colin Rafferty tries to agree: "But a physical object the monument—reminds us every time we encounter it, holds up the event we have forgotten so that we might recall what happened, so that we do not forget." He goes on to say, about commemorated places like Seneca Falls, "The site itself is proof. . . . *I'm here. This place is real. The things that happened actually had a place where they happened.*"[22]

But other scholars demur, taking up an aperçu by Robert Musil, the twentieth-century Austrian writer: "The most striking feature of monuments is that you do not notice them. There is nothing in the world as invisible as monuments. Doubtless they have been erected to be seen—even to attract attention; yet at the same time something has impregnated them against attention. Like a drop of water on an oilskin, attention runs down them without stopping for a moment."[23] For Kirk Savage, "monuments stand apart from everyday experience and seem to promise something eternal, akin to the sacred. Yet no matter how compelling they are, they can never fulfill that promise."[24] James Young captures my sense of the absent resonance I felt when visiting Seneca Falls: "the essential stiffness [that] monuments share with all other images: as a likeness necessarily vitrifies its otherwise dynamic referent, a monument turns pliant memory to stone. And it is this 'finish' that repels our attention, that makes a monument invisible. It is as if a monument's life in the communal mind grows as hard and polished as its exterior form, its significance as fixed as its place in the landscape."[25] Young cites the French theorist Pierre Nora: "The less memory is experienced from the inside, the more it exists through its exterior scaffolding and outward signs."[26]

I left Seneca Falls unmoved and uninspired, but maybe the problem was me. For the 150th anniversary of the first women's rights convention in 1998, nine very multicultural high school girls from the Bay Area went to Seneca Falls to perform a play that they had written as sixth graders for Women's History Month, under the sponsorship of Joan Mankin. Their journey was recorded for an award-winning documentary film titled *Seneca Falls*, which aired on PBS starting in 2010.[27] In demeanor and attitude, the young women stand as far as possible from afternoon tea, bonnets, bloomers, and even women's suffrage. The student who plays Stanton said, after visiting her home, "It's weird to think that she walked around in this house." Another described Seneca Falls as "the Mecca of our play." They were moved by the place: "Just this week, seeing these museums, listening to people speak, watching videos and everything, its even more of a wake-up call—but I have a long way to go. I need to learn about Black feminism." And another: "When I get back to San Francisco, I'm going to be all over the place with women's rights. I want to continue the fight." If, fifteen years later, these young women happened to catch President Obama's second inaugural address, they would have had no need to google "Seneca Falls."

———•———

I think Selma was God's chosen place.
«RICHIE JEAN JACKSON[28]»

At times history and fate meet at a single time in a single place to shape a turning point in man's unending search for freedom. So it was at Lexington and Concord. So it was a century ago at Appomattox. So it was last week in Selma, Alabama.
«PRESIDENT LYNDON B. JOHNSON[29]»

When a social group makes a concerted effort to begin with a wholly new start . . . there is a measure of complete arbitrariness in the very nature of any such attempted beginning.
«PAUL CONNERTON[30]»

I was reminded about the labile nature of commemorated birthplaces on my drive south to Selma, when I stopped in Pulaski, Tennessee, a small town just above the Alabama border. Its residents (pop. 7,641) know something about the vicissitudes of being commemorated as the start of an identity-based social movement—the Ku Klux Klan. In May or June 1866, in a one-story brick building on W. Madison Street off the courthouse square, five men met to invent the Klan.[31] In 1917, the United Daughters of the Confederacy put a bronze plaque on the front of the building, reading in part: "Ku Klux Klan organized in this the law office of Judge Thomas M. Jones" (followed by the names of the six organizers). The building still stands. In the 1980s and 1990s, Klansmen and their ilk made the birthplace a pilgrimage site, and "would come up to that building, kiss the plaque and bow down to it." Donald Massey bought the building in the 1980s, well aware of its fame but not sharing the ideology being commemorated, and in 1989, he took the plaque down, reversed it, and bolted it back up on the wall—no words showing, only a century's worth of blue-green patina. Massey said that it was like "turning your back on racism."[32] To be sure, "we are who our plaques say we are,"[33] but such reminders may be silenced—statues are occasionally taken down to erase an offensive truth about the past.

A place like Pulaski—or Selma—is "not a fixed point in space, but a point of departure for an endless multiplication of meaning."[34] These birthplaces get covered over by a palimpsest of later interpretations that variously recover once-lost details, alter the significance of the movement itself, or embed it all in a different narrative perhaps better suited to the culture and politics of the present. Selma-the-birthplace would like us to believe that it has a "unique access to the 'real'" history of African American civil rights, even as it "reflect[s] the difficulty attendant on such an ambition."[35] Historian Daniel J. Sherman continues: "The stories we seek in places remain fragmentary and inaccessible, not only because of lapses of memory, but because . . . activities that animate sites and cast them as repositories of meaning, of narratives [are] both apparent and tantalizingly concealed."[36]

Nobody forgets Selma. There before us is Rev. Dr. Martin Luther King Jr. heroically leading 8,000 of his followers across the Edmund Pettus Bridge in Selma on March 21, 1965, starting the march that would last five days, ending on the steps of the Confederate capital in Montgomery, where King would deliver a memorable address: "How long? Not long. Because the arc of the moral universe is long but it bends toward justice." Some of us remember watching it all unfold on television; younger generations might rely on Ava DuVernay's 2014 film *Selma*; a profusion of images, recordings, and firsthand accounts of the march are available online. Selma is thoroughly documented and easily retrievable from either personal memory, the archives, or endless retellings. It seems still to be part of our present, despite the passage of more than a half century. At the interpretive center just across from the Edmund Pettus Bridge, the park ranger asked me if I had noticed the sturdy but elderly black woman who passed me as I walked in: "She was arrested here many times before she had reached the age of fifteen." In a way, if President Obama had referenced any place other than Selma in his second inaugural address, we might all have scratched our heads.

For so many reasons, Selma is the ideal place for locating the birth of the African American civil rights movement. The place oozes symbolism, "fertile ground for this important event that would change America:"[37] the Edmund Pettus Bridge is named for a Confederate general and Grand Dragon of the Klan; in Dallas County, a vanishingly small percentage of African Americans were registered to vote; Sheriff Jim Clark and his deputies could be counted on to use their "cattle prods"[38] when facing protesters; East Selma, where blacks lived, "was isolated from" the city's "formal political center and its cultural zone."[39] Selma was a ripe place for protest.

Moreover, immediate events leading up to the march from Selma to Montgomery cast that moment in high relief: even before the bridge was crossed, everybody knew that this would be an irreversible turning point in American history. Selma had seen violence and death before. Mass media coverage of "Bloody Sunday" from the stillborn March 7 march fixed horrific images of police brutality in the minds of Americans north and south (and spurred sympathizers to join the movement).[40] Protester Jimmie Lee Jackson had been killed by an Alabama trooper less than a month before in a Selma café, and white minister James Reeb from Boston would be beaten to death after the second interrupted march on "Turnaround Tuesday" (March 9): "Jim's [Reeb] death galvanized . . . a nation that had hardly noticed . . . when Jimmy Lee Jackson, a local Negro, had been shot and killed during a similar demonstration."[41] Selma marked genuine sacrifice, and a willingness among protesters to endure the ultimate risk. Just as important, it worked: President Lyndon B. Johnson signed the Voting Rights Act a mere five months after the march.

However much Selma rings true as the birthplace of the African American civil rights movement, the chosen place can at the same time erode its own power to implant a single uncontested story in our memories. Did anything consequential happen before Selma or after? By selecting Selma as the place where those "pioneers began" the African American civil rights movement, Obama relegates earlier protests, marches, sit-ins, and rallies—occurring all over the South in the fifties and early sixties (and before)—to the movement's prehistory, devaluing (without intent, surely) their contributions to the cause. Those incremental precursors are made to culminate at Selma—and, perhaps more vitally, made to culminate in the heroic leadership of Martin Luther King: this was his show. Historian Yohuru Williams says that invoking Selma "frames the movement around the charismatic leadership of the Reverend Martin Luther King, Jr. but of course there were organizations and individuals involved in the quest for civil rights before that, including the NAACP dating back to the turn of the century . . . you've got W. E. B. DuBois . . . , you've got Marcus Garvey."[42] Benjamin Hedin writes that "many in the movement . . . begrudge [King's] memory for the way it hoards credit for triumphs won."[43]

Montgomery could have been chosen as birthplace of the movement, but the face of the 1955 bus boycott is Rosa Parks, not King (although King became the spokesperson for the boycott as head of the Montgomery Improvement Association). Birmingham is another starting place, but the enduring images are those of a bombed-out Sixteenth Street Baptist Church, where four little girls were killed on September 15, 1963, at the hands of the Klan. This tragedy came after the Children's Crusade on May 2, when Birmingham Commissioner of Public Safety Bull Connor ordered fire hoses and police dogs to be turned on the young marchers. The Children's Crusade was organized by James Bevel of the Southern Christian Leadership Conference (SCLC), not King.[44] Although King had spent time in the Birmingham jail (April 12–20, 1963), the Birmingham Campaign that year had been initiated by Fred Shuttlesworth, cofounder of the SCLC, who sparred with King over the decision to call a moratorium on street protests. Two years later, however, at Selma, King was firmly in charge of the movement, and became its charismatic face. Selma represents the apogee of King's heroism and command. After the march to Montgomery, the SCLC's subsequent Poor People's Campaign rekindled old movement disputes and exposed tactical differences between King and his rivals.[45] Against that ground, after King's murder three years later in Memphis, his martyrdom would be moved back to the scene of his greatest triumph: Selma.

There are risks in choosing King's prodigious accomplishments at Selma as models for activists today wishing to "carry on" the struggle for racial equality. Lionization of King at Selma obscures different lessons that could be more tractably drawn on as the struggle for equal rights wears on. King carefully orchestrated what happened at Selma, with a firmly centralized decision-making structure dependent on his personal charisma. As dramatized in DuVernay's film, the sequence of events at Selma resulted from King successfully playing a chicken game with President Johnson, mano a mano. Johnson initially requested that King call off the march, but King pushed on with plans for a protest that would force the president to act. Only after Turnaround Tuesday and Reeb's murder does Johnson see the political wisdom in sending to Selma several thousand military policemen and army troops to protect the protesters (and gets segregationist Governor George Wallace to call off the dogs). King was uniquely able to play the role of movement interface with those occupying the corridors of power in Washington. The implications for black activists today are ironic: Selma may not offer the best model for completing what the pioneers began there. #BlackLivesMatter could lose a lot of time, and a lot of ground, waiting for the next MLK—somebody with the presence and oratorical skills to put the whole movement on his or her back, and carry it into the smoke-filled rooms.

Obama could have chosen a birthplace that was less King-centric, suggesting different models for struggles today. At Greensboro, North Carolina, on February 1, 1960, four black college students took seats at the "Whites Only" lunch counter in Woolworth's—now on display at the Smithsonian's National Museum of American History (the building in Greensboro has become the International Civil Rights Center and Museum). The place seems commemoration-worthy, but King had little role to play in either the sit-in movement[46] or the coincident Freedom Riders movement.[47] These protests were organized largely by the Student Nonviolent Coordinating Committee (SNCC) and the Congress of Racial Equality (CORE), neither under King's control. Importantly, they relied far more on grassroots mobilization and bottom-up decision-making than King at Selma. Their members were typically younger than those drawn to the SCLC, more militant, and impatient with King's commitment to nonviolence. A more aggressive framing of the civil rights movement could have been signaled by locating its start at Greenwood, Mississippi, where, in 1966, Stokely Carmichael's speech was a "turning point" from "Civil Rights to Black Power": "We have to organize ourselves to speak from a position of strength and stop begging people to look kindly upon us. We are going to build a movement in this country based on the color of our skins that is going to free us from our oppressors and we have to do that ourselves."[48] King was not fond of the violent implications of Black Power. Imagine if Obama had implored his listeners to pursue the lead taken at Watts, Los Angeles, in August 1966? Recollections of incendiary riots, lootings, thirty-four deaths, and $40 million in property damage could have become a call to light the fire next time. King's passive resistance is not the only strategy available to movement leaders facing twenty-first-century challenges, but it comes off as just right *if Selma* is chosen as the start of something enduring, and these other birthplaces (and their lessons) are forgotten.

Selma is a politically safe birthplace for the African American civil rights movement, recalling the start of an unfinished struggle to extend Constitutional rights to a people long denied them—but without provocative and controversial implications for dealing with a new generation of challenges.[49] Touchier issues like black poverty rates, incarceration of young black males, racial health disparities, and police violence against blacks are sidestepped. After his Selma reference, President Obama says, "Our journey is not complete until no citizen is forced to wait for hours to exercise the right to vote," hinting at new voter identification requirements that could prevent or dilute the voting impact of African Americans.[50] Selma was and is about voting rights supposedly secured back then, but now threatened again—and so the place works uniquely well to excite "our generation" to fill King's huge shoes.

But who will step up? Political scientist Edmund Fong worries that in listing the three commemorated birthplaces, Obama unfolds a preordained "script set down in advance," "eviscerat[ing] any sense that they [activists today] were forging something new and revolutionary." He is pessimistic that Selma will inspire action: "Obama . . . drains from us the ability to reconsider these events in ways that might instill in us the possibility for action and reinvention." We are trapped into walking a path that somebody else blazed for us, "so why bother?"[51]

———•———

This link between place and self applies also to groups of selves and their collective identities. Place often defines a group and provides it identity.

«ROBERT DAVID SACK[52]»

"Stonewall" is *the* emblematic event in modern lesbian and gay history. . . . The 1969 riots are now generally taken to mark the birth of the modern gay and lesbian political movement—that moment in time when gays and lesbians recognized all at once their mistreatment and their solidarity.

«MARTIN DUBERMAN[53]»

Stonewall could be the odd birthplace out. Does a louche Greenwich Village gay bar really belong with hallowed Selma and historic Seneca Falls—as a birthplace commemorating "where pride began"? There was no doubt in Obama's mind that the LGBTQ community should be included among those groups who have been denied inalienable rights and who have suffered injustices because of their sexual orientations. To make the point persuasively, he needed to locate the beginning of their struggles for equal rights: women have Seneca Falls, African Americans have Selma, and gays have . . . By naming a gathering place on Christopher Street, gays have now been brought within the American story of extending by fits and starts basic civil rights to all people.

Commemorated birthplaces put a face on the collective identity of those people whose struggles for rights began there: "People produce places, and . . . they derive identities from them"; such material sites become "rallying points for a shared common memory and identity."[54] Cherished values of "diversity" and "inclusion" could in principle refer to all kinds of people or groups. By adding Stonewall to Seneca Falls and Selma, Obama in effect defines the relevant "we." Gays become a third group with a history of being discriminated against, a situation that demands redress if Obama's chosen narrative about self-evident truths is to be realized.

A look back on what happened at the Stonewall Inn in June 1969, with a recounting of the people who stood up then and there for justice, makes it seem improbable that this unglamorous place would get celebrated forty-four years later in a presidential inaugural address. The collective identity of gays and lesbians required a substantial makeover before Stonewall could effectively do its job as a truth-spot—to make us believe that members of the LGBTQ community are "created equal." The transformation began even before order was restored that night in Sheridan Square.

The very existence of a bar like Stonewall reflects how difficult it was in those days for gays and lesbians just to be the people that they are. The joint was owned by the Mafia, as were many gay bars at the time, which made regular payments to local law enforcement in order to prevent closure for illegally serving a clientele defined as "disorderly." The payoffs did not stop the cops from raiding gay bars with routine frequency (ostensibly for selling alcohol without a license), and shooing away most of the patrons into the night but taking some to jail for not wearing a sufficient number of articles of clothing that matched their biological sex. The Mafia ran Stonewall for money rather than for any commitment to the gay community, and even with police extortion, the Mob took in lots of money. Their profits were inflated by selling watered-down and falsely labeled cheap booze (insisting that patrons keep drinking it), along with assorted drugs. Chicken hawks trolled for gay boys (or cops posing as such, hoping to entrap). Stonewall was a rip-off dive bar: a grungy place, smelly, dingy, unsafe (no fire exit), "trashy, low, and tawdry," and always at risk of another raid.[55]

Yet the place was often packed, especially on weekend nights. Gays flocked there because it was "an oasis, a safe retreat from the harassment of everyday life, a place less susceptible to police raids than other gay bars and one that drew a magical mix of patrons ranging from tweedy East Siders to street queens."[56] For young gays living mainly on the street, dressed in all shades of effeminacy, Stonewall was home. It was the only gay bar in town where dancing was tolerated. Its black walls and restrained illumination made it inviting for those not necessarily eager to share their day identities. Nasty as it was, there were few alternatives for gay New York to find a place to meet like-minded people, relax, dress as they chose, dance, hook up, be themselves. Even at the end of the sixties, those who cruised the streets were regularly dispersed, prodded with billy clubs: "Keep moving, faggot, keep moving."[57] There were no community centers for homosexuals, few safe places other than the bars: the Mafia was all too eager to fill the void. Stonewall was, for good or ill, a testament to the discrimination, harassment, persecution, and clandestine existence that marked gay and lesbian life just a half century ago.

Stonewall is remembered now less for its sleaze than for one hot night in June 1969 when the "spark" for gay liberation was ignited. The place had been raided earlier that week, but the police arrived again as Friday night turned to Saturday morning—evidently bent on closing down the place for good. Stories abound about why this particular raid took place, just as there are endless debates over what exactly happened, who was materially involved, and what caused it all. Indeed, why would the cops bust a bar that was a reliable cash cow (as it was for the Mafia)? It was election season, and politicians pressured local precincts to show voters that they were effective in "cleaning up" New York City. Perhaps the police were pressured to close Stonewall because it had become notorious for yet another revenue stream enriching the Mafia owners: they extorted hush money from gay patrons who worked on Wall Street, for whom remaining safely closeted was worth almost any amount.[58]

Eyewitness accounts of the raid and its immediate aftermath converge around a few details: although most customers were allowed to leave the bar after their IDs were checked, the police held employees inside along with transsexuals and other especially effeminate gays. For whatever reason, those ushered out remained nearby instead of scattering, and the crowd became increasingly unruly as rumors spread that those held inside were being beaten. Bricks and bottles were thrown, paddy wagons arrived, someone tried to use lighter fluid to torch the entrance, windows were smashed at the bar and in police cars, the tactical police force arrived, some patrons fought back as they were herded toward police vans, some escaped, some were beaten. The resistance displayed that night at Stonewall was out of character for a population who had generally accepted such harassment by running away (and who had every good reason to avoid interventions that could expose their secrets). Evidently, a critical point in the escalation of the riots came when an apparent lesbian patron (women were generally sparse among Stonewall regulars, and her role remains challenged by eyewitnesses and historians alike) pleaded for her gay brothers to help as she was dragged roughly to the police van. Men who looked sufficiently manly were generally let out of the bar, and many of them left the scene; those with more feminine appearances were disproportionately detained and were more likely to swing back at a cop, struggle to break free, or heave a garbage can.

Most witnesses agree that those on the front lines of the riots were young, marginalized gays, street people, flame queens, and transvestites who may have had the most to lose if Stonewall was closed down for good.[59] For those who shed blood, Stonewall was a singular home and relatively safe haven, a place where they could hustle and cruise with less harassment than elsewhere. However, the spark ignited by the raid needed tinder and careful tending before the gay liberation movement could get under way. Here is where "the gay and lesbian community" began to change its complexion: "To talk about identity is to change or construct it, despite the dominant epistemology of identity, which specifies immutability."[60] Appropriation of the violent resistance began immediately, as activists Craig Rodwell and Fred Sargeant alerted the media that something newsworthy was happening down on Christopher Street. Unlike typical patrons of Stonewall, these activists possessed organizational savvy, social capital, and outward respectability—and the wherewithal to create something lasting out of the ephemeral unrest. They came from a more moderate generation of older gay activists, who (in retrospect) viewed Stonewall-the-bar as a potentially embarrassing and counterproductive locus for the birth of the gay revolution.[61] They were button-down men with ties, committed (for example) to pursuing gay rights in employment by displaying conformity to dominant American mores (except one). Some were present for the raid, others got there quickly—to watch a very different gay community get shoved, clubbed, and arrested: comparatively flamboyant young homeless street gays, queens of all kinds, trans people, and lesbian separatists whose rejection of dominant American values was displayed in their appearances. Can you imagine Obama citing Stonewall if the recalled memory was a chorus line of men with mascara kicking up their heels like Rockettes and chanting at the police: "We are the Stonewall girls / We wear our hair in curls / We don't wear underwear / We show our pubic hair . . ."[62] Moderate activists like Dick Leitsch realized, however, that the energy and community fomented at Stonewall could be put to good political use if public faces during the raid were tidied up.

Conversion of Stonewall into a respectable, lasting, and potent birthplace—"a marker of collective identity"[63]—began with the closing of the bar itself (by the owners), just four months after the raid. To replace the sordid site, moderate gay mobilizers created social movement organizations, sponsored dances not dependent upon Mafia protection, and spread the message of gay liberation mercilessly. While never quite forgetting the bar and the raid, they focused attention instead on the Christopher Street Liberation Day March to commemorate the first anniversary of Stonewall (which has now been reopened, festooned with rainbow flags)—distancing the budding movement from the seamier side of the riots, and sanitizing the story. The Gay Liberation Front (GLF) was formed first, but faltered quickly after fractious disagreements over whether to donate money (raised through gay dances) to the Committee to Defend the Black Panthers. Obama's easy concatenation of gays, women, and African Americans in 2013 belies a stormy and divisive history. Gays who favored donations to the Black Panthers argued that oppressed peoples of all stripes should work shoulder to shoulder for liberation (a intersectional position echoed in Obama's speech). Those who opposed donations pointed out that the Black Panthers had been, at times, "viciously antihomosexual"[64]—and recalled that King's SCLC tucked away important contributions by Bayard Rustin so that his homosexuality would not be a distraction in the pursuit of African American civil rights. Radical feminists found it difficult at first to accommodate lesbian separatists: Betty Friedan tagged them the "lavender menace," which was then embraced as a badge of honor by gay women. The immediate aftermath of Stonewall exemplifies "the dynamic and creative futility of saying 'we.'"[65]

The GLF was superseded by the Gay Activist Alliance, which became a stable and efficient organization for institutionalizing the march into an annual and global affair. Although these are referred to as the Stonewall gay pride parades, their direct connection to the original bar has become tenuous with time. West Coast gays pointed to Stonewall-like moments of oppression-cum-resistance that had taken place before the raid in July 1969. San Francisco declined to participate in Stonewall parades for several years, claiming place priority for starting the gay rights movement—they eventually joined forces, choosing to value a geographically united front over parochial pride.[66] Stonewall, not Compton's Cafeteria in the Tenderloin (riots happened there in August 1966), has become the brand name—but only after the Mafia, extortion, exorbitant swill, police raids, chicken hawks, and Rockette wannabes went sotto voce. Stonewall has become an intentionally faulty mnemonic device, but—it seems—a convincing one.[67]

It would be tempting but premature to conclude that all's well that ends well. Obama's reference to Stonewall was enabled not just by a salutary expansion of gay identities but also by seismic shifts in American public opinion toward increasing tolerance of alternative sexual orientations. He made it clear in his inaugural address that the next step in the struggle would be gay marriage (probably not foremost in the minds of those getting clubbed during the 1969 raid): "Our journey is not complete," he said, "until our gay brothers and sisters are treated like anyone else under the law, for if we are truly created equal, then surely the love we commit to one another must be equal as well." Two years later, the Supreme Court, in *Obergefell v. Hodges* (2015), would extend to same-sex couples the right to marry in all fifty states under the Fourteenth Amendment of the Constitution. On June 24, 2016, Obama created the Stonewall National Monument on Christopher Street in the Village, in order to commemorate in the most legitimizing way possible the birthplace of the movement for LGBTQ equality. Now, and for all time, gays would have their Selma, their Seneca Falls, a place for pride, and a place for all visitors to learn how sexual orientation once had been grounds for denying a wide range of civil rights.

Stop press! In March 2015, the Indiana Senate passed its version of the Religious Freedom Restoration Act, which was interpreted as allowing people to deny services to same-sex couples if that behavior ran contrary to their religious beliefs. A month later, under enormous public pressure, the bill was amended specifically to protect the rights of the LGBTQ community. Governor Mike Pence enthusiastically supported the original bill, which was consistent in spirit with his long-standing commitment to denying homosexuals protection under federal antidiscrimination laws—restoring the wedge between gays and both women and ethnic minorities. Pence became vice president a little over a year later. In March 2016, North Carolina's Governor Pat McCrory signed into law a "bathroom bill" insisting that individuals must use restrooms that match the sex listed on their birth certificate, in effect denying transgender people the right to choose the facilities that match their preferred sex. A week after its signing, again in response to outcry, part of the bill was repealed—but in February 2017, President Donald Trump "rescinded protections for transgender students that had allowed them to use bathrooms corresponding with their gender identity."[68] Interpretive signage and plaques displayed around the new truth-spot at the Stonewall National Monument in Greenwich Village still have a lot of work to do in order to make some recalcitrant Americans believe that the LGBTQ community indeed belongs among groups entitled to equal rights under God.

————•————

In this era of plural identities, we need civil times and civil spaces more than ever, for these are essential to the democratic processes by which individuals and groups come together to discuss, debate, and negotiate the past and, through this process, define the future.
«JOHN GILLIS[69]»

Why end the list with Stonewall and gays? Other birthplaces commemorate the struggles of unmentioned identity-based groups seeking full Constitutional rights (or, at least, justifiable political benefits): Little Bighorn or Wounded Knee for Native Americans, Manzanar for Asian Americans, Delano for Hispanic and Filipino farmworkers, the Triangle Shirtwaist Factory for organized labor, or Ellis Island for immigrants (likely to be the noisiest identity-based movement in the years ahead, amid calls for walls and deportation). It is hardly the case that these other struggles have already ended in total victory. Inaugural addresses are just as important for what gets left out—omitted truth-spots, missed stories.

President Trump gave his own inaugural address, of course, on January 20, 2017. He mentions three places by name, none of them birthplaces that commemorate the start of identity-based struggles for equal rights (not his thing). Only two of them are truth-spots. "Washington" becomes an untruth-spot, a place that misrepresents the Real America: "While triumphs have been celebrated in our nation's Capital, there was little to celebrate for struggling families all across our land." Those families live in the "urban sprawl of Detroit" and the "windswept plains of Nebraska," touchstones of what this country is all about. But any truth-spot can be appropriated for discrepant purposes, or undermined. "Detroit" can be made into a Phoenix of the New Economy, rebuilt not on the ashes of River Rouge and the Rust Belt manufacturing jobs making cars that enabled urban sprawl (the jobs President Trump hopes to recover from offshore)—but rebuilt by Quicken Loans, which brought thousands of good jobs to its downtown headquarters. "Nebraska" is so windswept that 2.77 percent of its energy comes from wind turbines, with a huge upside potential for growth (not Mr. Trump's favorite energy source). "Washington" is not destined to be an epistemic swamp forever: what a truth-spot it could become—a place where people gather to discuss dispassionately and decide in principled ways exactly which truths are indeed self-evident.

8

Ultra Clean Lab

Dirt is essentially disorder. There is no such thing as absolute dirt: it exists in the eye of the beholder. . . . Dirt is the by-product of a systematic ordering and classification of matter, in so far as ordering involves rejecting inappropriate elements.

«MARY DOUGLAS[1]»

Before entering Laura Wasylenki's clean lab in the Multidisciplinary Science Building II on the Bloomington campus of Indiana University, I had to put on a zip-up Tyvek bodysuit, complete with elastic bonnet for my thinning hair, and a pair of synthetic foam clogs. As I stepped onto a sticky mat at the threshold of the lab, Wasylenki pointed to a little ribbon blowing out from the lab space toward the changing room: "positive pressure air flow."[2] The place inside is white: white floors, white ceilings, white walls, white cabinets, white blinds, white fume hoods (the bench surfaces are black). The rare bit of color comes from Sesame Street characters pasted on the front of each exhaust hood: Big Bird, Cookie Monster, Bert, and Ernie have all found their way inside Wasylenki's clean lab—or, at least, paper images of them that are free of all metals or anything else that might corrode in the acidic atmosphere of the place. This is a *controlled* environment: nothing of the surrounding world gets inside that could possibly contaminate the experiments under way.

Wasylenki is a metal isotope geochemist, intensely curious these days about the characteristics of nickel in banded iron formations from the Late Archaean Eon about 2.4 billion years ago. Something very important happened then: the first significant accumulation of free oxygen in the earth's oceans and atmosphere—the "Great Oxidation Event," without which we would not be here. Scientists do not fully understand how and why this massively consequential change came about, but the increase in oxygen seems to be associated somehow with a corresponding decline in the amount of methane produced by microorganisms known as "methanogens." The "nickel famine" hypothesis suggests that methanogens need to consume nickel in order to survive, so the depletion of available nickel at that moment in geological time might have caused a decline in the amount of methane produced, which in turn brought on a more oxygenated state.[3]

It turns out that nickel atoms come in several weights. The atomic number for this element is 28, which means that each atom has 28 protons and electrons. However, the number of neutrons may vary, creating different isotopes of nickel: about two-thirds of naturally occurring nickel has 30 neutrons (nickel-58 is lighter in weight), another one-quarter has 32 neutrons (nickel-60 is the heavier isotope), and the remainder are relatively rare and even heavier isotopes 61, 62, and 64 (which together comprise only about 6 percent of naturally occurring nickel). Methanogens have a preference for the lighter isotope of nickel, and as they assimilate the lighter isotope at a faster rate than the heavier one, they "fractionate" the metal: more nickel-60 than nickel-58 is left behind. As the overall amount of available nickel declines (itself likely a result of the earth's cooling), and as the methanogens preferentially gobble up more and more of the lighter isotopes of nickel, the ratio of heavy to light nickel left behind in seawater and recorded in marine sediments should increase over time. Or, at least, that is Wasylenki's hypothesis.

How on earth can all that be examined experimentally—or, maybe the question should be, where? Ancient rocks laid down 2.4 billion years ago might record the story. Layers upon layers of iron oxides (ferrihydrites) were precipitated on the oceans' floor at about the time of the Great Oxidation Event. Outcroppings of these banded iron formations, or BIFs, may be found today in South Africa, Australia, and Canada. As they formed, the iron oxides incorporated bits of nickel that were left over after the methanogens finished eating. Even though the ancient iron oxides subsequently went through a "phase conversion" (becoming hematite, magnetite, and goethite), the amount and isotopic composition of the embedded nickel probably remains the same to this day. All Wasylenki needs is bits of BIFs from different periods of time, ranging from 3.8 to 1.8 billion years ago, each containing a little nickel. Luckily, other researchers studying related problems shared their samples of the ancient rocks with her. If she is right, the ratio of heavy to light nickel isotopes should increase as the pulverized nickel in iron-rich rock gets younger—that is, the layers from more recent years will contain proportionately more nickel-60.

But why the need for an ultra clean lab—which cost a hefty $730,000 for 440 square feet? There are two answers, one from nature, the other from the culture of metal isotope geochemists. Nickel is all around us. It has been used to make coins, rechargeable batteries, electric guitar strings, shampoo, detergents, gasoline additives, paint, and—as an alloy—to make steel and in electroplating processes that give car bumpers and kitchen appliances their shine. Who knows how much nickel I would have carried into Wasylenki's clean lab if I had not put on the moon suit, bonnet, and clogs? The sample quantities of nickel from the ancient rocks are miniscule: *any* extraneous nickel getting into the lab (or not carefully accounted for) would contaminate her measurements and calculations of isotopic ratios, completely wasting the experiment. The clean lab exists to keep all the nickel out, except for the bits of rock of experimental interest. In a moment, I'll describe how Wasylenki's lab manages to exclude unwanted nickel, and how she determines whether or not she has succeeded in that intensely "prophylactic" effort.

But when I first asked Wasylenki why she needed the clean lab, her answer came more from culture than nature: "because pretty much every isotope group in the world does their work in a clean lab." She earned her PhD in geology at Caltech in 1999, and in 2004, took a research scientist position at Arizona State University, before starting on the tenure track at Indiana in 2010. While in Tempe, "I learned about the culture of clean labs, that 'isotope groups just have clean labs, that's just how it is,' and if you don't have one then maybe you're not really in the game." Her explanation is genealogical rather than geochemical, the lore of this tribe: "This comes in some part from Clair Patterson [of Caltech—more in a moment about how he changed the world forever] who did some of the pioneering work on isotope geochemistry that had to be really clean. . . . And so part of it actually comes from Patterson's culture . . . and also Gerry Wasserburg's group had it at Caltech, and there are lots of rules about who goes in that room and whether they understand what they are doing. . . . And then from Wasserburg's group, it passed to Wasserburg's last PhD student Ariel Anbar, who is PI at the lab where I did my first isotope work at Arizona State. So part of that culture is pretty directly descended. I guess Patterson is Ariel Anbar's academic uncle." To be a bona fide member of this family, a player in this game, you've got to have a clean lab: "Everyone trusts Ariel because he came out of the Caltech lab, and everyone trusts the Caltech lab."

Excluding unwanted nickel is difficult and expensive. Everything that goes into the clean lab, except the samples, must be nickel-free: Wasylenki and her students, instruments and analytical apparatuses, reagents and resins, solutions and standards, floors and walls, air and water, me. No "dirt." All water that enters the clean lab is filtered through a Millipore Super-Q 18.2 megaohm-cm ionization unit (beats your Brita), and all air through Class 100 HEPA filters (essentially trapping all particles >0.3 microns in diameter). The room is dominated by four polypropylene (plastic, no metal!) laminar-flow exhausted clean hoods, like the one above your kitchen range but on steroids. The walls and ceiling panels are painted with several coats of epoxy paint (to keep the drywall intact and acid resistant), and Wasylenki tested its composition before it was applied. Evidently the coloring agent originally chosen by the architects "came back with barium and a few other metals . . . and zinc, and I knew I was going to work on zinc, so I didn't want zinc in the wall paint. . . . I ended up just asking them: the last two coats you put on the wall, just don't put any coloring agent at all. It's *white.*" The floor is vinyl (she tested its impermeability by dropping acid on it), and the light fixture frames are made of aluminum—not a metal of interest, and it won't rust. The metal pull chains for the window blinds were swapped out for plastic ones. In theory, the room itself has been eliminated as a source of experimental contamination. The same is true for the vials, tubes, columns, and beakers that come in contact with the sampled ancient rocks. All are made of Teflon or other plastics, and they are bathed in acid before use to remove impurities, in the Big Bird hood. Ultra clean.

But how can Wasylenki be sure that the lab is clean enough? The Holy Grail in this world is a "blank" of zero. A blank is an experimental procedure run without the vital sample in it, a kind of control or placebo. Wasylenki and her students conduct experimental procedures in stereoscope—*with* the sampled nickel and simultaneously *without*: "Hopefully, if you are doing this right, everything is clean and there isn't a contamination problem. You should have a couple nanograms of nickel there. Your sample is 3 micrograms, which is three orders of magnitude more. My student's going to put a couple randomly interspersed [blanks] in the samples and those should just come out uniformly very very low in nickel. If the blanks are high, now you have to start worrying that some of your results are bad."

The conversion of ancient rock into meaningful and uncontaminated data is the goal of everything that Wasylenki does in her clean lab. She will start off with 26 samples of nickel-harboring BIFs (arrayed by their geologic age), extracting and pulverizing them with a carbide-bit micro drill. The powder is dissolved in hydrochloric and nitric acids (distilled in-house, so that nothing unwanted gets into the process that way), creating a "digest," and then the nickel is separated from all other elements and purified, using ion-exchange column chromatography in the Ernie hood. The dissolved ancient rocks are dripped into a vertical tube with a resin that lets unwanted elements slip through (iron, manganese, chromium) while trapping the nickel—which is then itself eluted with a different acid solution and dried down in the Cookie Monster hood. All the while, blanks are checked for possible contamination: "This is why we have the clean room. This is the procedure . . . and it is absolutely critical that you not contaminate it with other stuff. This is the place."

Then the experimental process leaves the clean lab and goes downstairs for mass spectrometry, which will measure the nickel concentrations and isotopic ratios in the samples, using machines named The Count (which does just that) and Kermit. The nickel solutions get a final dilution in acid; then they are nebulized and ionized, and shot down a tube that has a prominent bend: "The light masses [isotopes] turn the corner more sharply than the heavy masses, and this is how they physically separate into ion beams, and then you have collectors at the end to measure how much of each isotope arrives." The anticipated result: a statistical ratio of heavy to light nickel, changing across geologic time. The process is plainly more complicated than all that, but these details are sufficient to make my point: the universe is excluded from this place of fact-making, except for those bits of nature that are of experimental interest—along with the contamination-free tools needed to make the desired observations (air, water, acids, balances, Teflon vials, resin beads, hot plates, and several scientists).

But are all these safeguards absolutely necessary? Wasylenki reflected back on her time at Arizona State: "It seemed really funny that there were some things that we did that were just overkill." The walls in that lab are covered by a plastic insert, at a far higher cost than the epoxy paint that Wasylenki chose for her lab in Bloomington. It "seemed just crazy to me, like just ridiculous overkill, given that other things were just a little bit sloppy, including dog hair appearing on the floor." "I had no evidence that the plastic walls actually made the blanks better." She wondered, too, about overkill in her own lab—especially at the point where samples leave the clean lab and go downstairs for isotope fractionation and counting: "We are now going to walk into the mass spec lab which has six machines in it, and isn't a clean room at all. We don't take our street shoes off and we don't change our clothes. . . . And you carry them through plain old air. . . . That's what seems funny to me: we've been so damned careful up here but then at the moment we are going to measure the thing, we are not so rigorous." Some research centers have put the mass spec machines inside clean labs: "If money hadn't been an issue, I would have done it." Moreover, the best-built clean lab cannot dictate "the human factors, the behavioral things." Some researchers do not report in their published papers the details of procedures that Wasylenki believes are vital for judging the validity of their measures: "You will find papers where people are not very explicit about the blanks. . . . If it's not reported, I don't know if they did it or not. . . . How did they clean their resin? How did they clean anything? Talk to me about all of your procedures, prove to me that the numbers you are putting in your results actually represent what was in your sample." About two years ago, the "whole metal isotope community" got together to discuss this problem and agreed "to push each other to be rigorous," a move of collective self-policing.

The very idea of "clean" is getting squishy. On the one hand, "clean" can be quantified: "I want that amount [of the metal in the blank] to be preferably three or four orders of magnitude lower than the smallest sample." Also, manufacturers of air and water filters rate their products in terms of the varying sizes of stuff filtered out. On the other hand, choices about the real requirements of an ultra clean lab are shaped by available budget, by what other scientists have done with their space—and then, once chosen, the built-in safeguards are overridden by practices that risk dirtying it all up again, practices not sufficiently described when findings are written up. Are some features of clean labs more for appearances (and perhaps bought-credibility) than geochemical necessity? Wasylenki noted: "The Chinese labs, partly because they have a lot of money for science right now, and partly due to smog, build more rigorous clean labs, and they work harder at having you cross multiple thresholds [before entering]. . . . I don't know of any labs in the US doing that except in the semi-conductor industry." The pursuit of "clean" is an ongoing and endless process: no physical spaces can secure absolute cleanliness in the face of human foibles—and indeed there are no "absolutes," as Mary Douglas said of dirt, only more or less tolerable degrees of clean, a judgment.

Wasylenki modeled her clean lab on those that came before her: "They are mostly alike. . . . They are pretty darned comparable." This is understandable: during the design phase, Wasylenki visited existing labs, recalled her experiences at Caltech and Arizona State, and relied on the architects for whom her lab was not their first rodeo. Other geochemists, elsewhere, have subsequently contacted Wasylenki for advice. There is mimesis in the design of clean labs, which makes sense in terms of maximizing ease of use. The world of metal isotope geochemistry is full of demographic churn, as in most sciences: researchers move a lot among labs, as grad students, postdocs, young professors (and they often do walk-throughs of facilities when they give colloquia away from home). A grad student visiting from Stanford was up and running experiments in Wasylenki's clean lab after only about fifteen minutes of orientation, which is typical: "If I go to someone else's clean lab, I can get oriented very rapidly because I know what to expect, and for the most part, little details will be different, but everything will function largely the same way."

Before reading Wasylenki's published scientific papers, I expected to find in them excruciatingly detailed accounts of exactly how her $730,000 white room kept the contaminating world at bay. Nada. I asked her if perhaps I had just overlooked descriptions of the place: "Nope. It is part of the lore. . . . The community is fairly small, and everybody knows everybody for the most part, everybody reading that paper knows, oh yeah, Laura is at IU and she built this clean lab there." Her lab is so clean that at the end of the day, when claims about natural reality are publicly asserted, it becomes invisible.

———•———

Recommendations are made to initiate studies of the biochemistry of lead in laboratory *sanctuaries* which exclude industrial lead contamination . . . which will relate to the issue whether to terminate the mining and smelting of lead.
«CLAIR C. PATTERSON[4]»

Laura Wasylenki met Clair C. Patterson when she arrived at Caltech for graduate studies shortly before his death in 1995. She suspects that his pioneering ultra clean lab was by then dismantled, after Patterson's retirement in 1992. He may be the most famous scientist you have never heard of. Consider this: at a time when most scientists agreed that planet Earth was about 3.3 billion years old, Patterson provided evidence in the early 1950s that it is in fact 4.55 billion years old (+/- 0.07 billion years)—and that number has stuck ever since. Consider this: at a time when authoritative scientists believed that levels of lead in the earth's environment had not changed much since the formation of the planet, and thus—as background—it posed little health or ecological threat, Patterson again proved them wrong by using the distinctive isotopic signature of anthropogenic lead to show that increased concentrations of lead were not a natural process but rather a consequence of industrialization (mainly from leaded ethyl in gasoline). All Patterson did was convince enough people that in the last 4.55 billion years, humans (starting in 6500 BC, in Anatolia) had spewed so much dangerous lead into the ecosystem that remedies were needed now. Thanks in part to him, gasoline no longer has lead, nor does paint, nor aerosol sprays, nor pesticides—and the tuna fish we eat have far less lead in their muscles than before Patterson, and they are canned without solder, which once contained lead.

You (and more than five million other viewers in 2014) might have met Patterson in Fox's documentary television series *Cosmos: A Spacetime Odyssey*, hosted by Neil deGrasse Tyson, where he is voiced by Richard Gere. Episode 7 is titled "The Clean Room," and focuses in part on what happens when a scientist speaks truth to power. Or maybe you met Patterson thinly disguised as Sam Beech (sound it out slowly, for a clue about his irascible, maverick, bulldog disposition) in Saul Bellow's 1982 novel, *The Dean's December*. Dean Albert Corde is informed by Beech: "We had been 'authoritatively assured' that lead levels were normal and tolerable. Far from it. Official standards are worse than incorrect; they are dangerously false. Investigations are conducted in laboratories themselves heavily contaminated. Only results obtained in ultra-clean sanctuary laboratories are dependable. These are few in number but only their evidence counts, and this evidence tells us that lead levels are about five hundredfold above natural prehistoric levels."[5]

Patterson initially faced tough sledding in making claims about anthropogenic sources of lead and the risks they posed. "They have been greeted with derisive and scornful insults from toxicologists, sanitary engineers and public health officials because their traditional views are challenged," Patterson said.[6] Critics "tried to paint him as a crank, and to ruin his career."[7] The reigning scientific authority on human risks from lead was Robert A. Kehoe, a physician based at the University of Cincinnati from 1924 to 1965, working for most of that time as director of the Kettering Lab.[8] The place was named after Charles F. Kettering, who, as a researcher and vice president at General Motors, patented tetraethyllead (TEL), which eliminated engine knock when added to gasoline. Kettering founded the Ethyl Corporation in 1923 to manufacture TEL, and hired Kehoe in 1924 to serve as chief medical consultant. After four decades of lead expulsion into the atmosphere from exhaust pipes of almost every car on the road, Kehoe testified on June 9, 1966, at the hearings of the

Subcommittee on Air and Water Pollution, chaired by Senator Edmund S. Muskie, that "there is no reasonable basis for anxiety concerning any potential threat that is offered to the public from the lead in the ambient atmosphere in the United States." Kehoe spoke with confidence: "Developing the information on this subject, I have had a greater responsibility than any other person in this country"; and cited his "methods of surveillance," "which are characterized by a high degree of technical precision." Kehoe tried to reassure the senators that lead has always been with us "in the surface of the earth, in its vegetation, in its animal life. . . . There is no way in which man has ever been able to escape the absorption of lead while living on this planet." Even during three decades of intensifying automobility, "there has been little or no change in the atmospheric conditions in respect to lead in Cincinnati."[9]

When Clair Patterson appeared before Muskie's subcommittee less than a week later, he faced this challenge: how to present his own decade-long research on lead, which showed dramatic and dangerous increases in lead concentrations all over the earth, from human-made sources, with enough credibility to persuade the senators that the mining and smelting of lead, and its use in gasoline and other products, should be outlawed or curtailed. Patterson succeeded (lead in gasoline was finally removed in 1987) because of his truth-spot in Pasadena: the ultra clean laboratory he built in 1953 at Caltech, the alpha place that spawned clean copies at Arizona State and eventually Indiana University Bloomington. Patterson's "theories and chemical analyses would have to be painstakingly perfect in every detail because his thesis was premised on his laboratory's being right and almost every other trace metal laboratory's being wrong."[10]

Patterson did not begin his scientific career with the intent to rid the world of lead pollution. Indeed, his original need for a clean lab stemmed from doctoral research at the University of Chicago in the late 1940s. Based on the assumption that meteorites were "leftover building materials from the early days of the solar system,"[11] and knowing that primordial uranium decays over time into different isotopes of lead, Patterson's adviser suggested that he "measure the isotopic composition and concentration of small quantities of lead"[12] in a sample from the Diablo Canyon meteorite—working "like an elemental egg timer."[13] In an oral history interview conducted in 1995, Patterson recalled: "And if we only knew what the isotopic composition of primordial lead was in the earth at the time it was formed, we could take that number and stick it into this marvelous equation we had. And you could turn the crank and, blip, out would come the age of the earth."[14] Not so fast: "Our experimental results didn't fit the calculations. Now, I tracked back and I found out there was lead coming from here, there was lead coming from there. . . . It was contamination of every conceivable source that people had never thought about before."[15] Patterson was working "in a very dusty laboratory in Kent Hall, one of the oldest buildings on campus,"[16] and "the lead around him was overwhelming the tiny lead samples he wanted to analyze."[17] Patterson embarked on what would become a lifetime of cleaning up. Everything in the lab was cleansed, glassware scoured and rinsed, platinum crucibles dipped in acid[18]—until the blanks finally came back at tolerable levels. Only then did the earth get scientifically older.

Lead is toxic for humans, whether ingested or inhaled, causing damage to the nervous system and adversely affecting cognitive functions—the ancient Greeks and Romans knew that. Upon discovering that there were considerable amounts of lead in just about everything around us, Patterson wondered if this had always been so. If not, what were the sources of new lead coming into the environment? Did possible increases in lead concentrations pose health risks? "I was forced to make the clean lab as a consequence of these discoveries."[19] Caltech provided generous space in North Mudd Hall, and in 1952, Patterson set about to build an "ULTRA CLEAN environment,"[20] the "first facility of its kind"[21] anywhere and destined to become (at least among metal isotope geochemists) "hallowed ground."[22]

The clean lab in Pasadena was remarkably similar to Wasylenki's lab at Indiana, built sixty years later, except in scale: all of Wasylenki's clean procedures happen in one room, at distinctive work stations identified by Muppets; Patterson had a clean suite: "Separate rooms are used for washing sample containers, purifying water and chemical reagents, preparing samples, and analyzing the samples."[23] Considerable retrofitting of Patterson's space was required: old pipes had lead in them, old electrical wiring used lead solder, the building-wide water supply had to be "passed through an ultra pure mixed bed resin column,"[24] old air flow was replaced by "an elaborate baffle system to pump in purified, pressurized air—when the door opened, air blew out rather than in"[25] (like Wasylenki's little ribbon). Walls were painted in acid-resistant epoxy: "It is convenient to check each item of paint or construction material to be used in the laboratory by rough emission spectrographic analysis *before* it is permanently used or installed."[26] Wasylenki followed those marching orders. Surfaces in the hoods must be acid-resistant plastic, not stainless steel, and cords for the electric hot plates must be Teflon coated.[27] Patterson estimated that "half of all activities in these laboratories is devoted to purification . . . and other contamination control procedures."[28]

Once built, the ultra clean lab must remain forever free of contaminants—no metal of interest gets inside unaccounted for. Weekly, the floors "are flooded with distilled water and . . . squeegeed down the drains."[29] One scientist's first introduction to Patterson and his lab began "by getting down on . . . [our] hands and knees together and cleaning the floor with Kimwipes, square centimeter by square centimeter."[30] The lab came with instructions "that listed each step of fifteen different procedures from washing equipment made of glass, Teflon, plastic, and polyethylene (each requiring a different process) to distilling water and purifying borax and other reagents."[31] Special attention was given to the changing room, where dusty humans prepared themselves by stripping "down to their underwear and put[ting] on Tyvek suits"[32] (I did not go that far). There should be a gelatin pad at the threshold of the clean lab (Wasylenki's sticky mat).[33] Caltech's Geology Division boasted that they had "the cleanest air in all of southern California,"[34] and for the growing family of metal isotope geochemists, Patterson and his lab became the "oracle of experimental technique."[35]

For all the expense and meticulous care in creating an ultra clean lab at Caltech, Patterson first needed to leave his sanctuary and enter a very dirty world to collect samples of nature that could reveal whether or not concentrations of lead had been changed by industrialization. His analytic strategy was similar to Wasylenki's studies of nickel. Present-day lead comes from three sources, and each has its own isotopic signature: it has been there primordially from the creation of the earth, it gets created from the decay of uranium, or it is introduced into the environment via human activity (smelting, making coins, lining plumbing, or running cars with leaded gasoline). By measuring the ratios among these different isotopes at different points in geological and historical time, Patterson can discern changes in the concentration of lead from anthropogenic origins. But where should he collect natural samples—and how?

Layers of ice in Greenland and Antarctica provide a stable record of whatever in the atmosphere settled down as new-fallen snow. After several cold excursions away from Pasadena, Patterson and his team found way more lead in ice near the surface than older stuff deeper down: "a 230-fold increase in lead concentrations in Greenland snow over the past 3000 years from the atmospheric deposition of industrial lead aerosols."[36] Patterson got "sicker than a dog"[37] aboard ships while collecting ocean water from various depths: he reported in 1963 that deep seawater had "three to ten times less lead than surface water,"[38] about 90 percent of it from auto emissions. He traveled to Mount Etna in Sicily, and to New Zealand and Hawaii, to find that volcanic emissions contributed insignificant quantities of lead into the atmosphere when compared to industrial sources.[39] Searching for a "pristine" spot for sampling nature far away from industrialization, Patterson trekked into the remote Kerrick

Meadow-Thompson Canyon area of Yosemite Park in the Sierra Nevada range. Still he found that 70,000 grams of lead were deposited annually on five square miles of the Canyon but only 250 grams "washed out in streams each year." The rest accumulated throughout the biomass—settling on the leaves of sedge, ingested by meadow mice, who were in turn eaten by pine martens.[40] Lead has accumulated that way in human bodies: "Then we . . . got ancient Indian bones that were thousands of years old, from two different sites in the southwestern United States, where I knew from archeological and anthropological information that there had been no metals or smelting or making of glazes for ceramics. And we analyzed . . . the enamels from the teeth, enamels from the long bone, enamels from the ribs": the amount of lead in modern skeletons was 1,000 times higher.[41]

Patterson's procedures for taking samples from field sites needed to be rather more careful than Linnaeus's gathering seeds and dried flowers from the Lapland countryside (chapter 3): properly folded sealed envelopes just would not do. Patterson knew there were three sources of contaminating lead that could taint his analyses, and two were handled by the filtering, blowing, purifying, washing, and acid-bathing in his ultra clean lab: lead seeping in from the ambient environment or dust on clothing, and lead introduced through the vials and reagents needed to prepare samples for mass spectroscopy. But a third possible source of lead contamination followed Patterson to "the ends of the earth":[42] the tools used to extract samples from their natural setting and the containers used for shipping them back to Caltech were inevitably drenched in lead from the start, above and beyond amounts at the field site before his arrival. In effect, Patterson needed to take a "mobile clean lab"[43] with him to the wild. One of his many collaborators recalled: "Scrupulous attention to the preparation of ultra-clean collection apparatus and the maintenance of its integrity . . . represents the essence of excellent field work."[44] To extract polar ice samples, "we sawed it out of the walls of this tunnel while we were wearing acid-clean plastic gloves and suits and using clean saws. Now, all of that equipment was cleaned back down here, in vats of acid. . . . And then it had to be all sealed up in plastic and flown up in these gigantic cargo planes."[45] The goal was to get "virgin"[46] ice, a special challenge because army engineers stationed in Greenland "smoked profusely and guzzled soda from lead-soldered cans and . . . sprayed their lead-contaminated urine, spit, and mucus around the tunnel."[47] On the high seas, the ship was "oozing lead all over the place as it moves through the water, so there's a local contamination problem"[48]—solved by collecting water ahead of the vessel, in a container that prevented water near the surface (more lead there) from contaminating samples taken from the deep.[49] In remote Thompson Canyon, he created "yet another laboratory—a natural one."[50] To extract muscle from a tuna fish properly, it took three people with knives and tweezers always dipped in acid.[51]

Having taken such pains to prevent contamination in collecting samples and in analyzing them at the clean lab back home, Patterson had good reason to be confident as he wrote the dissenting opinion in a 1980 National Research Council report: "There are no substances in the atmosphere, hydrosphere, or biosphere that are not contaminated with industrial lead to some degree."[52] He had been just as confident telling the Muskie subcommittee in 1965: "It can be shown from material balance considerations and from isotopic tracers that nearly all the lead in the atmospheres of American cities originates today from lead tetraethyl, and that 30 years ago, lead concentrations in these areas should have been about a hundred times less."[53] But why should Muskie or anybody else prefer this account to Robert Kehoe's counterassertion that most lead in human bodies "was derived via the natural food chain rather than from anthropogenic sources and as such the body burden of lead in the general population had not changed in decades."[54] All that stood between Patterson and Kehoe was the ultra clean lab at Caltech, capable of distinguishing with reliable precision naturally occurring lead (present at earth's creation, or decayed uranium) from auto emissions and other industrial uses of the metal.

From the mid-1960s to his death, Patterson told anybody who would listen that calculations of lead concentrations were wrong unless they were done in his own lab, or in another just as clean. Without proper controls for contamination, Kehoe's baseline measurements of lead concentrations were way too high, and when those numbers are assumed to describe the state of play at earlier historical moments, it is easy but erroneous to conclude that leaded ethyl did not add enough lead to worry about (or legislate against): "Patterson showed that . . . industrial samples once thought to be natural were actually greatly elevated above natural background."[55] Others' calculations were "due to underestimation of blank contamination."[56] French collaborator Claude Boutron wrote: "All heavy metals data for Antarctic and Greenland snow and ice obtained outside Pat's laboratory were erroneously high because of contamination problems."[57] Patterson told a 1975 House subcommittee, "Much of the analytical data regarding the occurrence of lead in the marine environment is inaccurate and misleading,"[58] but his data could be trusted "because his lab was cleaner than others."[59] He even tested that proposition, sending identical seawater samples to ten other labs and discovering that they found up to 100 times the 14 nanograms of dissolved lead that Patterson had found in his clean lab, because of contamination.

Still, Patterson could not allow the legislators to conclude that his measurements and calculations were absolutely unique to his ultra clean lab at Caltech, as if he was up to a little secret alchemy in a hermetically sealed place. Indeed, at a 1965 symposium sponsored by the US Public Health Service, Harvard physiologist Harry Heiman took note of the "geographic proximity of many pro-industry scientists to *Kehoe's* laboratory in Cincinnati, and he declared, 'It is extremely unusual in medical research that there is only one small group and one place in the country in which research in a specific area of knowledge is exclusively done.'"[60] As if by contrast, Patterson eagerly announced that his lab was open and available for emulation, and pleaded for federal support to build (or retrofit) more labs like his. George Tilton recalled: "He opened his laboratory to scientists from around the world and trained them in the techniques he had developed."[61] For Patterson, "they had to come to my laboratory from all over the world. . . . This was mecca"[62] (a truth-spot of a different sort). Come they did: following a 1981 conference at the Environmental Protection Agency, a "parade of key scientists visited Pasadena,"[63] "worshipful acolytes" built "carbon-copy" ultra clean labs at Carnegie-Mellon, UC Santa Barbara, and UConn, at the US Geological Survey in Denver, and in France and Japan—Patterson had become the "father of clean labs."[64] But he wanted more, asking the 1975 House subcommittee to support "constructing new types of labs."[65]

Patterson won. He and his ultra clean lab made almost everybody believe in the rise and threat of lead pollution. In the 1980 "alternative" National Research Council report, Patterson bragged: "ultra-clean laboratory techniques in various laboratories" have "become institutionalized," reducing "lead contamination during analysis more than a thousand-fold."[66] Today there are dozens if not hundreds of clean labs in Patterson's mold. Lead levels in human blood have declined since Patterson and Congress got the lead out of gasoline. One last thing about "Pat." He resented noise contamination in his office almost as much as lead in his clean lab, and he had Caltech double-insulate his doors, walls, ceilings, and windows. He thought and wrote in complete silence, leaving behind an "uncontaminated heritage for pure knowledge of science."[67] An acolyte remembers that Patterson preferred "to incubate his ideas alone,"[68] like Thoreau beside the Pond.

———•———

It is precisely the stripped down simplicity and invariability of labs—their placelessness—that gives them their credibility.

«ROBERT E. KOHLER[69]»

Places of this kind are outside of all places, even though it may be possible to indicate their location in reality.

«MICHEL FOUCAULT[70]»

What kind of place would you build if you sought universal assent for your experimental claims? If Laura Wasylenki finds empirical evidence to support the "nickel famine" hypothesis, the validity and credibility of her claim cannot appear to be dependent upon unique particulars of her clean lab in Bloomington, Indiana—even if, ironically, she and every other metal isotope geochemist knows that the necessary experiments could not have been properly conducted anywhere without a contaminant-free space like her 440 square feet of whiteness. Her goal (and Clair Patterson's too) is to make experimental discoveries into facts of nature rather than artifacts of a single experimental place. Local contingencies are the enemy of the universally true. But Wasylenki's ultra clean lab *is* a "local" thing, a bounded place with specific geographic coordinates and with a stringent material order built on-site. Her lab is unavoidably the local and particular provenance of claims seeking to be true everywhere and "as if" from anywhere. Place achieves placelessness—this is a paradox, and there are four ways to make sense of it: disengagement, transparency, standardization, and portability (each a component of Kohler's "placeless place"). Each path provides a clue about *how* the ultra clean lab lends legitimacy to experimental claims born inside.

1. Patterson (and Bellow's Sam Beech) described his ultra clean lab in Pasadena as a "sanctuary," perhaps not explicitly in an ecclesiastical sense (like Santiago de Compostela), or in the sense of a nature preserve (Walden Pond was a sanctuary for Thoreau), but rather as a place of refuge, a safe haven, a retreat. It was a place where he could explore experimentally the presence of lead on earth over time without risk of contamination. With an impervious seal between the experimental space and surrounding circumstances, the lab is fully disengaged from its situation. Most ordinary places have porous edges, allowing things and people to pass in and out, sometimes in unpredictable or undesired ways—unless built specifically to prevent such movement. Most ordinary places are promiscuous assemblages of stuff, inherently dirty and unavoidably contaminated—unless built ex-

plicitly to filter out the unwanted. Laura Wasylenki's lab is free of Bloomington air and water, free of limestone dust on the feet of those who cross the sticky mat, free of metals left in students' hair after shampooing: "stripped down simplicity." The lab is placeless in that it is clean apart from the encompassing place in which it sits, disconnected from the rest of Multidisciplinary Science Building II, the Indiana University campus, the city of Bloomington, the universe. To make us believe, this truth-spot is uprooted from its surrounds, severed from everything else at or near its location.

2. It is also a transparent place, not exactly open to the public (too many boiling acids), but accessible to cognoscenti.[71] I may have been the first person to step foot in Wasylenki's up-and-running clean lab who was not a metal isotope geochemist or trying to become one—other than the contractor, the architect, facilities manager, or maybe a snoopy colleague. Transparency of clean labs is key for the reproduction of a research culture that is profoundly rooted in this kind of place: students learn the ropes on-site, visitors get pointers as they design their own lab, everybody in the family comes to understand why the control of contamination is essential (and how to achieve it). Trust[72] is built through this accessibility and observability, as prospective and peer scientists get an eyewitness sense of the controlled environment in which everybody is expected to work. As in any family, there is of course both gossip and a wish to hide dirty laundry. Wasylenki told me that "labs have reputations," and after visiting one in particular, she found it "filthy" and got "worried about that." But during the interview, she explicitly asked me not to go into more detail, lest the identity of that wayward lab get revealed. Transparency allows for scrutiny: this family has a collective stake in demanding the immaculate of its members, to protect the shared credibility of their assertions.

3. Patterson's ultra clean lab was a prototype, not unlike what Henry Ford hoped his "industrial villages" would become—models for a mass-production society that would never lose its agrarian and small-town roots (chapter 4). He enjoyed far greater

success than Ford: Patterson brought acolytes to mecca and taught them how to be clean; he urged government agencies to provide funds to build labs like his; he disparaged any empirical claim resulting from experiments done in places that did not meet his exacting standards of cleanliness. Wasylenki's lab at Indiana is testament to Patterson's success, as are other copies now found anywhere metal isotope geochemists are at work: ultra clean labs are standardized in their design and engineering, all modeled more or less on the Caltech original and very slow to change. Their "invariability" across locations adds credibility to claims from any one of them, doing away with the specter of idiosyncrasy.[73] A scientist skeptical of Wasylenki's eventual findings about methane starvation could replicate her experiment, but only "if the configuration that produced it" in Bloomington is "reproduced" elsewhere.[74]

Standardization[75] is so important for the credibility of metal isotope geochemists (both entre nous and as a public-facing community making claims of huge policy and economic consequence) that the Caltech model clean lab has become normative. When Patterson told the National Research Council in 1980 that his experimental protocols had been "institutionalized," he made an astute sociological observation. As pioneer, Patterson created his prototype "first time through": he *chose* to filter, clean, rinse (and so forth), until his experimental blanks got low enough. Wasylenki and her peers have it different: Patterson's choice becomes their obligation. Sociologists Paul DiMaggio and Walter Powell suggest that "early adopters" are "commonly driven by the desire to improve performance," but "as an innovation spreads, a threshold is reached beyond which adoption provides legitimacy rather than improves performance."[76] Wasylenki's worries about overkill, and her appreciation that sometimes the physical space is cleaner than the practices inside, are indications that the normative obligation to mimic the Caltech-style lab goes beyond geochemistry and nature: it becomes a badge of membership or familial legitimacy, the totemic sacred space of the clan, the locus of its identity, an epistemic sine qua non. An enforced architectural isomorphism under those conditions is almost inevitable, insuring that any variations from Patterson's original will be small and incremental.

4. When Patterson left Pasadena to collect samples in Antarctica and Greenland, from various oceans and volcanoes, and in the wilderness at Yosemite Park, he did not exactly leave his lab behind. Wherever he went, he built a "mobile laboratory"[77] to insure that gathering samples from the field would not contaminate his results: anything or anyone that came into contact with the samples would need to be ultra clean. To be sure, the vicissitudes of the wild required compromise. The idea is to take just enough of the lab along so that samples brought home are as free from contamination as possible (and, once back at home base, all risks from Arctic temperatures or erupting volcanoes are gone, and nature can be safely recontextualized under the scrupulous controls).[78] The portable[79] clean lab is no longer cemented in place at North Mudd Hall, but is free to create an archipelago of impermanent truth-spots anywhere samples are sought. And when the lab arrives at a sampling site, it creates yet another kind of placelessness: only the thinnest sliver of Greenland is brought back to Southern California, and almost everything else about the place that makes it a place is left behind. Details about the collection sites seem to be rather unimportant: when I asked Wasylenki where the samples of ancient rocks she obtained from a colleague originally came from, she said that because her work is focused on "global" processes, "the exact locations do not actually matter" (Linnaeus, by contrast, paraded Lapland). Most ordinary places remain forever at the same longitude and latitude (setting aside plate tectonics!)—but not the clean lab, which could conceivably extend its authorizing purity anywhere.

One final irony: for all their necessity and obligation, ultra clean labs are rarely described in any detail in published scientific papers by metal isotope geochemists. This is a truth-spot that enables itself to disappear, and insists on it. To be sure, often-elaborate descriptions are found elsewhere: in grant proposals, in how-to manuals, in reminiscences, in Congressional testimony (where they are used to draw the line between true and false), and family gossip. But when experimental results are reported in the journals, the lab vanishes (along with other credentials routinely signifying legitimacy and membership that remain implicit and widely understood). In this small family of scientific specialists, where filiations across generations are respected, where novices get socialized in the clean lab of a mentor, where crossing the threshold in Tyvek establishes scientific bona fides, where confidence in others' results is grounded in a shared understanding of their truth-spot (which is essentially just like my truth-spot[80])—even to mention material conditions of the place could raise doubts and possibly cost trust: is there something wonky about that lab—and why? At the moment an experimental finding is officially reported, the ultra clean lab cannot appear to matter as much as it really does.

Coda

posit v. To put forward as a truth; postulate. [L *pōnere* (pp *positus*), to place]
«AMERICAN HERITAGE DICTIONARY[1]»

Could any place be a truth-spot? A gringo bartender who serves
up trendy mezcal, recalling his visit to a tiny village distillery
in out-of-the-way Oaxaca, told sociologist Sarah Bowen: "I was
outside, under a steel shack—you know, two fermentation tanks,
not even tanks, wooden tubs. And I'm [thinking]: this is the
truth. . . . This is the truth."[2] In a business where authentic and
exotic stuff carries a premium, finding and experiencing the place
where small-batch mezcal was made the old-fashioned way af-
firmed its value, its integrity, its reality—not so different from
rounding Mount Parnassus and getting that first glimpse of the
oracle site at Delphi, or finally reaching the end of the pilgrimage to Santiago de Compostela. The truth, it seems, is where
you find it.

But it really isn't as *voluntary* as all that—as if the designation
of a place as a truth-spot were completely in the eye of the believer. I want to shift the volition and responsibility and efficacy
from people to places—which exert themselves on bodies and
minds, sometimes convincing us that assertions from there are
true. There is something compelling about particular locations,

the materials encrusted there, the stories told about the place—
something insistent that "makes us believe," as Eudora Welty
put it, whether we happen to be looking for truth or not. Some
places persuade us of the truth even when we arrived there believing something contrary or in a state of doubt.

In principle, any place anywhere could be a truth-spot—but
not because an individual simply decides willy-nilly that the truth
happens right there. Rather, some places possess identifiable features that—in patterned ways—lend believability and authority
to claims or assertions associated with that spot. I am hesitant,
here at the end, to make a list of those place-features that make
people believe, which casual readers could then use as a checklist
for deciding whether this place or that is really a truth-spot. The
only way to know if a place is a truth-spot is to examine accounts
(claims, assertions, beliefs) somehow connected to the place, and
then ask: what exactly is it about this location—and its materiality, its narrations—that confers credibility on those accounts (remembering that credibility is never the upshot of place alone)?
There is no simple recipe for combining these three ingredients
of place into a surefire truth-spot, and mainly for that reason,
there can never be a definitive or finite list of "all" truth-spots.

This book promised an answer to a single question: how do
places make people believe? Edward Casey puts it this way: "But
how does truth happen there, in that there-place?"[3] My travels from Lapland to laboratories have been guided by an even
more general question: *what are places distinctively good at doing?*
Answers to that question have generated several recurrent patterns common to the truth-spots I have explored. These patterns
should not be read as generalizations found universally but sug-
gestions for how to think about the possible epistemic significance of a place. With that in mind, here is my list.

———•———

Places manipulate time. Places can be like time machines, not
in a hokey sci-fi teleporting sense, but by providing tangible,

resonating, and convincing evidence for assertions about how things were yesterday and how they will be tomorrow. Because of their durability (but not indestructability, as Delphi shows), some places persist through time as material reminders, capable of evoking memories that can be used to legitimate present-day political action (like Selma). But the past never sits still in such places: historically significant sites get made and remade in order to affirm today's preferred narrative about what happened back then (which says something about how Stonewall went from raunchy gay bar to National Monument in less than a half century). Societies endlessly build and curate places to commemorate the past so that whatever happened there will not be forgotten or confused. Busloads of tourists come away from Delphi convinced that the place was once the oracular center of the universe because they saw with their own eyes six columns excavated from the mountainside and then reerected and annotated by scholars asserting that it is the Temple of Apollo. Pilgrims to Santiago de Compostela feel the reality of their life-transforming ordeal as they pass by palpable mnemonic traces left by centuries of believers who made the path for them, creating obligations to sustain the transcendent possibilities of the Camino. Other places encourage people to accept the reality of a particular vision of the future. Standing there on Mount Parnassus, I had no grounds to doubt the oracle's prophecy about this book. Henry Ford put a soybean laboratory in Greenfield Village (and later moved it to the 1934 Chicago World's Fair) in order to show everybody how oil from a plant could be used in a car. That prototypal place translated an imaginary into a workable, material reality—and if enough people followed his lead, Ford's future would indeed come true (eight decades later, biodiesel fuel from soybean oil is commonplace).

Places gather together (or separate). The fundamental distinctions between near and far, between proximate and remote, between adjacent and apart, are a function of place. The relative location of things and people, the great or small distances between them, can build trust and confidence in accounts associated with a place—or, in other instances, can increase skepticism about their veracity. Linnaeus's system for classifying plants gained credibility as he moved among three distinct places separated by considerable distances (by contrast, Thoreau sought believability by staying home). Exotic Lapland was so far away from Leiden that its botanical experts were asked to trust Linnaeus's unrepeatable observations about a plant's natural growing conditions (and he made sure that they did, with reindeer boots). But Leiden becomes its own a truth-spot by reducing distances among experts who work in close quarters to decide the classification of plants, and by reducing the distances among plants collected from hither and yon, reassembled side by side in a garden for easy taxonomic comparisons. Copresence can produce credibility (like the scattered homes of American inventors brought together at Greenfield Village, or participants in a trial gathered up in an Eagleton courtroom but not before)—and so can geographic separation. Thoreau makes himself truthful through the solitude he constructs by living in a hut at a distance from gossipy Concord—in a way, like the objectivity attached to the Pythia's oracular pronouncements because of Delphi's distance from conniving Greek city-states. However, geochemist Clair Patterson could not have convinced Congress to ban lead from gasoline had he not been able to bring samples from the open sea or frozen poles back to Caltech, where they could be tightly colocated with the extremely sensitive measuring devices in his ultra clean lab. Things and people are spatially concentrated at some truth-spots, but at others they are kept well apart (which indicates the futility of seeking a consistent and universal set of place effects that lend believability to accounts, as if *only* "together" or *only* "apart" would work—it depends upon the particulars).

Places impose order (or remain messy). Places arrange in space things and people, building-in strict patterns of movement and interpersonal contacts that are sequenced by entrances, passages, barriers, and exits. The abundance of elevators and the outsize spaces for circulation at the Eagleton Courthouse in St. Louis remain curious until one realizes how much the pursuit of justice depends upon the staged physical segregations of people who play distinctive roles in a trial. Polluting contacts are prevented by a spatial order imposed by the federal *Design Guide*, not unlike the positive-pressure-air-flow doorway and sticky mat at the entrance to Laura Wasylenki's ultra clean lab in Bloomington. Her samples (once inside) move through an ordered sequence of analytical procedures that are precisely choreographed by the arrangement of Muppet-named workstations and instruments. Pilgrims walking the Camino to Santiago de Compostela follow yellow arrows and scallop shells, which mark the sacred way (the lineup of treasuries at Delphi does the same thing). But in other instances, credibility is won via the apparent absence of human attempts to impose material order on a place. Walden Pond and Lapland are wild and uncontrolled places come upon by two curious truth-seekers—found by them, not made, and the order they discover there belongs to the Creator. Thoreau and Linnaeus surrender to the pregiven reality of nature, and the order they create later in texts and taxonomies depends (for their credibility) upon an observed world itself "untouched" by human designs.

Places expose (or hide). Truth-spots succeed by putting on display the material grounds for accepting the legitimacy of a claim or belief—and (often simultaneously) by obscuring or disguising things that could compromise the constructed reality. Recalling Selma as the birthplace of the African American civil rights movement casts into high relief the unmatched role of Martin Luther King Jr., while hiding earlier sites of struggles that were not dependent upon King's charismatic authority and his preference for centralized decision-making. Ubiquitous glass at the Eagleton Courthouse materializes otherwise abstract values of openness and transparency that are central to the perceived legitimacy of judicial proceedings, even as walls and locked doors prevent the ordinary public from seeing what happens in judges' chambers, jury deliberation rooms, or holding pens for the accused in custody. Ford's Greenfield Village conceals (behind a fanciful assemblage of capitalist production before the assembly lines that made the museum possible) what Diego Rivera's "Detroit Industry" murals reveal: a manufacturing process dependent upon colossal machines that alienate the laborers who tend them.

Places are unique (or standardized). Affirmation of an account may depend upon its location at a place that is unlike any other place in the universe—or in a spot that is made from the template that creates identical places all over. Thoreau played both sides of this fence: Walden Pond was uniquely his own familiar home-ground, but he universalizes the place so that the realities he discovers in those particular woods are true anywhere and everywhere, even Zanzibar. Sometimes, however, the conditions of truth-making are present at just one location—you need to be *there*, and being *there* is convincing. Only Leiden possessed the supply of botanical experts and specimens needed to test the veracity of a young Swede's nascent system for classifying plants. Only at Santiago could the faithful pilgrim find certified remains of the apostle Saint James. Only at Seneca Falls can one visit the Wesleyan Chapel, where the feminist movement was born. These three examples suggest that uniqueness is not an inherent or permanent feature of a place, but rather a contested and hard-won achievement. Susan B. Anthony made Seneca Falls into the remembered birthplace of feminism in order to secure women's right to vote and her own legacy in that struggle. Distant Delphi provided grounds for its clients to conclude that prophecies received there were more reliable than those available at the corner oracle back home. However, Clair Patterson's ultra clean lab could not be a unique place without undermining the universal validity of his experimental findings about lead from automobile emissions. Standardization and multiplication of Patterson's laboratory (Wasylenki's lab is from the same mold, and there are many others) remove the worry that his observations depend upon idiosyncrasies found only inside those impermeable walls at Caltech. Standardization of many aspects of museum design and practice—for example, the re-placement of artifacts in persuasively annotated and beguiling displays—lends credibility to Greenfield Village and to Delphi's collection of statues housed in a building adjacent to the mountainside where they were found. Standardization of the design of federal courthouses prevents the delegitimizing supposition that the verdict in a trial might have gone the other way if the case had been tried in a courthouse with a different architecture. But if Saint James's genuine remains were cloned and distributed globally, why would the faithful walk to Santiago for the truth?

———•———

Truth-spot is a sensitizing concept, and does its job best not through abstraction but through extension. If, by now, you have begun to think about places that make people believe—truthspots not already considered in this book—then my work here is finished.

Veritas Filia ~~Temporis~~ Loci[4]

Notes

ORACULAR TOURISM

1. Eudora Welty, *The Eye of the Story: Selected Essays and Reviews* (New York: Vintage, 1983), 119.

2. Thomas F. Gieryn, "A Space for Place in Sociology," *Annual Review of Sociology* 26 (2000): 463–96.

3. Trevor J. Barnes, "Placing Ideas: Genius Loci, Heterotopia, and Geography's Quantitative Revolution," *Progress in Human Geography* 28 (2004): 565–95.

4. Steven Shapin, *A Social History of Truth: Civility and Science in Seventeenth-Century England* (Chicago: University of Chicago Press, 1994), 413.

5. Lawrence Durrell, "Delphi," in *Spirit of Place: Letters and Essays on Travel* (New York: E. P. Dutton, 1969), 273–77, at 275.

6. Michael Wood, *The Road to Delphi: The Life and Afterlife of Oracles* (New York: Farrar, Straus and Giroux, 2003), 99.

7. Vincent Scully, *Architecture: The Natural and the Manmade* (New York: St. Martin's Press, 1991), 59.

8. For Delphi details, I rely upon Michael Scott, *Delphi: A History of the Center of the Ancient World* (Princeton: Princeton University Press, 2014).

9. *Homeric Hymn to Apollo* 532–37, trans. Rodney Merrill, Center for Hellenic Studies, Harvard University, http://www.chs.harvard.edu/CHS /article/display/6294.

10. J. S. Morrison, "The Classical World," in Michael Loewe and Carmen Blacker, eds., *Divination and Oracles* (London: George Allen and Unwin, 1981), 87–114, at 100.

11. Margaret Foster, *The Seer and the City: Religion, Politics, and Colonial Ideology in Ancient Greece* (Berkeley: University of California Press, 2018).

12. Scott, *Delphi*, 117.

13. Sarah Iles Johnston, *Ancient Greek Divination* (Oxford: Wiley-Blackwell, 2008), 51.

14. Trevor Curnow, *The Oracles of the Ancient World* (London: Duckworth, 2004), 55.

15. Scott, *Delphi*, 70–73.

16. Thomas Barrie, *Spiritual Path, Sacred Place: Myth, Ritual, and Meaning in Architecture* (Boston: Shambhala, 1996), 179.

17. Julia Kindt, *Revisiting Delphi: Religion and Storytelling in Ancient Greece* (Cambridge: Cambridge University Press, 2016), 2.

18. Dean MacCannell, *The Tourist: A New Theory of the Leisure Class* (New York: Schocken, 1976), 137–38, 93.

19. Scott, *Delphi*, 218–19, 221.

20. Scott, *Delphi*, 249.

21. William Ridgeway, "The Relation of Archaeology to Classical Studies," *Proceedings of the Classical Association of Scotland* 6 (1908): 38–60, at 52.

22. Philipp Vandenberg, *The Mystery of the Oracles* (New York: Macmillan, 1982), 102.

23. Dominique Mulliez, "Delphi," in Panos Valavanis, ed., *Great Moments in Greek Archaeology* (Los Angeles: Getty Museum, 2007), 134–57.

24. Photios Petsas, *Delphi: Monuments and Museum* (Athens: Krene Editions, 1981), 18.

25. Georg Simmel, "The Ruin," in Kurt H. Wolff, ed., *Essays on Sociology, Philosophy, and Aesthetics* (New York: Harper and Row, 1959), 259–66.

26. Elena C. Partida, "The Treasuries at Delphi: An Architectural Study" (PhD diss., University of Birmingham, England, 1996), 25.

27. Scott, *Delphi*, 103.

28. John Urry and Jonas Larsen, *The Tourist Gaze 3.0* (London: Sage, 2011).

29. Barbara Kirshenblatt-Gimblett, *Destination Culture: Tourism, Museums, and Heritage* (Berkeley: University of California Press, 1998), 18.

30. Clifford Geertz, "Afterword," in Steven Feld and Keith Basso, eds., *Senses of Place* (Santa Fe: School of American Research Press, 1996), 259–62, at 259.

GROUND-TRUTHING AT WALDEN POND

1. John Steinbeck, *The Winter of Our Discontent* (New York: Viking, 1961), 51–52.

2. Stanley Cavell, *The Senses of Walden* (Chicago: University of Chicago Press, 1992), 19.

3. Henry David Thoreau, *Walden and Civil Disobedience* (New York: Penguin, 1986), 227. This may be the cheapest and most easily found print edition, which would have surely pleased its author. There are no significant textual variations between this version and far more expensive versions. Page references are hereafter embedded in the text of this chapter. *Walden* was originally published in 1854. Searchable versions are available online for free.

4. Laura Dassow Walls, *Seeing New Worlds: Henry David Thoreau and Nineteenth-Century Science* (Madison: University of Wisconsin Press, 1995), 4–7.

5. Kathryn Schulz, "Pond Scum: Henry David Thoreau's Moral Myopia," *New Yorker*, October 19, 2015.

6. Cavell, *Senses*, 11.

7. Ignacio Farías and Alex Wilkie, eds., *Studio Studies: Operations, Topologies, and Displacements* (New York: Routledge, 2016); Dora Thornton, *The Scholar in His Study: Ownership and Experience in Renaissance Italy* (New Haven: Yale University Press, 1997); Peter Galison and Caroline A. Jones, "Factory, Laboratory, Studio: Dispersing Sites of Production," in Peter Galison and Emily Thompson, eds., *The Architecture of Science* (Cambridge, MA: MIT Press, 1999), 497–540.

8. Martin Heidegger, "Why Do I Stay in the Provinces?," in Thomas Sheehan, ed., *Heidegger: The Man and the Thinker* (Chicago: Precedent Publishing, 1981), 27–30, at 28. Heidegger spent considerable time throughout his life at Todtnauberg, in a remote hut located in the mountains of the Black Forest in Germany. "He perceived greater authority in the bluntness of existence he found intensified by mountain terrain." Adam Sharr, *Heidegger's Hut* (Cambridge, MA: MIT Press, 2006), 65.

9. Steven Shapin, "'The Mind in Its Own Place': Science and Solitude in Seventeenth-Century England," *Science in Context* 4 (1991): 191–218, at 195.

10. Robert A. Gross, "'The Nick of Time': Coming of Age in Thoreau's Concord," in Kristen Case and K. Van Anglen, eds., *Thoreau at Two Hundred: Essays and Reassessments* (Cambridge: Cambridge University Press, 2016), 102–17, at 102.

11. Lawrence Buell, "Disaffiliation as Engagement," in Case and Van Anglen, *Thoreau*, 200–215, at 212.

12. Robert M. Thorson, *Walden's Shore: Henry David Thoreau and Nineteenth-Century Science* (Cambridge, MA: Harvard University Press, 2014), 9, 8.

13. Quoted in Samuel Arthur Jones, *Bibliography of Henry David Thoreau: With an Outline of His Life* (New York: De Vinne Press, 1894), 12.

14. Edward S. Casey, *Getting Back into Place: Toward a Renewed Understanding of the Place-World*, 2nd ed. (Bloomington: Indiana University Press, 2009), 242; cf. Casey, *The Fate of Place: A Philosophical History* (Berkeley: University of California Press, 1997).

15. Barry Lopez, *Arctic Dreams: Imagination and Desire in a Northern Landscape* (New York: Scribner's, 1986), 95.

16. Gary Snyder, *The Practice of the Wild* (New York: North Point Press, 1990), 18.

17. Irving L. Janis, *Victims of Groupthink: A Psychological Study of Foreign-Policy Decisions and Fiascoes* (Boston: Houghton Mifflin, 1972).

18. Lawrence Buell, *The Environmental Imagination: Thoreau, Nature Writing, and the Formation of American Culture* (Cambridge, MA: Harvard University Press, 1995), 111; Laura Dassow Walls, "Believing in Nature: Wilderness and Wildness in Thoreauvian Science," in Richard J. Schneider, ed., *Thoreau's Sense of Place: Essays in American Environmental Writing* (Iowa City: University of Iowa Press, 2000), 15–27, at 19.

19. Marilyn R. Chandler, *Dwelling in the Text: Houses in American Fiction* (Berkeley: University of California Press, 1991), 31–32.

20. David M. Robinson, *Natural Life: Thoreau's Worldly Transcendentalism* (Ithaca: Cornell University Press, 2004), 1.

21. Walls, *Seeing New Worlds*, 155.

22. Sherman Paul, *The Shores of America: Thoreau's Inward Exploration* (Urbana: University of Illinois Press, 1958), 293.

23. Alfred I. Tauber, *Henry David Thoreau and the Moral Agency of Knowing* (Berkeley: University of California Press, 2001), 6.

24. David M. Robinson, "The Written World: Place and History in Thoreau's 'A Walk to Wachusett'," in Schneider, *Thoreau's Sense*, 83–92, at 88.

25. Casey, *Getting Back*, 244.

26. Wes Jackson, *Becoming Native to This Place* (Washington, DC: Counterpoint, 1994).

27. Georg Simmel, *On Individuality and Social Forms* (1908; Chicago: University of Chicago Press, 1971), 145.

28. Cavell, *Senses*, 17.

29. H. Daniel Peck, *Thoreau's Morning Work* (New Haven: Yale University Press, 1990), 137.

30. Buell, *Environmental Imagination*, 263.

31. Thoreau is famous for puns like this: a "vagant" is a wanderer among many places.

32. W. Barksdale Maynard, *Walden Pond: A History* (Oxford: Oxford University Press, 2004), 332.

LINNAEUS'S CREDIBILIZING TRANSIT

1. Anna Pavord, *The Naming of Names: The Search for Order in the World of Plants* (London: Bloomsbury, 2005), 395–97.

2. Staffan Müller-Wille, "Collection and Collation: Theory and Practice of Linnaean Botany," *Studies in History and Philosophy of Biological and Biomedical Sciences* 38 (2007): 541–62.

3. Paul Lawrence Farber, *Finding Order in Nature: The Naturalist Tradition from Linnaeus to E. O. Wilson* (Baltimore: Johns Hopkins University Press, 2000), 9.

4. Pavord, *Naming*, 395.

5. Lisbet Koerner, *Linnaeus: Nature and Nation* (Cambridge, MA: Harvard University Press, 1999), 38, 26; Richard Drayton, *Nature's Government: Science, Imperial Britain, and the 'Improvement' of the World* (New Haven: Yale University Press, 2000), 16.

6. Bettina Dietz, "Contribution and Co-production: The Collaborative Culture of Linnaean Botany," *Annals of Science* 69 (2012): 551–69, at 559.

7. Pavord, *Naming*, 398.

8. Peter Dear, *The Intelligibility of Nature: How Science Makes Sense of the World* (Chicago: University of Chicago Press, 2006), 44–52.

9. Wilfrid Blunt, *Linnaeus: The Compleat Naturalist* (1971; London: Francis Lincoln, 2004), 121.

10. Phillip R. Sloan, "The Buffon-Linnaeus Controversy," *Isis* 67 (1976): 356–75, at 374.

11. Quoted in Blunt, *Linnaeus*, 119.

12. Londa Schiebinger, "Gender and Natural History," in N. Jardine, J. A. Secord, and E. C. Spary, eds., *Cultures of Natural History* (Cambridge: Cambridge University Press, 1996), 163–77, at 167; Schiebinger, *Nature's Body: Gender in the Making of Modern Science* (Boston: Beacon, 1993), 22–23.

13. Londa Schiebinger, *Plants and Empires: Colonial Bioprospecting in the Atlantic World* (Cambridge, MA: Harvard University Press, 2004).

14. Koerner, *Linnaeus*, 10, 82; see also 101–12.

15. Pavord, *Naming*, 395.

16. Koerner, *Linnaeus*, 16.

17. David N. Livingstone, *Putting Science in Its Place: Geographies of Scientific Knowledge* (Chicago: University of Chicago Press, 2003), 183.

18. Clifford Geertz, *Available Light: Anthropological Reflections on Philosophical Topics* (Princeton: Princeton University Press, 2000), 14.

19. Casey, *Getting Back into Place*, 237.

20. Livingstone, *Putting Science*, 41.

21. Staffan Mueller-Wille, "Joining Lapland and the Topinambes in Flourishing Holland: Center and Periphery in Linnaean Botany," *Science in Context* 16 (2003): 461–88.

22. Dorinda Outram, "New Spaces in Natural History," in Jardine, Secord and Spary, eds., *Cultures*, 249–65, at 263.

23. Quoted in Blunt, *Linnaeus*, 50.

24. Janet Browne, *Charles Darwin: Voyaging*, vol. 1 (Princeton: Princeton University Press, 1995).

25. Bruce Hevly, "The Heroic Science of Glacier Motion," in Henrika Kuklick and Robert E. Kohler, eds., *Science in the Field*, *Osiris* (second series) 11 (1996): 66–86.

26. James Clifford, "Spatial Practices: Fieldwork, Travel, and the Disciplining of Anthropology," in Akhil Gupta and James Ferguson, eds., *Anthropological Locations: Boundaries and Grounds of a Field Science* (Berkeley: University of California Press, 1997), 185–222, at 190, 212, 215.

27. Alix Cooper, "From the Alps to Egypt (and Back Again): Dolomieu, Scientific Voyaging, and the Construction of the Field in Eighteenth-Century Natural History," in Crosbie Smith and Jon Agar,

eds., *Making Space for Science: Territorial Themes in the Shaping of Knowledge* (London: Macmillan, 1998), 39–63, at 44, 47.

28. Nancy Scheper-Hughes, *Death without Weeping: The Violence of Everyday Life in Brazil* (Berkeley: University of California Press, 1992), xii.

29. Reid Helford, "Rediscovering the Presettlement Landscape: Making the Oak Savanna Ecosystem 'Real'," *Science, Technology and Human Values* 24 (1999): 55–79, at 57.

30. Paul Shankman, "The 'Fateful Hoaxing' of Margaret Mead: A Cautionary Tale," *Current Anthropology* 54 (2013): 51–70.

31. Stuart McCook, "'It May Be Truth, But It Is Not Evidence': Paul du Chaillu and the Legitimation of Evidence in the Field Sciences," in Kuklick and Kohler, *Science*, 177–197, at 179.

32. Patricia Fara, *Sex, Botany, and Empire* (New York: Columbia University Press, 2003), 25–27.

33. Clifford Geertz, *Works and Lives: The Anthropologist as Author* (Stanford, CA: Stanford University Press, 1988), 130.

34. Manuel Castells, *The Rise of the Network Society* (Oxford: Blackwell, 1996), 376–428.

35. Saskia Sassen, *The Global City*, 2nd ed. (Princeton: Princeton University Press, 2001).

36. Eric Weiner, *The Geography of Genius* (New York: Simon & Schuster, 2016).

37. Steven J. Harris, "Long-Distance Corporations, Big Sciences, and the Geography of Knowledge," *Configurations* 6.2 (1998): 269–304, at 288.

38. Harold J. Cook, *Matters of Exchange: Commerce, Medicine, and Science in the Dutch Golden Age* (New Haven: Yale University Press, 2007), 117–20.

39. Lorraine Daston, "The Sciences of the Archives," *Osiris* 27 (2012): 156–87.

40. Michel Foucault, *The Order of Things* (New York: Random House, 1970), 131, 137 (original French edition published in 1966 as *Les mots et les choses*).

41. Lorraine Daston and Peter Galison, *Objectivity* (New York: Zone Books, 2007), 59.

42. Blunt, *Linnaeus*, 103.

43. William T. Stearn, "The Influence of Leyden on Botany in the Seventeenth and Eighteenth Centuries," *British Journal for the History of Science* 1 (1962): 137–58, at 151.

44. Blunt, *Linnaeus*, 97.

45. Quoted in Blunt, *Linnaeus*, 100.

46. Stearn, "Influence of Leyden," 138.

47. David E. Rowe, "Making Mathematics in an Oral Culture: Göttingen in the Era of Klein and Hilbert," *Science in Context* 17 (2004): 85–129, at 97–98.

48. Deirdre Boden and Harvey Molotch, "The Compulsion of Proximity," in Roger Friedland and Deirdre Boden, eds., *NowHere: Space, Time, and Modernity* (Berkeley: University of California Press, 1994), 257–86, at 259, 267.

49. Norbert Schappacher, "Edmund Landau's Göttingen: From the Life and Death of a Great Mathematical Center," *Mathematical Intelligencer* 13 (1991): 12–18, at 16.

50. Livingstone, *Putting Science*, 23.

51. Koerner, *Linnaeus*, 29.

52. Andrea Wulf, *The Brother Gardeners: Botany, Empire, and the Birth of an Obsession* (New York: Knopf, 2009), 48.

53. Randall Collins, *The Sociology of Philosophies: A Global Theory of Intellectual Change* (Cambridge, MA: Harvard University Press, 1998), 26.

54. Andrew Barry, *Political Machines: Governing a Technological Society* (New York: Athlone, 2001), 177.

55. Koerner, *Linnaeus*, 39.

56. Thomas F. Gieryn, *Cultural Boundaries of Science: Credibility on the Line* (Chicago: University of Chicago Press, 1999), 287–98.

57. Christopher R. Henke, *Cultivating Science, Harvesting Power: Science and Industrial Agriculture in California* (Cambridge, MA: MIT Press, 2008), 133.

58. HRH The Prince of Wales and Bunny Guinness, *Highgrove: A Garden Celebrated* (London: Orion, 2014).

59. Quoted in Koerner, *Linnaeus*, 115.

60. Blunt, *Linnaeus*, 191.

61. Frans A. Stafleu, *Linnaeus and the Linnaeans* (Utrecht: International Association for Plant Taxonomy, 1971), 144.

62. Quoted in Blunt, *Linnaeus*, 157.

63. Adi Ophir and Steven Shapin, "The Place of Knowledge: A Methodological Survey," *Science in Context* 4 (1991): 3–21, at 15.

FORD'S POTEMKIN VILLAGES

1. Erving Goffman, *The Presentation of Self in Everyday Life* (New York: Random House, 1959), 254–55.

2. Sebag Montefiore, *Prince of Princes: The Life of Potemkin* (New York: St. Martin's Press, 2001), 382.

3. Quoted in Douglas Smith, ed., *Love and Conquest: Personal Correspondence of Catherine the Great and Prince Grigory Potemkin* (DeKalb: Northern Illinois University Press, 2004), 181.

4. Quoted in Steven Conn, *Museums and American Intellectual Life, 1876–1926* (Chicago: University of Chicago Press, 1998), 154.

5. Timothy Mitchell, "The World as Exhibition," *Comparative Studies in Society and History* 31 (1989): 217–36, at 225.

6. Michele Wehrwein Albion, ed., *The Quotable Henry Ford* (Gainesville: University Press of Florida, 2013), 101.

7. Quoted in Sten Rentzhog, *Open Air Museums: The History and Future of a Visionary Idea* ([Sweden]: Carlssons Jamtli, 2007), 124.

8. Albion, *Quotable Ford*, 103.

9. James S. Wamsley, *American Ingenuity: Henry Ford Museum and Greenfield Village* (New York: Harry N. Abrams, 1985), 27.

10. Albion, *Quotable Ford*, 153.

11. Miles Orvell, *The Death and Life of Main Street: Small Towns in American Memory, Space, and Community* (Chapel Hill: University of North Carolina Press, 2012), 30.

12. Quoted in Steven Watts, *The People's Tycoon: Henry Ford and the American Century* (New York: Random House, 2005), 422.

13. Jessie Swigger, *"History Is Bunk": Assembling the Past at Henry Ford's Greenfield Village* (Amherst: University of Massachusetts Press, 2014), 69.

14. David Maraniss, *Once in a Great City: A Detroit Story* (New York: Simon & Schuster, 2015), 86.

15. Michel Foucault, "Of Other Spaces," *Diacritics* 16 (Spring 1986): 22–27, at 26.

16. Paula Findlen, "The Modern Muses," in Susan A. Crane, ed., *Museums and Memory* (Stanford, CA: Stanford University Press, 2000), 161–178, at 177.

17. Sandra H. Dudley, "Encountering a Chinese Horse: Engaging with the Thingness of Things," in Dudley, ed., *Museum Objects: Experiencing the Properties of Things* (London: Routledge, 2012), 1–15, at 7.

18. Michael Baxandall, "Exhibiting Intention: Some Preconditions of the Visual Display of Culturally Purposeful Objects," in Ivan Karp and Steven D. Lavine, eds., *Exhibiting Cultures: The Poetics and Politics of Museum Display* (Washington, DC: Smithsonian Institution Press, 1991), 33–41, at 34.

19. Albion, *Quotable Ford*, 105 (my emphasis).

20. Conn, *Museums*, 154.

21. Spencer R. Crew and James E. Sims, "Locating Authenticity: Fragments of a Dialogue," in Karp and Lavine, *Exhibiting Cultures*, 159–75, at 163.

22. Richard Handler and Eric Gable, *The New History in an Old Museum: Creating the Past at Colonial Williamsburg* (Durham, NC: Duke University Press, 1997), 45.

23. Swigger, *"History Is Bunk,"* 52.

24. Diego Rivera, *My Art, My Life: An Autobiography* (New York: Citadel Press, 1960), 195.

25. Rivera, *My Art, My Life*, 183.

26. Quoted in Douglas Brinkley, *Wheels for the World: Henry Ford, His Company, and a Century of Progress, 1903–2003* (New York: Viking, 2003), 403.

27. Rivera, *My Art, My Life*, 183.

28. Albion, *Quotable Ford*, 64.

29. Rivera, *My Art, My Life*, 187.

30. Bertram D. Wolfe, *The Fabulous Life of Diego Rivera* (New York: Stein and Day, 1963), 306–7.

31. Albion, *Quotable Ford*, 65, 66.

32. Rivera, *My Art, My Life*, 188.

33. Patrick Marnham, *Dreaming with His Eyes Open: A Life of Diego Rivera* (New York: Knopf, 1998), 242.

34. Pete Hamill, *Diego Rivera* (New York: Abrams, 1999), 156.

35. Quoted in Linda Downs, "The Director and the Artist: Two Revolutionaries," in Mark Rosenthal, ed., *Diego Rivera and Frida Kahlo in Detroit* (New Haven: Yale University Press, 2015), 176–93, at 193.

36. Jeanine Head Miller et al., eds., *Telling America's Story: A History of The Henry Ford* (Virginia Beach: Donning, 2010), 49.

37. Richard Snow, *I Invented the Modern Age: The Rise of Henry Ford* (New York: Scribner, 2013), 4.

38. Albion, *Quotable Ford*, 165.

39. Albion, *Quotable Ford*, 20, 46, 42.

40. Albion, *Quotable Ford*, 176.

41. Quoted in Howard Segal, *Recasting the Machine Age: Henry Ford's Village Industries* (Amherst: University of Massachusetts Press, 2005), 11.

42. Watts, *People's Tycoon*, 433.

43. David L. Lewis, *The Public Image of Henry Ford: An American Folk Hero and His Company* (Detroit: Wayne State University Press, 1976), 281.

44. Albion, *Quotable Ford*, 175, xv.

45. Segal, *Recasting the Machine Age*, 33.

46. Robert W. Rydell, *World of Fairs* (Chicago: University of Chicago Press, 1993).

47. Dolores Hayden, *Seven American Utopias: Architecture of Communitarian Socialism, 1790–1975* (Cambridge, MA: MIT Press, 1976).

48. Stanley Buder, *Pullman: An Experiment in Industrial Order and Community Planning, 1880–1930* (Oxford: Oxford University Press, 1970).

49. Jeffrey N. Wasserstrom, *Global Shanghai, 1850–2010* (London: Routledge, 2009).

50. Andrew Ross, *The Celebration Chronicles: Life, Liberty, and the Pursuit of Property Value in Disney's New Town* (New York: Ballantine, 1999).

51. Miller, *Telling America's Story*, 70.

52. Albion, *Quotable Ford*, 100.

53. Quoted in Linda Bank Downs, *Diego Rivera: The Detroit Industry Murals* (New York: Norton, 1999), 34.

54. Rivera, *My Art, My Life*, 198–99.

55. Jerry Herron, "Modern Racket," in Rosenthal, *Diego Rivera*, 164–75, at 172.

56. Wolfe, *Rivera*, 307.

57. Rivera, *My Art, My Life*, 190.

58. Quoted in Tom Mackaman and Jerry White, "Diego Rivera's 'Battle of Detroit,'" *World Socialist, International Committee of the Fourth International*, October 3, 2013, wsws.org.

59. Downs, *Rivera*, 171.

60. Herron, "Modern Racket," 164.

61. Downs, *Rivera*, 65.

62. Mark Rosenthal, "Diego and Frida: High Drama in Detroit," in Rosenthal, *Diego Rivera*, 18–123, at 86.

63. Downs, *Rivera*, 22.

64. Rivera, *My Art, My Life*, 195.

65. Rosenthal, "Diego and Frida," 102; cf. Alex Goodall, "The Battle of Detroit and Anti-Communism in the Depression Era," *The Historical Journal* 51 (2008): 457–80.

66. Quoted in Downs, *Rivera*, 177.

67. Downs, *Rivera*, 181.

68. Rosenthal, "Diego and Frida," 103.

69. Jean Baudrillard, *Selected Writings*, ed. Mark Poster (Stanford: Stanford University Press, 1988), 172.

70. Rosenthal, "Diego and Frida," 101.

71. Downs, "The Director," 188.

72. Herron, "Modern Racket," 173.

73. Downs, *Rivera*, 146.

74. Downs, *Rivera*, 131.

75. Rosenthal, "Diego and Frida," 69.

76. *World Socialist, International Committee of the Fourth International*, October 3, 2013, wsws.org.

77. Rosenthal, "Diego and Frida," 51.

78. Marnham, *Dreaming*, 240; Rosenthal, "Diego and Frida," 98.

79. Marnham, *Dreaming*, 243.

80. Downs, *Rivera*, 184.

81. Simon J. Knell, "Museums, Reality, and the Material World," in Knell, ed., *Museums in a Material World* (London: Routledge, 2007), 1–28, at 26.

82. Crew and Sims, "Locating Authenticity," 163.

TRAPDOOR TO THE TRANSCENDENT

1. William Langland, *Piers Plowman: A New Translation of the B-Text*, trans. A. V. C. Schmidt (Oxford: Oxford University Press, 1992), 65.

2. Alain de Botton, *The Architecture of Happiness* (New York: Pantheon, 2006), 107.

3. Shirley MacLaine, *The Camino: A Journey of the Spirit* (New York: Simon and Schuster, 2000).

4. Roger Stalley, "Sailing to Santiago: Medieval Pilgrimage to Santiago de Compostela and Its Artistic Influence in Ireland," in Alex Norman and Carole M. Cusack, eds., *Religion, Pilgrimage, and Tourism* (London: Routledge, 2015), 2:175–93, at 181.

5. Nancy Louise Frey, *Pilgrim Stories: On and off the Road to Santiago* (Berkeley: University of California Press, 1998), 4–5.

6. Eric Weiner, "Where Heaven and Earth Come Closer," *New York Times*, March 9, 2012.

7. Constance Mary Storrs, *Jacobean Pilgrims from England to St. James of Compostela: From the Early Twelfth to the Late Fifteenth Century* (Santiago de Compostela: Xunta de Galicia, 1994), 38.

8. [Aimery Picaud?], *Liber Sancti Jacobi* (Book 5), also known as *Codex Calixtinus*, trans. William Melczer as *The Pilgrim's Guide to Santiago de Compostela* (New York: Italica Press, 1993); orig. date ca. 1135.

9. Katherine Lack, *The Cockleshell Pilgrim: A Medieval Journey to Compostela* (London: Society for Promoting Christian Knowledge, 2003).

10. Francis Davey, ed. and trans., *The Itineraries of William Wey* (Oxford: Bodleian Library, 2010).

11. Domenico Laffi, *A Journey to the West: The Diary of a Seventeenth-Century Pilgrim from Bologna to Santiago de Compostela*, trans. James Hall (Santiago de Compostela: Xunta de Galicia, 1997); orig. date 1681.

12. Walter Starkie, *The Road to Santiago: Pilgrims of St. James* (Berkeley: University of California Press, 1965).

13. Paulo Coelho, *The Pilgrimage* (1987; New York: Harper, 1995).

14. Jack Hitt, *Off the Road: A Modern-Day Walk down the Pilgrim's Route into Spain* (New York: Simon & Schuster, 1994).

15. MacLaine, *Camino*.

16. Conrad Rudolph, *Pilgrimage to the End of the World: The Road to Santiago de Compostela* (Chicago: University of Chicago Press, 2004).

17. Hape Kerkeling, *I'm Off Then: Losing and Finding Myself on the Camino de Santiago* (2006; New York: Free Press, 2009).

18. Sonia Choquette, *Walking Home: A Pilgrimage from Humbled to Healed* (Carlsbad, CA: Hay House, 2014).

19. Victor Turner, "Pilgrimages as Social Process," in Turner, *Dramas, Fields, and Metaphors* (Ithaca: Cornell University Press, 1974), 166–230, at 196.

20. Turner, "Pilgrimages," 195.

21. Horton (and Marie-Hélène) Davies, *Holy Days and Holidays: The Medieval Pilgrimage to Compostela* (Lewisburg, PA: Bucknell University Press, 1982), 53.

22. Sean Slavin, "Walking as Spiritual Practice: The Pilgrimage to Santiago de Compostela," in Norman and Cusack, *Religion*, 4:283–99, at 290; Neil J. Smelser, *The Odyssey Experience: Physical, Social, Psychological, and Spiritual Journeys* (Berkeley: University of California Press, 2009), 11; Frey, *Pilgrim Stories*, 73.

23. Coelho, *Pilgrimage*, 116.

24. Rudolph, *Pilgrimage*, 34.

25. Choquette, *Walking Home*, 75.

26. Lack, *Cockleshell Pilgrim*, 25.

27. Hitt, *Off the Road*, 3, 43, 3.

28. Kerkeling, *I'm Off*, 32, 99; Rudolph, *Pilgrimage*, 36.

29. Adrian Ivakhiv, "Nature and Self in New Age Pilgrimage," in Norman and Cusack, *Religion*, 1:293–318, at 306.

30. Lack, *Cockleshell Pilgrim*, 131.

31. MacLaine, *Camino*, 117, 92; Choquette, *Walking Home*, 163.

32. Rudolph, *Pilgrimage*, 38–39, 18.

33. Victor Turner and Edith Turner, *Image and Pilgrimage in Christian Culture* (New York: Columbia University Press, 1978), 31.

34. Smelser, *Odyssey*, 12; Thomas DeGloma, *Seeing the Light: The Social Logic of Personal Discovery* (Chicago: University of Chicago Press, 2014), 97.

35. MacLaine, *Camino*, 243.

36. Kerkeling, *I'm Off*, 86, 109, 267.

37. Liliane Voyé, "Popular Religion and Pilgrimages in Western Europe," in William H. Swatos Jr. and Luigi Tomasi, eds., *From Medieval Pilgrimage to Religious Tourism* (Westport, CT: Greenwood, 2002), 115–35, at 131.

38. Choquette, *Walking Home*, 51, 71, 141.

39. Coelho, *Pilgrimage*, 121.

40. Coelho, *Pilgrimage*, 253.

41. Lack, *Cockleshell Pilgrim*, 154.

42. Frey, *Pilgrim Stories*, 164, 182, 164, 155, 170.

43. MacLaine, *Camino*, 162, 121.

44. Choquette, *Walking Home*, 267.

45. Hitt, *Off the Road*, 62, 168, 253.

46. Kerkeling, *I'm Off*, 75.

47. Luigi Tomasi, "Homo Viator: From Pilgrimage to Religious Tourism via the Journey," in Swatos and Tomasi, *From Medieval Pilgrimage*, 1–24, at 6.

48. Jonathan Sumption, *The Age of Pilgrimage: The Medieval Journey to God* (1975; Mahwah, NJ: HiddenSpring, 2003), 256.

49. "Memorials to Pilgrims Who Died on the Camino," *Amawalker* (blog), May 21, 2015, http://amawalker.blogspot.com/2012/08/memorials -pilgrims-who-died-on-camino.html.

50. Choquette, *Walking Home*, 91.

51. Frey, *Pilgrim Stories*, 114.

52. Kerkeling, *I'm Off*, 115.

53. Choquette, *Walking Home*, 70.

54. Rudolph, *Pilgrimage*, 19.

55. Laffi, *Journey*, 122–23.

56. Hitt, *Off the Road*, 224.

57. Sumption, *Age of Pilgrimage*, 288.

58. Kerkeling, *I'm Off*, 75, 106.

59. MacLaine, *Camino*, 150.

60. MacLaine, *Camino*, 142.

61. Laffi, *Journey*, 143–44.

62. Lack, *Cockleshell Pilgrim*, 142.

63. MacLaine, *Camino*, 219.

64. Choquette, *Walking Home*, 312.

65. Hitt, *Off the Road*, 191.

66. Kerkeling, *I'm Off*, 278, 279.

67. Robert A. Scott, *Miracle Cures: Saints, Pilgrimage, and the Healing Powers of Belief* (Berkeley: University of California Press, 2010), 80.

68. Kerkeling, *I'm Off*, 5.

69. Hitt, *Off the Road*, 137.

70. Choquette, *Walking Home*, 164.

71. Barbara Nimri Aziz, "Personal Dimensions of the Sacred Journey: What Pilgrims Say," *Religious Studies* 23 (1987): 247–61, at 248.

72. Hitt, *Off the Road*, 216.

73. [Picaud?], *Liber*, 88–89.

74. Hitt, *Off the Road*, 210.

75. Sumption, *Age of Pilgrimage*, 241; Ian Reader, *Pilgrimage: A Very Short Introduction* (Oxford: Oxford University Press, 2015), 47.

76. Starkie, *Road*, 103.

77. Davey, *Itineraries*, 213.

78. Kerkeling, *I'm Off*, 227–28.

79. Frey, *Pilgrim Stories*, 112.

80. Hitt, *Off the Road*, 77.

81. Mircea Eliade, *The Sacred and the Profane* (New York: Harcourt, 1957), 25–26.

82. Alex Norman and Carole M. Cusack, "General Introduction," in Norman and Cusack, *Religion*, 1:1–11, at 1.

83. Émile Durkheim, *The Elementary Forms of the Religious Life* (1912; New York: Free Press, 1995), 44, 36.

84. Eliade, *Sacred*, 24–27.

85. Scott, *Miracle Cures*, 87.

86. Lack, *Cockleshell Pilgrim*, 138.

87. Turner, "Pilgrimages," 210, 226.

88. Starkie, *Road*, 249, 252.

89. Kerkeling, *I'm Off*, 128.

90. Laffi, *Journey*, 129.

91. Starkie, *Road*, 207.

92. John Brierley, *A Pilgrim's Guide to the Camino de Santiago*, 13th ed. (Forres, Scotland: Findhorn Press, 2016), 110.

93. Rudolph, *Pilgrimage*, 76.

94. Stalley, "Sailing to Santiago," 187.

95. Sumption, *Age of Pilgrimage*, 250.

96. Reader, *Pilgrimage*, 48.

97. Hitt, *Off the Road*, 91.

98. Kerkeling, *I'm Off*, 97.

99. Hitt, *Off the Road*, 165.

100. Coelho, *Pilgrimage*, 129.

101. MacLaine, *Camino*, 69.

102. Kerkeling, *I'm Off*, 143.

103. Choquette, *Walking Home*, 140.

104. Hitt, *Off the Road*, 229, 179ff.

105. Hitt, *Off the Road*, 238.

106. Coelho, *Pilgrimage*, 55.

107. Frey, *Pilgrim Stories*, 124.

108. Barbara Abou-El-Haj, "Santiago de Compostela in the Time of Diego Gelmirez," in Norman and Cusack, *Religion*, 2:145–74, at 164.

109. [Picaud?], *Liber*, 124–25.

110. Rudolph, *Pilgrimage*, 6.

111. Hitt, *Off the Road*, 208.

112. Rudolph, *Pilgrimage*, 20.

113. Kerkeling, *I'm Off*, 52.

114. Hitt, *Off the Road*, 2.

115. Choquette, *Walking Home*, 250.

116. Sumption, *Age of Pilgrimage*, 163.

117. Jill Dubisch, *In a Different Place: Pilgrimage, Gender, and Politics at a Greek Island Shrine* (Princeton: Princeton University Press, 1995), 36.

118. Hitt, *Off the Road*, 144.

119. Heather Blair, *Real and Imagined: The Peak of Gold in Heian Japan* (Cambridge, MA: Harvard University Press, 2015), 37.

120. James J. Preston, "Spiritual Magnetism: An Organizing Principle for the Study of Pilgrimage," in Norman and Cusack, *Religion*, 1:112–29, at 121.

121. Starkie, *Road*, 1.

122. Choquette, *Walking Home*, 120, 194.

123. Coelho, *Pilgrimage*, 65.

124. Hitt, *Off the Road*, 105, 35.

125. Kerkeling, *I'm Off*, 58–59.

126. Coelho, *Pilgrimage*, 178.

127. Kerkeling, *I'm Off*, 326.

128. MacLaine, *Camino*, 221, 60, 85.

129. Rudolph, *Pilgrimage*, 47.

130. Frey, *Pilgrim Stories*, 7, 125.

131. Hitt, *Off the Road*, 43, 230.

132. Henry Miller, *Big Sur and the Oranges of Hieronymus Bosch* (New York: New Directions), 6 (with thanks to Belden C. Lane, *Landscapes of the Sacred: Geography and Narrative in American Spirituality* [Baltimore: Johns Hopkins University Press, 2002], 12).

133. Langland, *Piers*, 44, 59–60, 66.

134. Lutz Kaelber, "The Sociology of Medieval Pilgrimage: Contested Views and Shifting Boundaries," in Swatos and Tomasi, *From Medieval Pilgrimage*, 51–74, at 64.

THE WHOLE TRUTH AND NOTHING BUT

1. Inscription, John Joseph Moakley United States Courthouse, Boston; Brandeis was admitted to the bar at St. Louis's Old Courthouse in 1878.

2. Don E. Fehrenbacher, *The Dred Scott Case: Its Significance in American Law and Politics* (New York: Oxford University Press, 1978), 250.

3. Fehrenbacher, *Dred Scott Case*, 276.

4. Matt Apuzzo, "Ferguson Police Routinely Violate Rights of Blacks, Justice Dept. Finds," *New York Times*, March 3, 2015.

5. Janell Ross, "How Black Lives Matter Moved from a Hashtag to a Real Political Force," *Washington Post*, August 19, 2015.

6. Inscription, Thomas F. Eagleton United States Courthouse, St. Louis.

7. Judith Resnik and Dennis Curtis, *Representing Justice: Invention, Controversy, and Rights in City-States and Democratic Courtrooms* (New Haven: Yale University Press, 2011), 12.

8. Martha J. McNamara, *From Tavern to Courthouse: Architecture and Ritual in American Law, 1658–1860* (Baltimore: Johns Hopkins University Press, 2004).

9. Robert J. Moore Jr., *The Old Courthouse* (St. Louis: Jefferson National Parks Association, 2004), 3.

10. Moore, *Old Courthouse*, 6.

11. Moore, *Old Courthouse*, 24.

12. Resnik and Curtis, *Representing Justice*, 15, 154, 171, 158.

13. Upon the completion of each new federal courthouse, the GSA issued a booklet extolling its virtues in text and artful full-color photographs. I draw on these booklets as idealized versions of what both architects and judges thought they were doing when they designed and built the new buildings. I shall refer to each as "GSA booklet," followed by the city where the courthouse is located. The complete set of booklets is available via the Design Excellence Monograph Library at gsa.gov. So, for the Cobb epigraph: GSA booklet, Hammond, IN, 2.

14. Bob Schwartz, HOK architect, interview by author, St. Louis, September 1, 2016.

15. Anne Maass et al., "Intimidating Buildings: Can Courthouse Architecture Affect Perceived Likelihood of Conviction?," *Environment and Behavior* 32 (2000): 674–83.

16. Resnik and Curtis, *Representing Justice*, 159.

17. All quotations from Steve Brubaker come from my interview with him, Chicago, October 6, 2016.

18. *U. S. Courts Design Guide*, Section 3-1. Current version is available at http://www.gsa.gov/graphics/pbs/Courts_Design_Guide_07.pdf.

19. GSA booklet, St. Louis, 5, 24.

20. *Design Guide*, Section 2-6.

21. GSA booklet, St. Louis, 24.

22. GSA booklet, Seattle, 5, 3.

23. GSA booklet, Orlando, 4–5.

24. GSA booklet, St. Louis, 12.

25. Quoted in Justice Douglas P. Woodlock, "Drawing Meaning from the Heart of the Courthouse," in Steven Flanders, ed., *Celebrating the Courthouse: A Guide for Architects, Their Clients, and the Public* (New York: Norton, 2006), 155–167, at 160.

26. Justice Stephen C. Breyer, "Foreword," in Flanders, *Celebrating the Courthouse*, 9–12, at 10.

27. Woodlock, "Drawing Meaning," 161.

28. GSA booklet, Phoenix, 8.

29. Resnik and Curtis, *Representing Justice*, 134, 138.

30. George A. Davidson, "The Lawyer's Perspective," in Flanders, *Celebrating the Courthouse*, 168–75, at 170.

31. *Design Guide*, Section 3-5.

32. *Design Guide*, Section 3-10.

33. Woodlock, "Drawing Meaning," 161.

34. *Design Guide*, Section 4-15.

35. *Design Guide*, Section 1-3.

36. *Design Guide*, Sections 3-3, 3-4.

37. *Design Guide*, Section 6-3.

38. *Design Guide*, Section 3-4.

39. Sybille Bedford, *The Faces of Justice: A Traveller's Report* (New York: Simon and Schuster, 1961), 19.

40. *Design Guide*, Sections 5-3, 5-6.

41. Linda Mulcahy, *Legal Architecture: Justice, Due Process, and the Place of Law* (Oxford: Routledge, 2011), 9.

42. John Brigham, *Material Law: A Jurisprudence of What's Real* (Philadelphia: Temple University Press, 2009), 161.

43. Yi-Fu Tuan, *Space and Place: The Perspective of Experience* (Minneapolis: University of Minnesota Press, 1977), 102.

44. I wasn't there. This hypothetical reconstruction probably describes Judge Perry's court on the twelfth floor more accurately than the special courtroom on the third floor actually used for the public comment session.

45. Todd S. Phillips, "Courthouse Design at a Crossroads," in Flanders, *Celebrating the Courthouse*, 202–23, at 207.

46. Thomas Scheffer, Kati Hannken-Illjes, and Alexander Kozin, "How Courts Know: Comparing English Crown Court, U.S.-American State Court, and German District Court," *Space and Culture* 12 (2009): 183–204, at 185.

47. *Design Guide*, Sections 4-13, 4-14.

48. Davidson, "Lawyer's Perspective," 169.

49. Jordan Gruzen et al., "The Geometry of a Courthouse Design," 83–109 in Flanders, *Celebrating the Courthouse*, 83–109, at 98.

50. Mulcahy, *Legal Architecture*, 77–78.

51. *Design Guide*, Sections 4-3, 4-4.

52. GSA booklets: Boston, 8; Seattle, 11; Jackson, MS, 7.

53. Breyer, "Foreword," 11.

54. Resnik and Curtis, *Representing Justice*, 17.

OBAMA'S THREE BIRTHPLACES

1. Barack Obama, Second Inaugural Address, January 21, 2013.

2. Steven F. Lawson, *Running for Freedom: Civil Rights and Black Politics since 1941*, 4th ed. (New York: Wiley Blackwell, 2015), 380.

3. Keith H. Basso, *Wisdom Sits in Places: Landscape and Language among the Western Apache* (Albuquerque: University of New Mexico Press, 1996), 101.

4. Sally G. McMillen, *Seneca Falls and the Origins of the Women's Rights Movement* (Oxford: Oxford University Press, 2008), 3.

5. Colin Rafferty, *Hallow This Ground* (Bloomington: Indiana University Press, 2015), 156.

6. Sanford Levinson, *Written in Stone: Public Monuments in Changing Societies* (Durham: Duke University Press, 1998), 87.

7. James E. Young, *The Texture of Memory: Holocaust Memorials and Meaning* (New Haven: Yale University Press, 1993), 6–7.

8. David Lowenthal, *The Past Is a Foreign Country* (Cambridge: Cambridge University Press, 1985). The title of Lowenthal's book is a quotation from L. Hartley, a twentieth-century British writer.

9. Louise Michelle Newman, *White Women's Rights: The Racial Origins of Feminism in the United States* (New York: Oxford University Press, 1999).

10. McMillen, *Seneca Falls*, 81.

11. Ellen Carol DuBois, *Feminism and Suffrage: The Emergence of an Independent Women's Movement in America, 1848–1869* (Ithaca: Cornell University Press, 1978), 19, 55.

12. Quoted in DuBois, *Feminism and Suffrage*, 59.

13. McMillen, *Seneca Falls*, 196.

14. Lisa Tetrault, *The Myth of Seneca Falls: Memory and the Women's Suffrage Movement, 1848–1898* (Chapel Hill: University of North Carolina Press, 2014), 70–72; Ellen Carol DuBois, "The Limitations of Sisterhood: Elizabeth Cady Stanton and Division in the American Suffrage Movement, 1875–1902," in DuBois, *Woman Suffrage and Women's Rights* (New York: New York University Press, 1998), 160–75.

15. Judith Wellman, *The Road to Seneca Falls: Elizabeth Cady Stanton and the First Woman's Rights Convention* (Urbana: University of Illinois Press, 2004).

16. Daniel J. Sherman, *The Construction of Memory in Interwar France* (Chicago: University of Chicago Press, 1999), 215.

17. McMillen, *Seneca Falls*, 96.

18. Joanne H. Wright, "Getting to the Root of Patriarchy: Radical Feminism's Quest for Origin," in Wright, *Origin Stories in Political Thought: Discourses on Gender, Power, and Citizenship* (Toronto: University of Toronto Press, 2004), 127–58.

19. Wellman, *Road to Seneca Falls*, 14.

20. DuBois, *Feminism and Suffrage*, 41.

21. Maurice Halbwachs, *The Collective Memory* (1950; New York: Harper & Row, 1980), 140.

22. Rafferty, *Hallow This Ground*, 10, 36, 65 (the last quotation pertains to his visit to Treblinka, the Nazi extermination camp in Poland).

23. Quoted in Daniel J. Sherman, "Art, Commerce, and the Production of Memory in France after World War I," in John R. Gillis, ed., *Commemorations: The Politics of National Identity* (Princeton: Princeton University Press, 1994), 186–211, at 206.

24. Kirk Savage, *Monument Wars: Washington, D.C., the National Mall, and the Transformation of the Memorial Landscape* (Berkeley: University of California Press, 2009), 6–7.

25. Young, *Texture of Memory*, 13.

26. Young, *Texture of Memory*, 5.

27. DVD available through Louise Vance Productions, senecafalls-film.org.

28. See Richie Jean Sherrod Jackson, *The House by the Side of the Road: The Selma Civil Rights Movement* (Tuscaloosa: University of Alabama Press, 2011).

29. Lyndon B. Johnson, Address to Congress, March 15, 1965, pro-posing the Voting Rights Act.

30. Paul Connerton, *How Societies Remember* (Cambridge: Cambridge University Press, 1989), 6.

31. Elaine Frantz Parsons, *Ku-Klux: The Birth of the Klan during Reconstruction* (Chapel Hill: University of North Carolina Press, 2015), 27.

32. Quoted in Edward Walsh, "An Old Plaque Is Turned Around—And Ku Klux Klan Marches." *Washington Post*, January 26, 1993.

33. Rafferty, *Hallow This Ground*, 41.

34. David Chidester and Edward T. Linenthal, "Introduction," in Chidester and Linenthal, eds., *American Sacred Space* (Bloomington: Indiana University Press, 1995), 1–42, at 18.

35. Sherman, *Construction of Memory*, 9.

36. Sherman, *Construction of Memory*, 215–16.

37. Jackson, *House*, 26.

38. Sheyann Webb and Rachel West Nelson, *Selma, Lord, Selma: Girlhood Memories of the Civil-Rights Days* (Tuscaloosa: University of Alabama Press, 1980), 49.

39. Craig Evan Barton, "Duality and Invisibility: Race and Memory in the Urbanism of the American South," in Barton, ed., *Sites of Memory: Perspectives on Architecture and Race* (Princeton: Princeton Architectural Press, 2001), 1–12, at 8.

40. David J. Garrow, *Protest at Selma: Martin Luther King, Jr., and the Voting Rights Act of 1965* (New Haven: Yale University Press, 1978), chap. 4.

41. Orloff W. Miller, quoted in Richard D. Leonard, *Call to Selma: Eighteen Days of Witness* (Boston: Skinner House Books, 2002), 137.

42. Yohuru Williams, "Civil Rights in America: Seneca Falls, Selma, Stonewall and Beyond," *NewVisionsNewVoices* (radio program, Charles Dutton, host), February 2014, https://soundcloud.com/newvi

sionsnewvoices/civil-rights-in-america-seneca-falls-selma-stonewall-and -beyond; see Williams, *Rethinking the Black Freedom Movement* (New York: Routledge, 2016).

43. Benjamin Hedin, *In Search of the Movement: The Struggle for Civil Rights Then and Now* (San Francisco: City Lights Books, 2015), 59.

44. Glenn T. Eskew, *But for Birmingham* (Chapel Hill: University of North Carolina Press, 1997).

45. Taylor Branch, *The King Years: Historic Moments in the Civil Rights Movement* (New York: Simon & Schuster, 2013), 165–72.

46. Iwan Morgan and Philip Davies, eds., *From Sit-Ins to SNCC: The Student Civil Rights Movement of the 1960s* (Gainesville: University Press of Florida, 2012).

47. Raymond Arsenault, *Freedom Riders: 1961 and the Struggle for Racial Justice* (Oxford: Oxford University Press, 2006).

48. For the Carmichael quotation, see http://www.encyclopedia. com/doc/1G2-3401804839.html.

49. Clarence Lang, *Black America in the Shadow of the Sixties: Notes on the Civil Rights Movement, Neoliberalism, and Politics* (Ann Arbor: University of Michigan Press, 2015).

50. The Editors of Black Issues in Higher Education, eds., *The Unfinished Agenda of the Selma-Montgomery Voting Rights March* (New York: John Wiley, 2005).

51. Edmund Fong, *American Exceptionalism and the Remains of Race: Multicultural Exorcisms* (New York: Routledge, 2015), 74.

52. Robert David Sack, *Homo Geographicus* (Baltimore: Johns Hopkins University Press, 1997), 135.

53. Martin Duberman, *Stonewall* (New York: Dutton, 1993), xvii.

54. Brian S. Osborne, "Landscapes, Memory, Monuments, and Commemoration: Putting Identity in Its Place," *Canadian Ethnic Studies* 33 (2001): 39–77, at 42, 51.

55. David Carter, *Stonewall: The Riots That Sparked the Gay Revolution* (New York: St. Martin's Press, 2004), 74; Duberman, *Stonewall*, 181.

56. Duberman, *Stonewall*, 182.

57. Duberman, *Stonewall*, 82.

58. Carter, *Stonewall*, 262.

59. Carter, *Stonewall*, 163.

60. Richard Handler, "Is 'Identity' a Useful Cross-Cultural Concept?," in Gillis, *Commemorations*, 27–40, at 30.

61. Carter, *Stonewall*, 212.

62. Lillian Faderman, *The Gay Revolution: The Story of the Struggle* (New York: Simon & Schuster, 2015), 181–82.

63. Carole Blair, Greg Dickinson, and Brian L. Ott, "Introduction: Rhetoric/Memory/Place," in Dickinson, Blair, and Ott, eds., *Places of Public Memory: The Rhetoric of Museums and Memorials* (Tuscaloosa: University of Alabama Press, 2010), 1–54, at 25.

64. Faderman, *Gay Revolution*, 211.

65. Rudy J. Koshar, "Building Pasts: Historic Preservation and Identity in Twentieth-Century Germany," in Gillis, *Commemorations*, 215–38, at 231.

66. Elizabeth A. Armstrong and Suzanna Crage, "Movements and Memory: The Making of the Stonewall Myth," *American Sociological Review* 71 (2006): 724–51, at 741.

67. Armstrong and Crage, "Movements and Memory," 746.

68. Jeremy W. Peters, Jo Becker, and Julie Hirschfeld Davis, "Trump Rescinds Rules on Bathrooms for Transgender Students," *New York Times*, February 22, 2017.

69. John R. Gillis, "Introduction—Memory and Identity: The History of a Relationship," in Gillis, *Commemorations*, 3–24, at 20.

ULTRA CLEAN LAB

1. Mary Douglas, *Purity and Danger: An Analysis of Concepts of Pollution and Taboo* (London: Routledge & Kegan Paul, 1966; Penguin, 1970), 12, 48.

2. Quotations in this section (unless otherwise noted) come from the author's interview with Laura Wasylenki on December 30, 2015.

3. K. O. Konhauser et al., "Oceanic Nickel Depletion and a Methanogen Famine before the Great Oxidation Event," *Nature* 458 (2009): 750–53.

4. Clair C. Patterson, "An Alternative Perspective—Lead Pollution in the Human Environment: Origin, Extent, and Significance," in National Research Council, *Lead in the Human Environment* (Washington, DC: National Academy Press, 1980), 265–349, at 273 (my emphasis).

5. Saul Bellow, *The Dean's December* (New York: Harper and Row, 1982), 138–39.

6. Quoted in George R. Tilton, "Clair Cameron Patterson, 1922–1995," in *Biographical Memoir* (Washington, DC: National Academy Press, 1998), 11.

7. Herbert L. Needleman, "A Convulsive Clear Consciousness: Clair Patterson and Human Lead Exposure," in Cliff I. Davidson, ed., *Clean Hands: Clair Patterson's Crusade against Environmental Lead Contamination* (Commack, NY: Nova Science, 1999), 93–103, at 94.

8. Christian Warren, *Brush with Death: A Social History of Lead Poisoning* (Baltimore: Johns Hopkins University Press, 2000).

9. Senate Committee on Public Works, Subcommittee on Air and Water Pollution, Hearings, June 7–15, 1966, "Air Pollution—1966," 89th Cong. 225, 205, 204, 206, and 211 (1966) (statement of Robert A. Kehoe).

10. Sharon Bertsch McGrayne, *Prometheans in the Lab: Chemistry and the Making of the Modern World* (New York: McGraw-Hill, 2001), 179.

11. Bill Bryson, *A Short History of Nearly Everything* (New York: Broadway Books, 2003), 156.

12. Tilton, "Patterson," 5.

13. Lydia Denworth, *Toxic Truth: A Scientist, a Doctor, and the Battle over Lead* (Boston: Beacon, 2008), 5.

14. Clair C. Patterson, Oral History Interview, March 5, 6, 9, 1995, Archives, California Institute of Technology, Pasadena, 16.

15. Patterson, Oral History, 17.

16. Tilton, "Patterson," 6.

17. McGrayne, *Prometheans*, 171.

18. Denworth, *Toxic Truth*, 14.

19. Patterson, Oral History, 19.

20. Robert Sharp, "Vignettes of Clair Patterson," in Davidson, *Clean Hands*, 47–53, at 49.

21. Cliff I. Davidson, "Clair Patterson: More Than Thirty Years of Research on Environmental Lead," in Davidson, *Clean Hands*, 61–77, at 64.

22. Dorothy M. Settle, "Some Remembrances from Almost Three Decades of Working with Patterson," in Davidson, *Clean Hands*, 31–36, at 31.

23. Davidson, "Clair Patterson," 64.

24. Clair C. Patterson and Dorothy M. Settle, "The Reduction of Orders of Magnitude Errors in Lead Analyses of Biological Materials and Natural Waters by Evaluating and Controlling the Extent and Sources of Industrial Lead Contamination Introduced during Sample Collecting, Handling and Analysis," in Philip D. LaFleur, ed., *Accuracy in Trace Analysis: Sampling, Sample Handling, Analysis—Volume 1*, NBS

Special Publications 422, Proceedings of the 7th Materials Research Symposium, NBS, October 7–11, 1974 (Washington, DC: U.S. National Bureau of Standards, 1976), 321–51, at 336.

25. Denworth, *Toxic Truth*, 19.

26. Patterson and Settle, "Reduction," 341.

27. Patterson and Settle, "Reduction," 335.

28. Patterson, "Alternative Perspective," 295.

29. Patterson and Settle, "Reduction," 341.

30. Cliff I. Davidson, "Introduction," in Davidson, *Clean Hands*, xvii–xxxiv, at xxvi.

31. Denworth, *Toxic Truth*, 20.

32. Denworth, *Toxic Truth*, 19.

33. Patterson and Settle, "Reduction," 340.

34. Sharp, "Vignettes," 49.

35. William F. Fitzgerald, "Clean Hands, Dirty Hands: Clair Patterson and the Aquatic Biogeochemistry of Mercury," in Davidson, *Clean Hands*, 119–37, at 120.

36. A. Russell Flegal, "Introduction: Clair Patterson's Influence on Environmental Research," *Environmental Research, Section A* 78 (1998): 65–70, at 66.

37. Patterson, Oral History, 31.

38. Tilton, "Patterson," 10.

39. Denworth, *Toxic Truth*, 169.

40. Denworth, *Toxic Truth*, 108–10.

41. Patterson, Oral History, 49.

42. McGrayne, *Prometheans*, 180.

43. Denworth, *Toxic Truth*, 168.

44. Fitzgerald, "Clean Hands," 128.

45. Patterson, Oral History, 34.

46. Patterson and Settle, "Reduction," 328.

47. McGrayne, *Prometheans*, 181.

48. Patterson, Oral History, 39.

49. Thomas M. Church, "From Meteorites to Man: The Patterson Geochemical Heritage," in Davidson, *Clean Hands*, 3–29, at 19.

50. Denworth, *Toxic Truth*, 108.

51. Patterson and Settle, "Reduction," 331–32.

52. Patterson, "Alternative Perspective," 310.

53. *Senate Committee on Public Works, Subcommittee on Air and Water Pollution, Hearings, June 7–15, 1966, "Air Pollution—1966,"* 89th Cong. 314 (June 15, 1966) (statement of Clair C. Patterson).

54. Jerome O. Nriagu, "Automotive Lead Pollution: Clair Patterson's Role in Stopping It," in Davidson, *Clean Hands*, 79–92, at 84.

55. Davidson, "Introduction," xxi.

56. Tilton, "Patterson," 10.

57. Claude F. Boutron, "Analyzing Polar Ice and Snow for Heavy Metals and Other Trace Elements: Two Decades of Fruitful Interaction with Clair Patterson," in Davidson, *Clean Hands*, 105–17, at 108.

58. *House of Representatives Committee on Science and Technology, Subcommittee on Environment and the Atmosphere, Hearings on September 17–26, 1975, "Environmental Effects of Dumping in the Oceans and Great Lakes,"* 94th Cong. 87 (September 18, 1975) (statement of Clair C. Patterson).

59. Herbert L. Needleman, "Clair Patterson and Robert Kehoe: Two Views of Lead Toxicity," *Environmental Research, Section A* 78 (1998): 79–85, at 81.

60. McGrayne, *Prometheans*, 187.

61. Tilton, "Patterson," 16.

62. Patterson, Oral History, 41.

63. McGrayne, *Prometheans*, 193.

64. Denworth, *Toxic Truth*, 123, 19.

65. *House of Representatives Committee on Science and Technology, Subcommittee on Environment and the Atmosphere, Hearings on September 17–26, 1975, "Environmental Effects of Dumping in the Oceans and Great Lakes,"* 94th Cong. 87 (September 18, 1975) (statement of Clair C. Patterson).

66. Patterson, "Alternative Perspective," 294.

67. Church, "From Meteorites," 26.

68. Sharp, "Vignettes," 52.

69. Robert E. Kohler, *Landscapes and Labscapes: Exploring the Lab-Field Border in Biology* (Chicago: University of Chicago Press, 2002), 7; see Edward Relph, *Place and Placelessness* (London: Pion, 1976).

70. Michel Foucault, "Of Other Spaces," *Diacritics* 16 (Spring 1986): 22–27, at 24.

71. Jan Golinski, *Making Natural Knowledge* (Cambridge: Cambridge University Press, 1998), 84; Graeme Gooday, "The Premisses of Premises:

Spatial Issues in the Historical Construction of Laboratory Credibility," in Crosbie Smith and Jon Agar, eds., *Making Space for Science: Territorial Themes in the Shaping of Knowledge* (London: Macmillan, 1998), 216–45, at 224–25.

72. Steven Shapin, *A Social History of Truth* (Chicago: University of Chicago Press, 1994), 21.

73. Steven Shapin, "Here and Everywhere: Sociology of Scientific Knowledge," *Annual Review of Sociology* 21 (1995): 289–321, at 308.

74. John Law and Annemarie Mol, "Situating Technoscience: An Inquiry into Spatialities," *Environment and Planning D: Society and Space* 19 (2001): 609–21, at 611.

75. David Livingstone, *Putting Science in Its Place: Geographies of Scientific Knowledge* (Chicago: University of Chicago Press, 2003), 21, 142, 176.

76. Paul J. DiMaggio and Walter W. Powell, "The Iron Cage Revisited: Isomorphism and Collective Rationality in Organizational Fields," *American Sociological Review* 48 (1983): 147–60, at 148.

77. Bruno Latour, *Pandora's Hope: Essays on the Reality of Science Studies* (Cambridge, MA: Harvard University Press, 1999), 46, 43, 67.

78. Karin Knorr Cetina, *Epistemic Cultures: How the Sciences Make Knowledge* (Cambridge, MA: Harvard University Press, 1999), 27.

79. Brian Gee, "Amusement Chests and Portable Laboratories: Practical Alternatives to the Regular Laboratory," in Frank A. J. L. James, ed., *The Development of the Laboratory* (New York: American Institute of Physics, 1989), 37–59.

80. Edward S. Casey, "How to Get from Space to Place in a Fairly Short Stretch of Time: Phenomenological Prologomena," in Steven Feld and Keith H. Basso, eds., *Senses of Place* (Santa Fe, NM: School of American Research Press, 1996), 13–52, at 45.

CODA

1. *The American Heritage Dictionary of the English Language*, paperback ed. (1980), s.v. "posit."

2. Sarah Bowen, *Divided Spirits: Tequila, Mezcal, and the Politics of Production* (Oakland: University of California Press, 2015), 151.

3. Edward S. Casey, *The Fate of Place: A Philosophical History* (Berkeley: University of California Press, 1997), 265.

4. "Truth Is the Daughter of ~~Time~~ Place" (with apologies to Aulus Gellius, Leonardo da Vinci, Francis Bacon, and many others).